Take Back Your Life!
Using Microsoft® Office Outlook® 2007 to Get Organized and Stay Organized

Sally McGhee
John Wittry

PUBLISHED BY
Microsoft Press
A Division of Microsoft Corporation
One Microsoft Way
Redmond, Washington 98052 6399

Library of Congress Control Number: 2007924646

Printed and bound in the United States of America.

3 4 5 6 7 8 9   QWT   2 1 0 9 8

Distributed in Canada by H.B. Fenn and Company Ltd.

A CIP catalogue record for this book is available from the British Library.

Microsoft Press books are available through booksellers and distributors worldwide. For further information about international editions, contact your local Microsoft Corporation office or contact Microsoft Press International directly at fax (425) 936-7329. Visit our Web site at www.microsoft.com/mspress. Send comments to mspinput@microsoft.com.

Microsoft, Excel, Groove, MapPoint, OneNote, Outlook, PowerPoint, SharePoint, Windows, and Windows Live are either registered trademarks or trademarks of Microsoft Corporation in the United States and/or other countries. Other product and company names mentioned herein may be the trademarks of their respective owners. Take Back Your Life! is a trademark of McGhee Productivity Solutions, Inc.

The example companies, organizations, products, domain names, e-mail addresses, logos, people, places, and events depicted herein are fictitious. No association with any real company, organization, product, domain name, e-mail address, logo, person, place, or event is intended or should be inferred.

Acquisitions Editor: Juliana Aldous Atkinson
Developmental Editor: Sandra Haynes
Project Editor: Lynn Finnel
Editorial Production: Custom Editorial Productions, Inc.
Copy Editor: Christina Palaia
Cover Design: Tom Draper Design

Body Part No. X13-23794

Table of Contents

Part Three

Creating an Integrated Management System— The Processing and Organizing Phase

Chapter Seven

Setting Up Your Action System. 130

Chapter Eight

Creating Meaningful Objectives. 144

Chapter Nine

Processing and Organizing Categories: (none) 172

Part Four

Creating an Integrated Management System—The Prioritizing and Planning Phase

Chapter Twelve

Acknowledgments

This book is the culmination of an extraordinary journey of listening, learning, and sharing. John and I feel honored to be walking this path and to have written this book together.

Over the years we've worked with many special individuals who've impacted our lives both professionally and personally. We'd would like to thank: Jinny and Tim Ditzler, Ben Cannon, Mark and Nancy Duarte, John Roger and John Morton, Stephen McGhee, Graham Alexander, Sir John Whitmore, Werner Erhard, Dean Acheson, Cam Greig, and Alan Platt.

We're deeply grateful to Russell Bishop, who many years ago created a company called Productivity Development Group (PDG) and hired David Allen and Sally McGhee. Some of the philosophies in this book are consistent with the philosophies created during that time.

Special acknowledgment goes to our team at MPS who are extremely passionate about serving our customers and 'walking the talk.' The content of this book is a reflection of their commitment to excellence and finding the best possible solutions.

None of this was possible without the support of our family and friends who stood by our commitment to this project and supported us in maintaining work-life balance.

And most importantly we owe an abundance of gratitude to all of our clients who've been, and still are, the feeding ground for our ongoing inspiration, learning, and creation.

Who Is This Book For?

This book is for individuals using Microsoft Office Outlook who are interested in increasing personal productivity and work-life balance: board members, chief executive officers, vice presidents, senior managers, and managers all the way down through individual contributors. These people are also mothers, fathers, husbands, wives, and college students. Most of us are dealing with conflicting priorities, too little time, too much information, and a desire to live a more balanced life and have more impact on those around us.

While this book is specifically focused towards users of Office Outlook 2007, if you're working with earlier versions such as Office Outlook 2000, 2002, and 2003, you'll still be able to apply all the principles and philosophies from this book. Just be aware that the instructions and screen shots are specific to Outlook 2007. And for those of you who've read the first book in our *Take Back Your Life* series, you'll be happy to know we've upgraded the existing material and created new chapters with brand new content. As you can imagine, our clients are constantly challenging us to improve our material; therefore, we think you'll find this book even more useful than the first one.

Why a Book About Productivity?

We have a passion for productivity, work-life balance, and contributing. We believe that the quality of life for many of our clients can be improved and that, in order for this to happen, well-targeted education combined with technology is essential. We wrote this book to share what we've learned in the hope it positively impacts your lives and the lives of those around you.

Over the years, we've discovered that many of our clients don't really know what productivity or balance is or how to use Outlook to improve it. Productivity is an interesting topic, and, from our perspective, it is often entirely misunderstood. When asked, our clients state that productivity is "managing time more effectively, producing a certain number of widgets within a specific timeframe, getting more things done, or being more effective." However, in the corporate world, true productivity begins in the board room and impacts entire organizations; from achieving bottom line objectives to greater work-life balance for employees. Millions of dollars can be saved while key results are highlighted and increased. And in our personal lives, true productivity becomes the cornerstone for work-life balance and an increased sense of well being.

For productivity to thrive in an organization or in an individual, it requires a fundamental paradigm shift redefining what productivity is. Productivity is not about getting more things done. It's about getting the *right* things done. When you think about getting the *right* things done, it challenges you to identify *what* the right things are. In most cases, the appropriate reference point will be your business and personal objectives. This then leads to the question: do you have these clearly in your line of sight? Are they in alignment with your team's objectives, your department's objectives, and ultimately the board's objectives? And do your personal objectives support your family's goals?

In the absence of aligned Meaningful Objectives, decisions are made without direction and in a vacuum. The volume of information we receive becomes the enemy, and there's no reference point for making decisions about what to do and what not to do. Our environment appears reactive and we feel like we're merely coping and surviving during the day instead of proacting and causing our day to happen.

When a company creates and cascades objectives from the board room down to the individual contributor level and when families agree on goals, powerful alignment is created. Objectives become the foundation for making decisions about what to do and what not to do. Individuals are empowered to do the *right* things instead of just *doing* things. This is one of the first and most critical shifts to creating a sustainable culture of productivity.

The philosophies in this book revolve around your Meaningful Objectives, both professional and personal. You will be using them as your reference point for collecting information, decision making, organizing, planning, and prioritizing. Therefore, increasing productivity is dependent on you having clear, specific, and compelling objectives. From this vantage point, you can then work on how you manage your time and actions to most effectively accomplish your objectives while remaining in balance.

Whether you lead a company or a team, whether you're an individual contributor, a husband or a wife, you can increase your personal productivity and create work-life balance. And in terms of impacting others, I'm sure you're aware that creating change is easier to do when you're leading by example. Therefore, this book is focused towards the individual and assisting you to make these changes first. As your staff and friends see you demonstrating balance and achieving your objectives, they'll be intrigued and want to know how you did it. At that point you can contemplate how to create change with your team and company. That'll be the next book!

How to Use This Book

Increasing productivity and work-life balance involves both setting up a system to support you in managing your life and making well thought out behavioral changes. It's important to be aware that setting up your system, which we will refer to as an Integrated Management System (IMS), takes an initial investment of time, as does changing behaviors. However, once your system is set up, it's easy to maintain and will bring great rewards. As you know, changing habits, although tough at first, can be very satisfying in the long run.

We encourage you to be patient while reading this book and while applying the methods and models outlined. There's no hurry and you're better off thoroughly understanding the concepts before you implement them. As Ghandi said, "Speed is irrelevant if you do not know where you are going." From a place of understanding, you'll be empowered to customize your system to your work style, circumstances, and personality. It's better to slow down and understand the concepts than rush through them.

The good news is that as you implement these concepts we're confident you'll see significant results both at work and home. Below are some recent client results. These are average figures taken six weeks after completing a client engagement with three hundred people. Something to look forward to!

Client Results from a Fortune 100 Consumer Products Company

- 6.5 more hours per week spent on activities directly relating to objectives
- 32 percent less time spent "doing e-mail"
- 63 percent decrease in the number of messages in their e-mail inboxes
- 18 percent less time spent looking for information each day
- 30 percent improvement in perception of work-life balance

Part One of the book, "Laying the Foundation for Productivity—Using an Integrated Management System," redefines productivity and introduces the Integrated Management System (IMS), detailing what it is and how to use it to increase your effectiveness both at home and work. Parts Two, Three, and Four of the book walks you through exactly how to set up and use your IMS day to day.

Clients often share with us that it took time and on-going practice to fully integrate all of the methods and models outlined in this book. They describe what took place over time as a lifestyle change. To assist you with this integration and deepening of the material, we invite you to visit our Web site at *www.mcgheeproductivity.com* and go to the products section. In this section you'll find a variety of tools and learning aids specifically designed to support you in refining, reinforcing, and expanding your productivity skills. It does take discipline and support to fully integrate theses philosophies; however, the rewards will speak for themselves.

Part One

Laying the Foundation for Productivity— Using an Integrated Management System

In this part

Part One:
Laying the
Foundation for
Productivity—
Using an
Integrated
Management
System

Take Back Your Life!

Chapter One

Changing Your Approach Changes Your Results

Part One:
Laying the
Foundation for
Productivity—
Using an
Integrated
Management
System

Increasing productivity is actually not that difficult to do. In fact it can be quite simple once you learn what to do and how to do it. The key is creating an environment in which you can routinely focus on and complete activities that link to and drive your meaningful objectives. Sounds simple enough; however, for some of us it is not quite that easy. So, what makes it complicated? Well, many things: consistent interruptions, an overwhelming volume of information, cell phones, pagers, instant messaging, conflicting priorities, broken agreements, other people, fire drills—and the list goes on.

Notice that most of these items are external obstacles and distractions. External obstacles are relatively easy to handle after you know how, and we offer you various solutions in this book to address them. We think you'll be pleased with how quickly you can implement the solutions and how immediate the results will be.

The hardest part of the change process is not dealing with external issues but rather our internal limiting beliefs. These beliefs affect the way we think about our productivity, and they dictate our attitudes and approaches, and in some cases, they can persuade us we are going to fail before we even start! What makes them so hard to change is twofold. Number one, they are unconscious: we literally don't know we have these beliefs, and yet they drive our lives and impact how successful we are at creating and sustaining positive change. Number two is we believe they are the truth, that they are real, which is why we call them beliefs.

Part One:
Laying the
Foundation for
Productivity—
Using an
Integrated
Management
System

Take Back Your Life!

We've discovered over the years that if you don't become aware of and change these unconscious beliefs, the positive behavioral changes you make cannot be sustained. Positive changes slowly fall apart under the power of your limiting points of view.

Sally: When I first started my career I noticed a phrase I kept using under my breath. I would quietly grumble, "I should be able to do all the things I want." I clung to this belief because I wanted it to be true. I was working long hours, I was stressed out and tired, and in the end I didn't have time to get it all done. My work was beginning to suffer, and my family life and body were affected. Without realizing it, I was letting my own limiting belief hold me hostage and force me to sacrifice the things I cared about most. "I should be able to do all the things I want" was simply not true. It was driving me to work harder to get it all done, and I was failing, which was very disappointing. I began justifying why I wasn't getting it all done, believing that I should be able to.

As you know, there are only 24 hours in a day. No matter how well you manage them, you can't increase them to 25. Conversely, no matter how poorly you manage them, you can't reduce them to 23. However, I did not manage my life from a 24-hour calendar; I managed my life from a to-do list. Each day, I decided what I was going to do, and then started a marathon to get the list completed. Everything was taking longer than I thought. I was running myself ragged and breaking agreements. But "by George," I should be able to get that list finished.

I kept hearing myself say, "I just don't have the time to do it all." This was the reality, and yet I kept thinking I should be able to get it all done, which drove me to continue to try. It was the perfect pattern: my belief justified my approach and my approach justified my belief. To an observer, I was banging my head against a brick wall and wondering why I had a headache! I resisted using a calendar, I was stubborn, and I was righteous about my belief because, honestly, there just isn't enough time in the day—but that is no excuse for not getting it all done, right?

Finally, in reaction to some feedback from my team and family, I hired a productivity coach. Surprise, surprise, the coach wanted me to schedule my activities on a calendar to ensure I actually had the time to complete them. At first, it was humiliating and humbling because activities took much longer than I expected and I couldn't cram as much into the day as I was used to doing.

Over time, I began to learn how to plan a day during which I could actually complete everything and get home on time—that was a new concept for me. I came to respect the calendar. I realized there really are only 24 hours in a day and I can only do what 24 hours will allow. After years of struggling against my limiting belief, my life began to turn around. I realized a simple truth: there will always be more to do than I can do and I will never, ever get it all done. Once I realized this, I became a lot more strategic about what I

Chapter One: Changing Your Approach Changes Your Results

Part One:
Laying the
Foundation for
Productivity—
Using an
Integrated
Management
System

decided to do and made sure I plannedthese activities on my calendar to get them done.

With this new approach, I started to keep my agreements and moved back into my integrity. I was a lot more discerning about what I agreed to do, and I gradually began to take back my life. I created unstructured quality weekends with family and friends, I fulfilled a life-long dream to buy a horse, and I reduced my work week to four days, only to see my business grow by 40 percent. Now I embrace my new belief, "Working with my calendar allows me to do what I truly want to do," rather than the familiar statement "I should be able to get it all done." As a result, I'm productive and my life is a place of self-expression and joy. This is what I want to help you to achieve for yourself.

10 Beliefs That Limit Productivity

When clients start to make positive changes toward improving their productivity, they often bump up against their unconscious limiting beliefs and find making the changes hard. Therefore, it is a good idea to acknowledge the limiting beliefs ahead of time so that you can begin the process of turning them around (moving them from the 'unconscious' to the 'conscious'). Limiting beliefs, unconscious by nature, are usually buried beneath statements with which most of us are familiar. We want to help you clarify yours by offering 10 of the most common statements we hear from our clients and the limiting beliefs that often accompany them.

Familiar statement

- There's too much information coming at me too fast, and I can't keep up.

Possible limiting beliefs

- I should be able to handle all the information that's coming at me.
- I have to handle the volume to be a good person (a good employee, or a valuable team member).

Familiar statement

- I get too many interruptions.

Possible limiting beliefs

- Interruptions are a necessary part of my day-to-day experience.

Part One:
Laying the
Foundation for
Productivity—
Using an
Integrated
Management
System

Take Back Your Life!

- I must respond to all requests to be a responsible team player.
- My boss expects me to respond to requests within a few minutes of their communication.
- It's my job to help others.

Familiar statement

- I don't have the discipline to be organized.

Possible limiting beliefs

- I am an easygoing person—I'm not a disciplined person.
- I'm too lazy to be organized.
- Discipline is no fun.
- I don't want to be disciplined.
- Discipline is a bad thing.

Familiar statement

- I have to keep everything.

Possible limiting beliefs

- As soon as I get rid of it, you just know I'm gonna need it.
- Someone will ask me for it, and so I must keep it.
- It is my job to keep records of everything.
- I will get in trouble if I don't have it on hand.

Familiar statement

- It takes too much time to get productive.

Possible limiting beliefs

- My job is more important than the effort it takes to implement a new system.
- The upfront effort won't pay off in the long run.
- It is not worth the extra time.

Chapter One: Changing Your Approach Changes Your Results

Part One:
Laying the
Foundation for
Productivity—
Using an
Integrated
Management
System

Familiar statement

- I can't find what I need when I need it.

Possible limiting beliefs

- My system doesn't work, and so I rely on memory.
- I am not an organized person.
- My memory is getting worse.
- With the new search functions, I don't need to organize my files.

Familiar statement

- Organization cramps my freedom and creativity.

Possible limiting beliefs

- It is not possible to be creative and organized at the same time.
- Being organized is too rigid.
- Organization cramps creativity.
- Being organized is left brain and I am a right-brain person.

Familiar statement

- I'm no good with technology.

Possible limiting beliefs

- Technology is hard to learn, and I am not a technical person.
- Technology always breaks down and can't be trusted.
- Technology is complicated.

Familiar statement

- There's not enough time in the day!

Possible limiting beliefs

- I should be able to do everything I want to do in a day.
- I have to do whatever is requested of me.
- I can't get it all done.

Part One:
Laying the
Foundation for
Productivity—
Using an
Integrated
Management
System

Take Back Your Life!

Familiar statement

■ I'm not organized by nature.

Possible limiting beliefs

■ Organization is a gene that's passed down the family line, but I didn't get it!

■ I'm an easygoing person.

■ I'm lazy and undisciplined.

■ It is too hard to get organized.

■ I don't want to be organized because, then, I would have to be responsible.

If you've tried to make positive changes in your life before and those changes have not lasted, you can be sure there's an unconscious limiting belief that's keeping you stuck. Take a moment and evaluate if any of the limiting beliefs in the preceding list resonate with you. It's only when you can acknowledge these beliefs and bring them to your conscious awareness that you can set about changing them and improving and sustaining the results.

Did you know beliefs can transform spontaneously without any conscious effort on our part? For this to occur, new ideas that make us question our old beliefs must be introduced into our experience. When something influences the nature of our beliefs, casting doubt, it begins to break down old beliefs and creates a place for a new belief to be introduced and to blossom. By understanding this process, you can start to alter your own limiting beliefs.

The first step in this process is challenging the foundation of your belief, questioning its roots and casting doubt on its validity. Doubt creates an opening, a crack in which your unconscious mind starts to explore the possibility of a new belief. In other words, new beliefs are formed when you have gathered enough evidence to discredit or disqualify the old belief. No one questioned whether a man could run faster than a 4 minute mile before it happened. We all believed that was an unbreakable barrier. Then Roger Bannister broke it. Suddenly what was true before was now disproved, disqualified and discredited and a new belief about human potential began to be formed. As you can probably imagine, doubt can come from many different places: a trusted friend, a scientist, a doctor, a historian, or an authority figure. You might experience doubt simply from watching a movie or read-

Part One:
Laying the
Foundation for
Productivity—
Using an
Integrated
Management
System

ing a book that challenges your point of view. After this sort of distrust is introduced, you begin to wonder what is and is not true. Over time, you will find yourself consciously and unconsciously collecting evidence from various places to annihilate your old beliefs and justify your new ones. Eventually, the new beliefs become solidified, and when this occurs they drop into your unconscious mind and you begin living your life as if these beliefs are the truth—at least for now.

Sally: In my life, on occasion I sometimes still hear my old belief trying to cast its web of doubt: "You should be able to get it all done." However, I've learned to manage this false belief, and when it rears its ugly head I respond to it differently. I tell myself, "I will never ever get it all done, therefore I need to be more strategic and focus on the important things first." I've gotten smarter about saying 'no' and planning from my calendar and not from my to-do list. Changing this belief resulted in tremendous freedom and peace of mind for me.

We are going to take a look at each familiar statement and its limiting beliefs one by one. In each section, we list one limiting belief, we suggest a new belief, and then we provide several external solutions you can implement to improve your results. The new beliefs we offer are simply suggestions to help guide you; it is important that you create your own new beliefs and that they are unique and inspire you to make positive changes. Creating these new beliefs ensures that the external solutions you implement hold up over time. This is a critical step in maintaining and sustaining your productivity in the future.

1. There's Too Much Information Coming at Me Too Fast, and I Can't Keep Up

Limiting belief

- I should be able to handle all the information that's coming at me.

New belief

- There is a way to be in control of my e-mail, and I can regularly have an empty Inbox.

Part One:
Laying the
Foundation for
Productivity—
Using an
Integrated
Management
System

Take Back Your Life!

Solutions

- ■ The volume of e-mail isn't really the issue; *how you process and organize the volume* is. Learning how to use the "Four Ds for Decision Making" can transform this belief. (See Chapter 9 for more details on the Four Ds.)

Each year we receive more and more data from a growing array of devices that can be accessed from an increasing number of locations. It's both exciting and overwhelming at the same time. If you're not careful, the quantity of data starts to drive you instead of the other way around. Remember, the whole idea here is for you to be in charge and take back your life.

Jeff Price, vice president at a mortgage company, asked us how he could handle his overwhelming volume of e-mail. When we asked how many messages he wanted to organize, he grimaced and rolled his eyes, "1,500!" As we watched Jeff process and organize his e-mail, we noticed that he opened messages and commented to himself, "This doesn't make sense. I can't handle this right now. It's too complicated, and I'll look at it later." He then proceeded to close each e-mail message and let it reside in his Inbox! When you handle your e-mail this way, it doesn't take long to accumulate 1,500 messages in your Inbox.

For Jeff to process his e-mail more effectively, we taught him how to use the Four Ds for Decision Making. This model helped Jeff make strategic decisions for each and every e-mail, allowing him to empty his Inbox. All Jeff needed was a little education about how to process and organize his e-mail more effectively.

Over the last several years, we've heard an increasing number of statements from sources such as clients, newspapers, business magazines, and even television about the volume of e-mail and how the volume is decreasing productivity, increasing stress, and creating reactive unfocussed environments. The people who are making these comments present convincing arguments, and it sure sounds like e-mail is a huge problem. However, as you might be beginning to realize, the problem is not e-mail but *how we approach working with e-mail.* We've allowed it to become an issue and we've allowed ourselves to become the problem!

Our company has thousands of clients who consistently end their work days with empty Inboxes! We have statistics to prove that with the right kind of education, you can reduce the number of messages in your Inbox by 81 percent, and you can reduce the volume of messages you receive by 50

Part One:
Laying the
Foundation for
Productivity—
Using an
Integrated
Management
System

percent. The Four Ds for Decision Making is a powerful model that will help you successfully manage your e-mail.

2. I Get Interrupted Too Many Times

Limiting belief

■ Interruptions are a necessary part of my day-to-day experience.

New belief

■ I create boundaries that allow me to manage interruptions successfully and get my work done.

Solutions

■ You can reduce the number of interruptions you receive and get your "real work" done during the day. The solution is to implement personal boundaries that allow you and your staff to create scheduled, uninterrupted work time.

We all are interrupted throughout the day, but are all interruptions completely necessary?

Consider the following situation: Ben Smith, a financial manager, is working on a Microsoft Office Excel worksheet in his office. Kathie Flood, a team member, walks in to ask a question about the company's health policy. Ben stops what he's doing and navigates to an intranet site to answer her question. When Kathie leaves, he must find his place in the Excel worksheet and start over. Joel, another team member, pops his head in the door and says, "Got a minute?" "Sure," Ben replies, and leaves his worksheet once again. By the time Joel leaves, Ben has lost 30 minutes and now must attend a meeting, postponing work on the worksheet until he has a free evening or weekend.

Because Ben consistently allowed these interruptions, he actually trained his staff that it was OK to disturb him. Some of these interruptions were necessary, but not all of them were. Unfortunately, interrupting Ben had become a habit for his team.

The solution is for Ben to meet with his staff so that he can create new expectations and ask for their help in supporting him. Subsequently, Ben called a meeting and let his team members know he wanted to have more uninterrupted work time during the day. He explained that he'd set up a recurring two-hour "work time" appointment on his calendar, and during

> Small things done consistently in strategic places create major impact.

Part One:
Laying the
Foundation for
Productivity—
Using an
Integrated
Management
System

that time he wanted team members to avoid interrupting him or booking other meetings. Ben was pleased at how respectful and supportive his staff was of this request. They understood his predicament and wanted to support him in making positive changes.

Our statistics show that by creating and reinforcing boundaries you can reduce your time dealing with interruptions by as much as 61 percent, allowing you to get more of your work done during the day.

3. I Don't Have the Discipline to Be Organized

Limiting belief

- I am an easygoing person—I'm not a disciplined person.

New belief

- Discipline is a decision, not a personality trait, and therefore I can be organized and use a system effectively.

Solutions

- Discipline is a skill that you already possess; you demonstrate it every day. The key to discipline is creating the appropriate motivation to make the specific changes you want. This enthusiasm then drives you to be disciplined.

Later in this book, we will help you set up an *Integrated Management System* that will improve your productivity and quality of life. This system requires discipline to maintain, and so being motivated to maintain it is an important and necessary step for your success.

There are two kinds of motivation: "away from" and "toward." The first is when you are motivated "away from" something you consider to be negative, and the other is when you are motivated "toward" something you consider to be positive. Both work equally well, although they're quite different. "Away from" motivation starts when you're sick and tired and tired and sick of an area in your life. Maybe you're fed up with processing e-mail in the evenings, frustrated listening to your to-do's rattling around your head, and weary of working long hours. This kind of negative energy can be a compelling driver of change.

"Toward" motivation requires some digging on your part. Ask yourself the question, "Why do I want to improve my productivity and work/life balance?

Part One:
Laying the
Foundation for
Productivity—
Using an
Integrated
Management
System

What is the benefit to me?" When you answer these questions, keep asking yourself, "Why?" until you find the underlying motivation. Remember to keep it positive. Don't list what you don't want, such as stress or overwhelm. List the positive side of those: you want more relaxation and ease, or more focus and control. It is very important to let your mind know what experience you want to have rather than the ones you don't want. When a child walks across the kitchen floor with a glass of milk in hand and you say, "Don't spill the milk," the child spills the milk. You see a picture of spilling the milk in your mind before you can utter the word *don't*. By then, it is too late. Instead, say to the child, "Walk slowly and carefully, and hold the glass with two hands," and watch what happens.

You'll know when you've found your "toward" motivation because you'll feel more inspired to make changes. When you discover that core desire, nothing will stop you from getting what you want.

When you start to use Microsoft Office Outlook in a more disciplined way, you'll find remarkable freedom. You'll create quality time at home, reduce your e-mail quantity, honor your agreements, and feel more relaxed and in control.

4. I Have to Keep Everything

Limiting belief

- As soon as I get rid of it, you just know I'm gonna need it.

New belief

- I don't need most of what I keep, and so I am letting go and trusting my new system in which the Delete key is my friend.

Solutions

- OK, prepare yourself. On average, the clients we work with throw away 50 percent of their stored information, and they feel lighter and happier, and have more time.

Our clients invest huge sums of energy filing and finding data. Of course, some of this filing is entirely appropriate, but we've discovered that a large proportion of it isn't. So, if you're a "keeper"—and you know who you are— hold on to your hats!

Part One:
Laying the
Foundation for
Productivity—
Using an
Integrated
Management
System

Take Back Your Life!

You keepers are a proud and experienced breed! There's nothing quite like laying your hands on a file that no one else can find. It justifies all of your filing and keeping efforts. Every department has a keeper who retrieves critical documents no one else can find. You probably know who the keeper is in your department!

Keepers learned to be keepers. At some point in their lives, they made a decision to hang on to information, and they've been hanging on to it ever since. If you're a keeper, you might recognize yourself in one of these statements:

- I got badly burned when I couldn't lay my hands on an important document. Now, I'm afraid to let go of information.

- I want to be able to back up the decisions I make, and so I keep everything.

- If my system crashes, I want backup data.

- I felt so good when no one else could find "that document" and I could. As a result, I decided to keep everything so that I could continue to feel useful.

At some point, you made a decision about keeping, and that decision has been driving you ever since. These beliefs are very powerful, but they may not support you in your current situation.

For example, we worked with a doctor who needed help managing the paperwork in his office. We asked him if there were any other areas we needed to clean up while we were there. He said, "Yes," and promptly showed us a room that looked like a storage closet full of boxes. He said, "That was my old office, and when it got filled up, I moved into another room!" We were a little surprised and realized this was a bigger project than we originally thought! He told us, "I'm a doctor, and I might need this information to save someone's life." It was a powerful justification. The only problem was that he had stopped being able to find anything a long time ago!

We ordered a dumpster and spent two days getting rid of 80 percent of his papers. After we finished working together, the doctor said to us, "You know, when I first started, I was scared I wouldn't be a good doctor, so I kept all of this information to help me feel more confident. Now I know I'm a good doctor, and I don't need all of it any more!" We will always remember this man because it took a great deal of courage for him to let go of all those papers he'd been holding on to for so many years.

Part One:
Laying the
Foundation for
Productivity—
Using an
Integrated
Management
System

We don't know your reasons for being a keeper, but it's worth taking a long, hard look to determine whether they are still good reasons that apply today and whether they still serve you.

The truth is, most people use only 15 percent of what they file, and this makes the other 85 percent ineffective. By clarifying what is useful and letting go of the rest, you can reduce your filing and save valuable time and energy that you can direct to more meaningful tasks.

5. It Takes Too Much Time to Get Productive

Limiting belief

- My job is more important than the effort it takes to implement a new system.

New belief

- I'm happily investing in my system, and my productivity is increasing.

Solutions

- You can save one to two hours a day using an Integrated Management System. This fact alone more than justifies the upfront investment required to set it up.

Following are a few examples of how people trip themselves up by not taking the time to set up an effective system.

- Writing a to-do list, and then rewriting it a week later on another list, and then on another.

- Opening an e-mail message, reading the message, closing the message, and then not doing anything with it right then and there only to open and read it again tomorrow.

- Going to the store to pick up something like dog food, only to arrive at the store and forget the brand name you wanted.

- Finding yourself at the office in need of the proposal you wrote for a meeting, and remembering you left it at home.

- Needing to read the *Leadership and Self-Deception* book at home, only to find that you left it at the office.

- Arriving at a meeting to find that you don't have the notes you need.

Part One:
Laying the
Foundation for
Productivity—
Using an
Integrated
Management
System

Take Back Your Life!

- Walking out of a meeting and remembering a critical point you wanted to raise during the meeting. Too late now!

These are just a few examples of how people waste time by not having an Integrated Management System to help them remember what, where, and when.

Here are some interesting statistics: on average, customers spend two to three hours a day working with e-mail and 60 minutes a day finding and filing information. After setting up an Integrated Management System, they spend one to two hours a day working with e-mail and 10 minutes a day finding and filing information. That's a savings of one hour and 50 minutes a day, which is almost 12 weeks a year! These time savings are nothing short of extraordinary.

Now, multiple those savings by the number of people on your team, and then expand that to the number of people in your organization. The results will really take your breath away! The bottom line is: You can't afford not to create an effective Integrated Management System.

6. I Can't Find What I Need When I Need It

Limiting belief

- My system doesn't work, and so I rely on memory.

New belief

- Reference systems are easy to set up and they save me time.

Solutions

- Setting up a Reference System is a skill that anyone can learn, and it's a skill that can save you 50 minutes a day.

Today there are so many places to store information that it's easy to fall into the trap of wanting to use all the tools you have at your disposal. You may be storing information in multiple and duplicate locations, such as in Personal Folders, the Inbox, the My Documents folder, Archive Folders, the Sent Items folder, or Offline folders, to mention just a few. Can you feel your head spinning thinking about where to find that critical document?

Robert Brown, an account manager at a telecommunications company, was having problems keeping track of the information he needed. He had

Chapter One: Changing Your Approach Changes Your Results

Part One:
Laying the
Foundation for
Productivity—
Using an
Integrated
Management
System

papers all over his desk, 1,023 messages in his Inbox, and 106 documents in his My Documents folder. A surprising 80 percent of the e-mail in his Inbox was reference material. He didn't know where else to put it, and so he kept it in his Inbox. That might sound familiar to you.

Robert wanted to clean up his e-mail first, and so we coached him through creating an *E-mail Reference System* in his Personal Folders list. The first step was creating a folder hierarchy. Robert created 10 top-level folders that related specifically to his Meaningful Objectives, and he created additional subfolders that related to his Supporting Projects. He then dragged his e-mail messages from his Inbox into these new reference folders, and by the end of the process, he could barely contain his smile. He grinned and said, "I had no idea how easy it would be to file and find information based on my objectives."

Robert then created a *Document Reference System* in his My Documents folder, and also a *Paper Reference System* in his file cabinet using the same folder hierarchy that he used in his E-mail Reference System.

Robert duplicated the same folder hierarchy across all his storage locations: Personal Folders, My Documents, and paper. This made it easy for him to remember where to file and find his data. Robert didn't realize how simple it was to set up a Reference System that mapped directly to his objectives. All he needed was a little coaching to point him in the right direction. He did all the rest himself.

Most of you weren't taught how to set up an effective Reference System. When you have one, you'll be amazed at how simple it is to find and file information and how much time you'll save.

7. Organization Cramps My Freedom and Creativity

Limiting belief

- It is not possible to be creative and organized at the same time.

New belief

- It is possible to be organized and spontaneous; in fact organization promotes my experience of freedom and creativity.

Part One:
Laying the
Foundation for
Productivity—
Using an
Integrated
Management
System

Solutions

- Organization actually fosters and supports creativity and spontaneity.

You may find your creativity disrupted by the nonstop flood of reminders spinning around your head:

- Call Kevin for his birthday.
- Review the P&L worksheet.
- Call Northwind Traders about the meeting schedule.
- Review the Microsoft Office PowerPoint slide deck.
- Decide on a Valentine's Day present.

Imagine if you could clear your mind of all these lists and transfer them to Outlook. This would create space for new ideas and creative thinking.

Being disorganized can also stifle your creativity. Imagine you're an artist and decide to paint the autumn colors in Aspen, Colorado. You drive for three and a half hours from Denver to Aspen to find the perfect spot. When you arrive, you realize you've forgotten to pack your paint brushes. That can make being creative really hard! Preparation does support creativity.

Another example has to do with scheduling. It can be frustrating when your calendar is booked and there is no time left to be spontaneous. However, if you preplan, you can block out large chunks of time with no organized events. This provides downtime in which you can be impulsive and spur-of-the-moment. Having an IMS also allows you to know who to renegotiate with when something spontaneous arises and is a true priority.

After you've set up your Integrated Management System, you'll find that it supports your creativity and spontaneity. The best result is being able to close your system, knowing that everything's taken care of so that you can relax and let go!

8. I'm No Good with Technology!

Limiting belief

- Technology is hard to learn, and I am not a technical person.

Part One:
Laying the
Foundation for
Productivity—
Using an
Integrated
Management
System

New belief

- I can learn to use technology, and it supports me in being productive and effective.

Solutions

- Using technology is a skill anyone can learn with the right education. You'll be surprised at the personal satisfaction that comes from using technology more effectively.

For many of us, technology is frustrating because we expect it to be intuitive. When computers don't respond the way we want, we get irritated. We've heard clients yelling profanities at their computers and have seen people walloping their PCs in hopes of intimidating the computers into cooperating. Needless to say, neither technique works.

Some of us spend hours trying to figure out how to use Tasks, set up Internet connections, and deal with errors. We wonder if we're ultimately saving any time at all. Fortunately, just a little bit of technical education can go a long way!

Katie Jordan, vice president of a finance company, was a paper-based organizer who loved her papers. She used Outlook only for e-mail because she hadn't been able to figure out how to use it effectively to track her objectives, projects, meeting agendas, and tasks.

She tried using tasks, reminders, and flagging e-mail messages, but always gave up in frustration. However, when Katie's company decided to move all of its paper-based systems to digital systems, Katie knew it was time to get some help with Outlook because she could no longer avoid it.

After a full day of coaching, Katie managed to eliminate at least two-thirds of her papers, transferring the contents into Outlook. She learned how to set up Categories to track all of her objectives, projects, meeting agendas, and tasks. Katie also learned how to insert e-mail messages into tasks and calendar appointments, and how to drag e-mail directly into her To-Do list. She was consistently amazed at what Outlook could do and reluctantly admitted that her new Integrated Management System might even work better than her old, paper-based system. This was a huge step forward for Katie, given how frustrated she'd been with technology and how much she had loved her paper.

Part One:
Laying the
Foundation for
Productivity—
Using an
Integrated
Management
System

Take Back Your Life!

What Katie was missing in her previous attempt to switch to Outlook was the right type of education. Most technical training classes focus on individual features and benefits that help you use the basic software, but they don't help you use Outlook to increase productivity and improve your work/life balance. After you've set up your Integrated Management System and learned how to use it, you can increase your overall usage of Outlook features by as much as 50 percent.

9. There's Not Enough Time in the Day!

Limiting belief

- I should be able to do everything I want to do in a day.

New belief

- I can't do everything, but by working effectively with my calendar I can get the most important things done.

Solutions

- Lack of time is seldom the issue. The real issue is working in cooperation with your calendar and deciding what you can do given the amount of time you have.

As you know, managing your time with Olympian skill doesn't create more hours in the day. We all have the same 24 hours, and so the issue isn't managing time—it's managing what you can do in the time you have. We always say to our clients, "You can't do everything, but you can do anything, as long as it fits into your calendar." Therefore, you have to be very careful about the choices you make.

Phil Spencer, an executive in a software company, explained he didn't have enough time in the day to get his job done. We gently reminded him that he couldn't create any more time and that the issue was more along the lines of how he was managing his commitments.

Phil kept his to-do lists in multiple locations—in e-mail, on a calendar, on paper, in an Excel worksheet, on a running list in his head, and on a few sticky notes stuck here and there. Phil first needed to learn how to centralize and prioritize this list. Then, he needed to find out how to schedule items effectively on his Outlook Calendar so that he would know what he could and couldn't do.

Part One:
Laying the
Foundation for
Productivity—
Using an
Integrated
Management
System

Phil transferred his various commitments into the Outlook Task list. He then compared the list with the available time on his Calendar and, right away, saw what the problem was. He was overcommitted and had more to do than time would allow. One more overachiever trying to expand his daily 24-hour quota!

Phil had to make some tough decisions because he couldn't complete all his agreements in the time he had. He was going to have to reprioritize, renegotiate, and, in some cases, cancel his commitments. Even though these were hard decisions, Phil had a much clearer idea now of what he could and couldn't do.

It was a humbling experience for Phil, but now he has a system that supports him in being realistic so that he can make well-informed decisions. This was a powerful change. It put Phil in a position of control instead of reaction, and it increased his sense of personal integrity, honesty, and self-esteem.

10. I'm Not Organized by Nature

Limiting belief

- Organization is a gene that's passed down the family line, but I didn't get it!

New belief

- I can learn to be organized and have fun with it.

Solutions

- Organization is an exceptionally simple skill that you *can learn* just like any other. In fact, it's a skill that's easier to pick up than are most of the skills you learned in your current career!

Consider for a moment: organization techniques were not taught in school. Most of us learned what we know today about organization through trial and error, picking up tips and tricks here and there, often coming up with stopgap solutions that haven't served us effectively in the long run.

Part One:
Laying the
Foundation for
Productivity—
Using an
Integrated
Management
System

Take Back Your Life!

Sally: When I was little, my dad used to tell me, "If you could forget to put your head on in the morning, you would!" I was incredibly scatterbrained and disorganized. I left for school each day with very good intentions, but always forgot to bring something I needed. I realized that I was relying on memory to keep track of things, and that clearly wasn't working. I quickly learned that if I was going to be more successful and feel more in control of my life, I needed to be more organized. I started using a paper organizer to write things down. It was the only way for me to remember things consistently! It made a significant difference, and so I continued learning about productivity, going to various time-management courses, and trying different systems.

I never found a system that quite fit all my needs, and so in 1989, I designed and manufactured my own system. Today, these organization skills are just part of who I am. Clients have referred to me as an "Olympic Gold Medal organizer." However, my closest friends know my history better! The fact that I wasn't organized drove me to develop my system and gain the ability to be organized.

Organization is a skill that you can learn. Give yourself the time to be a student and learn new techniques. These techniques can help improve your life and may be among the greatest gifts you can give yourself.

Making Changes Involves Letting Go

When clients embark on the journey of letting go of limiting beliefs and embracing new positive ones that open up doors, it can often involve a high degree of trust and courage. Making changes is not always easy to do; however, the rewards are big.

Change. It has the power to uplift, to heal, to stimulate, surprise, open new doors, bring fresh experience, and create excitement in life. Certainly it is worth the risk.
—**Leo Buscaglia**

Linda Mitchell, a program manager at a software company, had 3,983 e-mail messages in her Outlook Inbox. One of her goals while we coached her was to gain control of her e-mail so that she could get to zero and start with a clean slate. Linda was fed up with having to manage so much e-mail and fed up with her compulsion to keep everything—everything without which, she feared, she could not operate. Her belief was she could not be effective if she did not keep everything.

Linda created a new belief: "I am letting go and trusting my system." By the end of the session, Linda had successfully reduced her volume of e-mail by half. When we posed to her the question, "What are you willing to let go of to eliminate the remaining e-mail messages?" the thought of eliminating the remaining 1,991 messages was more than Linda could bear. She was not

Part One:
Laying the
Foundation for
Productivity—
Using an
Integrated
Management
System

quite ready for that level of letting go. However, a week later, we received this e-mail message from her:

Dear Sally,

Yesterday, I deleted every single e-mail in my Inbox. I sent a message to all my staff and customers and informed them that my mail had been deleted and if there was anything I'd missed to get back to me ASAP!

Three months later she e-mailed us again.

Dear Sally,

I feel great. I have 25 e-mails in my Inbox and nothing happened as a result of deleting the backlog of 2,000 messages! I took the leap and it worked! I realize that I can do my job without keeping so much information. My system works; what a relief!

Letting go and changing behaviors require a leap of faith and a great deal of courage. Linda wanted to gain control of her e-mail, and to do so she had to change her approach and her beliefs. She took a risk and she let go—it was not a rational thing to do, and she did not think her way into it, she just let go. As you go through this book and implement your system in certain places you will need to have courage and simply let go.

In this chapter, you've probably learned that *often the problems we identify aren't the problems that truly need fixing!* The problems lie within us and in how we approach certain situations in our lives. As we change our own inner beliefs and implement different solutions, we produce different results. As Jim Rohn says, "I used to say, 'I sure hope things will change.' Then, I learned that the only way things are going to change for me is when I change."

One of our favorite expressions is "If you always do what you've always done, you'll always get what you always got." If you're not as productive as you'd like to be, if your e-mail setup is not working for you, and if you don't have the life balance you want, you're going to have to do some things differently. Now is the perfect time to pick up your courage and make some positive changes.

I used to say, "I sure hope things will change." Then, I learned that the only way things are going to change for me is when I change.
—**Jim Rohn**

Part One:
Laying the
Foundation for
Productivity—
Using an
Integrated
Management
System

Take Back Your Life!

Chapter Two
Defining Productivity

Part One:
Laying the
Foundation for
Productivity—
Using an
Integrated
Management
System

In this chapter, we introduce a new and powerful way to redefine productivity and work/life balance. Without clarifying these terms, it can be difficult to improve them. After you understand these definitions, you'll be surprised how simple the concepts are and how quickly you can implement solutions to produce immediate results. In this chapter, we also introduce the McGhee Productivity Solutions (MPS) Cycle of Productivity and the McGhee Productivity Solutions (MPS) Action Hierarchy Model, both of which diagram how to create and generate a culture of productivity. And last, we introduce the Integrated Management System (IMS) that assists you on an individual level to implement the MPS Cycle of Productivity. (You'll have the opportunity to set up your IMS in Chapter 7.)

What Is Productivity?

Productivity seems like a generic term, one that is easy enough to define, but it actually means very different things to different people. For example, when we ask clients what productivity means, we get a variety of different responses:

- Getting more done
- Doing what I said I would do
- Being more strategic
- Using my resources wisely
- Experiencing work/life balance
- Meeting my objectives effectively

Part One:
Laying the
Foundation for
Productivity—
Using an
Integrated
Management
System

Take Back Your Life!

- Feeling in control and relaxed
- Delegating effectively
- Spending more time being proactive, not reactive
- Going home each day feeling complete
- Completing more things on my list
- Spending more time with my kids
- Procrastinating less
- An empty Inbox

When you review these comments carefully, you'll discover that there's an underlying theme that links them all together. That theme is "action" or "getting things done."

Therefore, you might define productivity in its simplest form as **completing actions**. However, you can cheerfully complete actions until you are blue in the face (and some of you are) and still not experience what we define as true productivity. We're sure you've had days that were really busy but on reflection, you didn't feel as effective as you wanted to be.

Productivity is not about getting more things done; it's actually about getting the right things done. However, most of our clients are still working with an unconscious belief—"I've got to get it all done!" This belief is extremely powerful and drives our clients to create habits and routines to support it. Instead of starting work at 9 AM, they're now starting work at 8 AM—to get more done! Instead of leaving work at 5 PM, they're now leaving work at 6 PM—to get more done. Instead of waking up at 6 AM, they're now waking up at 5 AM—to process more e-mail. They're purchasing smart phones so they can do e-mail during meetings, on planes, and at stop lights—to get more done. These habits ultimately have a negative impact on people's lives: they cause broken agreements with family members and coworkers, deteriorating relationships, declining health, decreased quality-of- life and well-being.

The truth is, you'll always have more to do than you *can* do, and you'll never ever get it all done. To emphasize this point: you will NEVER, EVER get it all done. Let that sink in for a moment.

Therefore, it's time to let go of the unconscious belief "I've got to get it all done!" because it won't bring you any success. All it will do is drive you to keep changing your habits to get more done and feel overwhelmed!

Part One:
Laying the
Foundation for
Productivity—
Using an
Integrated
Management
System

Once you let go of this belief, you'll naturally be more discerning about what you choose to do: *Focusing on activities that make the biggest impact, activities that affect your ultimate goals and objectives.* You'll find yourself relaxing, being more focused, saying no, and living in greater balance.

Remember *productivity is not about getting it all done. It's about getting the right things done.* This is a critical shift in thinking to make before you can start being more productive.

Meaningful Objectives

When we observe clients who are extremely productive, we find that simply completing a list of actions isn't enough for them. What's important is that their actions are linked and driven by **Meaningful Objectives**. These clients rarely do anything that *doesn't* relate to one of their objectives. Their Meaningful Objectives are their North Star, their guiding light, and their reference point for success or failure.

Their individual business Meaningful Objectives roll up to a department **Unifying Goal**(s), which is the most important achievement a department can accomplish. The Department Unifying Goal(s) then rolls up to an overall organization Unifying Goal(s), which is the most important focus for the company. This cascading of objectives, up and down the organization, creates a high degree of alignment and focus and makes individual objectives more meaningful. And on a personal level, an extremeley productive person's Meaningful Objectives roll up to a family vision creating alignment and focus at home.

The word *meaningful* is important because without meaning, your objectives become dry and nothing more than text on a to-do list that you might (or might not) look at every now and then. You won't be motivated to work on your objectives, but you'll feel guilty when you don't.

We often say to our clients, "Your productivity is only as good as your objectives." It's very important to have Meaningful Objectives because productivity is impossible to direct and measure without them.

Meaningful Objectives are the first core principle we use in this book to assist you in increasing your productivity.

If you don't have clear objectives, you can easily fall into the trap of completing actions just for the sake of doing something. You'll feel as though you're getting a lot done, but deep down you know you aren't being as effective as you can be.

Part One:
Laying the
Foundation for
Productivity—
Using an
Integrated
Management
System

After you learn how important Meaningful Objectives are to true productivity, you begin to realize that *getting things done* has little to do with productivity and *completing actions that link to and drive your Meaningful Objectives has everything to do with productivity.*

Productivity: Completing actions that link directly to and drive your Meaningful Objectives

Understanding this definition is critical because it is the foundation on which this book is written.

You'd be amazed at how many people we have coached, at every organizational level, who didn't have Meaningful Objectives either for themselves or for their direct reports. (Not many people have Unifying Goals for their teams, either.) In the case where clients do have objectives in place, they are often unclear, not measurable, and do not fit the definition of a Meaningful Objective. Identifying objectives that are meaningful and clarifying them so that they're specific and measurable are critical steps in helping you manage your life. As Lily Tomlin once said, "I always wanted to be somebody. I guess I should've been more specific!"

Following are a few examples of Meaningful Objectives:

Sales Sell $3 million worth of online learning products by December. (Mark receives a 5 percent commission on revenue when he makes this goal, and money is a major motivator for him.)

Career development Complete certification program for coaching at the senior management level by May 1. (Joe has dreamed of providing effective coaching services at this level for many years.)

Health Run Pikes Peak in less than my personal best time of 3 hours and 15 minutes. (Bob suffered a mild heart attack two years ago, and so this represents a major accomplishment for him.)

Home Build a 500-square-foot dog run. (Susan wants to protect her landscaping from her two rather large, 11-month-old puppies.)

When you create Meaningful Objectives, be discerning as to how many you can handle at one time. It is easy to fall into a trap of having too many objectives, a problem that can have a cumulative, negative effect on your life, similar to having no objectives. When you have too many objectives, you may feel that no matter how productive you are, it's never enough. You miss deadlines, you experience an unusual number of emergency situations, your work is mediocre, your life isn't in balance, and your priorities conflict. You are back to surviving and coping.

You've got to think about the big things while you are doing the small things, so that all small things go in the right direction.
—**Alvin Toffler**

Part One:
Laying the
Foundation for
Productivity—
Using an
Integrated
Management
System

It's normal to want to please others and demonstrate that you're part of the team by expanding the scope and/or number of your objectives. But in that context, it's also easy to overcommit. Your intentions are honorable, but your results may not be so glowing. You may end up working long hours to ensure that your performance at work isn't harmed, but the consequence can be that your personal life suffers. When you have too many objectives, ultimately something goes out of balance.

We also recommend that you create personal Meaningful Objectives at the same time that you create business objectives. By doing so, you can integrate both areas, ensuring that they support each other, that your objectives are realistic and create a sense of well-being and balance.

Also, be sure to create your Meaningful Objectives in alignment with your boss and your team so that you're not producing them in a vacuum. Ultimately, the creation process starts in the board room with the mission, vision, and values of a company, cascades down to a department or division as a Unifying Goal, passes to the individual as a Meaningful Objective, and then works back up, creating corporate alignment and collaboration. The same process can be used in your personal life such that your personal objectives are aligned with your vision and integrated with your family's objectives as well.

By managing both the number and the quality of your objectives, you can maintain equilibrium. By integrating them with your boss and your family, you can create alignment and cooperation. In Chapter 8, you will be creating your personal and business Meaningful Objectives.

Strategic Next Actions

Productivity: Completing actions that link directly to and drive your Meaningful Objectives.

This definition is extremely close to being complete; however, over the years we have noticed another situation that impedes our clients' productivity. We found that many clients add tasks to their to-do lists that they couldn't complete, but they'd learn this only when it came time to take action. At that point, they'd realize that a to-do item involved multiple steps and couldn't be finished without several other preceding actions. In many cases, they realized these tasks weren't the most strategic to accomplish anyway.

On the other hand, our most productive clients spend considerable time planning and thinking through their tasks. They ensure that each task they've listed is the most strategic action they can take and that it doesn't

Part One:
Laying the
Foundation for
Productivity—
Using an
Integrated
Management
System

Take Back Your Life!

have any dependencies. (A **dependency** is any additional step that must be completed before you can begin the task.) We refer to actions that link to Meaningful Objectives and have no dependencies as **Strategic Next Actions (SNA)**.

When you take the time to create Strategic Next Actions, watch out, because your productivity will soar! Use of Strategic Next Actions is the second core principle you'll be working with throughout the book.

After we discovered the importance of Strategic Next Actions, we expanded our definition of productivity to consistently completing Strategic Next Actions that link to and drive your Meaningful Objectives. This statement encapsulates what we see our successful clients doing. After you incorporate these two principles, Meaningful Objectives and Strategic Next Actions, into your Integrated Management System, you'll be enthusiastic about how powerful they are and how much value you'll receive.

Productivity: Consistently completing Strategic Next Actions that link to and drive your Meaningful Objectives.

Work/Life Balance

It's important to have a personal reference point for balance; otherwise, you can't create or maintain it. The American Heritage Dictionary defines **balance** as "A weighing device, consisting essentially of a level that is brought into equilibrium by adding known weights to one end while the unknown weights hang from the other." Our definition of balance is:

Balance: A consistent focus or influence that creates a sense of well-being.

If you're not feeling good and you're out of sorts, you need to find a way to increase your sense of well-being and bring yourself back into balance so that the scales are equally weighted. We hear you saying, "Easier said than done!" and you're correct. The challenge is to determine what you can do to increase your well-being.

When you review your personal and business Meaningful Objectives, focus on them collectively and ask yourself, "Can I maintain a sense of well-being as I complete these? Do these objectives promote my happiness?" It's important to include both personal and business objectives because you can't create balance in a vacuum; you need to evaluate the whole picture and not just a piece of it. After you've done this a few times, you'll start to discover the areas on which you need to focus to create balance for yourself.

Part One:
Laying the
Foundation for
Productivity—
Using an
Integrated
Management
System

Balance is subtle and it's different for each one of us. Sometimes all it takes to acquire it is one great vacation with your family, consistently exercising three times a week, or having unstructured time on weekends. The most unexpected events can create a high degree of well-being, and so bringing your life back into balance doesn't necessarily require time-consuming activities. It does require quality activities such as being alone for a day, getting a massage, or reading a great book. You may not immediately recognize which activities hold the most quality for you, but by trying different things, you'll find out.

We're all so busy "getting things done" that we often don't think about what we need to do to create balance as a consistent focus and experience. *Balance* might seem like an inappropriate word to use in conjunction with work, and many of our clients think that if they approach work with balance, they'll slow down, get less done, lose their edge, and ultimately reduce their productivity.

However, we see our most productive clients using balance to *increase* productivity, not *decrease* it. When they exercise early in the morning, they start their day being more centered and having a clearer head. When they make time during the week to watch a sports game or go to the theater, they awake the next morning with the great idea they've been searching for. Sometimes we see clients working long hours for days back to back, but then they balance that work with a three-day vacation or take time in the middle of the week to play golf or work in the yard.

It's important to identify what allows you to successfully create balance. The key is to review your personal and business objectives simultaneously while asking yourself, "What do I need to do to maintain balance?" Chapter 8 discusses how to accomplish this goal in detail.

The MPS Cycle of Productivity

Over the years, we've noted that our most successful clients perform a distinct set of behaviors over and over, achieving their objectives effectively while maintaining balance. The MPS Cycle of Productivity is a very simple, four-step model that highlights these behaviors and supports our definition of productivity.

Productivity: Consistently completing Strategic Next Actions that link to and drive your Meaningful Objectives.

Part One:
Laying the
Foundation for
Productivity—
Using an
Integrated
Management
System

Take Back Your Life!

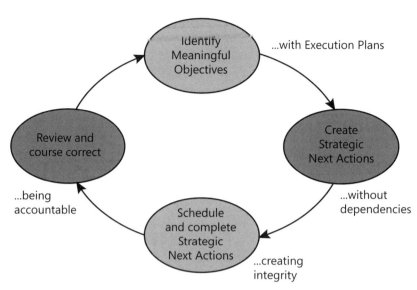

Figure 2-1   The MPS Cycle of Productivity demonstrates how to create and maintain an environment of productivity.

The MPS Cycle of Productivity illustrates the following:

- Identifying Meaningful Objectives . . . with Execution Plans
- Creating Strategic Next Actions . . . without dependencies
- Scheduling and completing Strategic Next Actions . . . creating integrity
- Reviewing and course correcting. . . being accountable

Imagine for a moment that your organization's board of directors has identified the objectives that must be accomplished for the company to succeed. These objectives are integrated with the company's mission, vision, and value and are communicated throughout the organization. To accomplish the objectives, each division of the company then creates its own Unifying Goals, ensuring they're in alignment with the board's directives. Then, individual employees in the company determine the Meaningful Objectives that roll up and down with their boss and their direct reports. The process of creating Meaningful Objectives cascades throughout the company to the individual contributors.

Picture everyone completing Strategic Next Actions that link to and drive their Meaningful Objectives, which unlock Unifying Goals that in turn achieve the company mission and vision. That is a productivity culture: people in the right places doing the right things to support the overall company

Part One:
Laying the
Foundation for
Productivity—
Using an
Integrated
Management
System

objectives, all operating from a place of integrity and accountability. This is a powerful and inspiring environment to be in.

Step One: Identifying Meaningful Objectives...with Execution Plans

Identifying your Meaningful Objectives is the first step in the MPS Cycle of Productivity. Whether you're a stay-at-home parent, a college student, a small business owner, or a worker in the corporate world, identifying clear Meaningful Objectives for both your business and personal life is essential. Without them, productivity can't occur.

Objectives assist you in measuring progress, making course corrections, and focusing on strategic activities. They're powerful filters that support you in making effective decisions.

Most of us receive a nonstop flood of information, all of which requires our immediate attention. If the information you receive directly relates to your objectives and assists you in moving forward, the decision to take action is clear. However, if the information doesn't relate to an objective, you must evaluate how to handle it because working on actions that don't link to objectives isn't productive. You'll learn more about renegotiating and disengaging from activities that do not link to objectives in Chapter 9.

After you have clarified your objectives, the next step is to create Supporting Projects for each one so that you know what resources are required. Then, you can calculate how much of your time is necessary to complete the objectives. Without Supporting Projects, it's easy to say yes to things without knowing what is involved, and then when you find out what's involved, you wish you'd done a bit more planning up front. Supporting Projects empower you to make effective decisions on whether or not to take on new commitments or to renegotiate current ones. This is good information to know!

Without Meaningful Objectives and Supporting Projects, it's easy to become directionless and fall into the trap of "any road will do," which is not a very satisfying long-term strategy. Although it takes time to clarify objectives and make plans to accomplish them, the value you receive from having objectives and plans is enormous. Take the time to create objectives and plans on the front end because, ultimately, this will save you time on the back end.

Part One:
Laying the
Foundation for
Productivity—
Using an
Integrated
Management
System

Take Back Your Life!

Step Two: Creating Strategic Next Actions...Without Dependencies

The next step in the MPS Cycle of Productivity is to create Strategic Next Actions that link to your Meaningful Objectives. You must ensure that these actions drive your objectives forward and that they don't have any dependencies. They are not Strategic Next Actions if they have dependencies and are not linked to objectives. If actions have dependencies, we call them Tasks; this is a key distinction. You can only move forward in the MPS Cycle of Productivity by accomplishing a Strategic Next Action, *an action that can physically be completed in one, simple step.*

The Case of Henry and the Car

Consider the case of Henry Miller, a client whose objective was to sell his car so that he could buy the one he really wanted. To accomplish this, he needed to define a Strategic Next Action, which he thought was to fix the brakes on his old car. That action seemed pretty simple until we had a conversation with Henry.

"Henry, what do you need to do to fix the brakes?" was our question. He replied, "Take my car to the dealership on Broadway." Then, we asked him, "What do you need to do to take your car to the dealer?" He answered, "Book an appointment to have them look at the brakes." Then, another question, "What do you need to do to book the appointment?" he said, "Go online to look up the phone number." In other words, Henry's Strategic Next Action wasn't to get the brakes fixed on his car, but to get on the Internet and get the phone number for the dealership.

Henry found that the action of fixing his brakes had multiple dependencies. To fix the brakes, he needed to take the car to the dealer; to take the car to the dealer, he had to book an appointment; to book an appointment, he needed the phone number; and to get the phone number, he needed to look it up on the Internet. As mentioned earlier, if an action has multiple dependencies, we define it as a **Task**. If an action has no dependencies and is linked to an objective, we call it a **Strategic Next Action**.

Henry's actual Strategic Next Action was "Go online and get the phone number for the dealer on Broadway." It is important to notice the distinction between a Task and a Strategic Next Action because they are *not* the same thing. Understanding this distinction can increase your ability to get more of the right things done while saving time.

Chapter Two: Defining Productivity

Part One:
Laying the
Foundation for
Productivity—
Using an
Integrated
Management
System

The story of Henry and his car is just a small example of how seemingly "simple" actions can end up having multiple, unexpected dependencies when you examine them closely. When we look at our clients' to-do lists, we find that 80 percent or more of the items on their lists are made up of actions that have dependencies; in other words, their lists are made up of Tasks. This makes for a to-do list that is unrealistic and that *can't be done*. When our clients realize they cannot do a Task, because Tasks have dependencies, and can in fact only do Strategic Next Actions, because Strategic Next Actions don't have dependencies, their productivity begins to improve. This is a powerful distinction, and after you start separating your actions in this way, you'll be amazed at how easy it is to keep the MPS Cycle of Productivity going and achieve your Meaningful Objectives.

Step Three: Scheduling and Completing Strategic Next Actions...Creating Integrity

After you decide what your Strategic Next Actions are, you can move to the third step in the MPS Cycle of Productivity, which is **scheduling and completing** these actions on the calendar. This step supports you in keeping your agreements and maintaining integrity. Reliability and integrity are important values to live by and are integral to creating a productivity culture.

Most clients we work with are profuse "creators": they write long lists and agree to numerous activities. The problem lies in their ability to complete what they've agreed to do. Even though their day contains only 24 hours, they don't plan their activities to fit in that time frame. They say yes to obligations and sincerely believe everything will work out—but without realistic scheduling, they sacrifice balance, break agreements, and lose integrity. Therefore, understanding how to manage your calendar and schedule SNAs so that you can do what you said you would do is critical because nothing restores integrity faster than keeping your word. We talk more about creating and maintaining integrity in Chapter 12.

Our company's statistics prove that there's a 75 percent greater chance an action will be completed if it's scheduled on your calendar rather than simply tracked on your To-do List or in your head. Placing an SNA on your calendar ensures that you see it and have the time to complete it. When it's on your To-do List, you may not look at it, and if you don't allocate time to do it, it probably won't get done.

When you begin to schedule your Strategic Next Actions on your calendar, you dramatically increase the likelihood that you'll complete these actions.

Part One:
Laying the
Foundation for
Productivity—
Using an
Integrated
Management
System

Take Back Your Life!

This kind of completion releases energy and gives you the motivation and inspiration to continue moving forward.

You just might be one of those people who are starved for completion. Your objectives span months or years, giving you no daily sense of achievement. By redirecting your focus to implementing a Strategic Next Action without a dependency, you can experience a daily sense of accomplishment that leads to renewed energy.

Step Four: Reviewing and Course Correcting...Being Accountable

Because our clients are so busy *reacting* to the world around them, they rarely take time to stop and *proactively* review progress towards completing objectives and ensuring they're on track. Their time is spent reacting to the volume of information they receive and desperately trying to keep their heads above water.

Step four is a proactive step that involves pulling yourself away from the day-to-day to review your objectives and ensure they're on track. We're going to use a common analogy here about airplanes to support understanding this step. An airplane is technically on course only 25 percent of the time. The pilot spends 75 percent of her time course correcting to ensure the plane reaches its destination successfully. That is a lot of course correction! If you apply this analogy to your objectives, 75 percent of the time you need to be course correcting to achieve your goals.

Step four is a time to course correct and involves reviewing your Strategic Next Actions and evaluating whether they have moved you closer to your Meaningful Objectives. If they did, you can create a subsequent Strategic Next Action to continue the MPS Cycle of Productivity. However, if completing an action didn't move you forward , you must create an alternative Strategic Next Action to course correct.

In either scenario, you're acknowledging completion and reviewing progress toward your Meaningful Objectives.. In other words, this is a time to pause and review "off-course" and "on-course" feedback for yourself. Ask yourself, "Am I completing the actions necessaryto stay on track toward my objectives? This can be a tough question to ask and answer. You need to slow down to ask it and review the situation honestly and proactively. After you find the answer, you can then take the necessary steps to correct your course or acknowledge that you are on track and what you are doing is working.

Part One:
Laying the
Foundation for
Productivity—
Using an
Integrated
Management
System

Acknowledgment is critical because it's the fuel that motivates you and your team and allows you to recognize if you are on track and moving toward your objectives. Much like piloting a plane you must continually adjust to ensure you reach your destination. Regular reviews are essential because with them, if you are off course, you can adjust early and reduce your time spent and resources used. If you wait too long to adjust direction, the adjustment you do make must be much bigger and can take much longer and use more resources.

By using the MPS Cycle of Productivity, you can simultaneously maintain your focus on the big picture while completing small, tactical steps. All your actions drive you toward the completion of your Meaningful Objectives, which enables you to be strategic and use your time and resources wisely. If you continually create and complete Strategic Next Actions that link to and drive your Meaningful Objectives, you can achieve your goals easily and gracefully. Don't know about you, but that sure sounds good to us!

Although this is a simple concept, it delivers profound results. As my grandma used to say, "It's a cinch by the inch and hard by the yard." Turns out she was right!

Introducing the MPS Action Hierarchy Model

The MPS Action Hierarchy Model demonstrates how to create an environment in which productivity, alignment, and focus thrive. Start at the top of the model shown in Figure 2-2. The board creates missions, vision, and values that drive company focus. Each division creates its own Unifying Goals in alignment with the board. From these Unifying Goals, Meaningful Objectives are created and broken down into Supporting Projects, Tasks, and Subtasks. From the Subtasks, Strategic Next Actions are created.

Part One:
Laying the
Foundation for
Productivity—
Using an
Integrated
Management
System

Take Back Your Life!

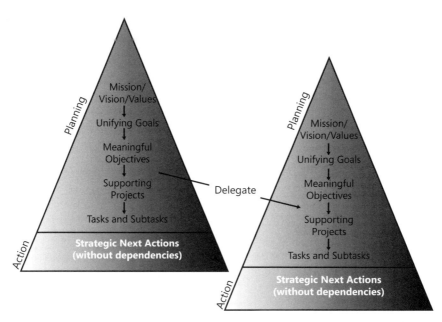

Figure 2-2   The MPS Action Hierarchy Model shows you how to align Strategic Next Actions with Mission, Vision, Values, and Unifying Goals.

When you bring together the MPS Cycle of Productivity and the MPS Action Hierarchy Model, you can begin to see how you can create an environment in which productivity can take place. In this environment, employees can cause and create their Meaningful Objectives and move from the old model of coping and surviving to a new culture of thriving.

Imagine if every department had Unifying Goals and every individual in your company had clear Meaningful Objectives, focused on completing Strategic Next Actions, and regularly reviewed off-course/on-course feedback. Each time someone completes a Strategic Next Action, that person would unlock a dependency that was keeping one of the subtasks inactive. As individuals continue through the MPS Cycle of Productivity, consistently completing Strategic Next Actions, they'd eventually unlock their Subtasks completely, and then their Tasks, and then their Supporting Projects, and then their Meaningful Objectives, and eventually the Unifying Goals of their division. Finally, the Mission, Vision, and Values of the company would be achieved.

Obviously, achieving company goals requires completing many cycles of action. If you stay focused on the MPS Cycle of Productivity and consistently complete Strategic Next Actions that link to and drive Meaningful Objectives, you're on your way to a much more focused, aligned, and pro-

Part One:
Laying the
Foundation for
Productivity—
Using an
Integrated
Management
System

ductive environment. This is the foundation and philosophy for the IMS that you will soon set up. The idea is for you to use your IMS to track Meaningful Objectives, Supporting Projects, and Strategic Next Actions so that you know what cycles of action must be completed to move toward accomplishing your Meaningful Objectives. Without an IMS set up this way, you will find it a challenge to continually manage this cycle.

Even if you're not on the board and cannot drive how the entire company runs, you can work at your own level and create an environment in which you can be productive and in which you can positively influence the people around you.

From one perspective, changing culture is simply a numbers game; this concept is clearly demonstrated by the 100th Monkey Phenomenon. When a critical number of people start demonstrating specific behavioral changes, there is a tipping point at which the culture will flip such that everyone demonstrates these behaviors. This phenomenon shows that when enough of us are aware of something, all of us become aware of it. This type of change starts with one person. Perhaps you are that person...

What Gets in the Way of Productivity?

Productivity sure sounds easy. All you have to do is stay focused on your Meaningful Objectives and complete the associated Strategic Next Actions. Our clients stare in amazement at the MPS Cycle of Productivity and say, "Wow! That sure sounds easy. So, why does it seem so hard in real life?"

The truth is, of course, that our lives are never that simple! When we're working with a company, community, or family, we have many internal and external distractions and obstacles that make it more challenging to maintain focus on the MPS Cycle of Productivity. Take a look at the following list and see if you can relate to any of these obstacles and distractions.

- Unrelenting interruptions
- Unclear and confusing objectives
- Too many objectives
- Changing and conflicting priorities
- Too many fingers in the pie
- Unexpected fire drills
- Overwhelming volume of information

Part One:
Laying the
Foundation for
Productivity—
Using an
Integrated
Management
System

Take Back Your Life!

- Technical problems
- Not being able to say no
- Not having the right training to do the job
- Miscommunications and misunderstandings
- Lack of focus and alignment
- People who don't do what they say they'll do

When you add four or five of these distractions and obstacles into your day, achieving productivity becomes challenging. It's easy to get sidetracked, to react, to lose focus, to spin your wheels. Many people say some of the following statements in response to obstacles:

- "I don't have the time to slow down and think about what I'm doing. I just need to get it done!"
- "Getting my objectives done is my night job!"
- "I don't have time to be productive!"

Do any of these sound familiar? When you are stuck at this level of distraction, you are operating from the old model of coping and surviving, which is very distinct from the new model of causing, creating, and thriving. The key is to stay focused on the new model and to use your IMS to help you do this.

Introducing the Integrated Management System

An Integrated Management System (IMS) supports you in maintaining your focus so that you can successfully achieve your Meaningful Objectives and avoid getting caught up in distractions or obstacles. Your IMS tracks and manages all of your relevant personal and business information in one central location. You use it to record your Unifying Goals, Meaningful Objectives, Supporting Projects (Tasks, Subtasks), and Strategic Next Actions. With this data in a central location, you can manage your objectives, evaluate where you are against the plan, and determine what needs to happen to keep you moving forwarding the MPS Cycle of Productivity. The system is centralized and flexible, tracks both your personal and business information, and can synchronize with your smart phone or personal digital assistant (PDA) so that all of this information is available 24 hours a day, seven days a week.

Part One:
Laying the
Foundation for
Productivity—
Using an
Integrated
Management
System

Setting up an IMS in Microsoft Outlook is an enlightening process for most of our clients. Although they've been using Outlook for many years, they never realized the value it could offer. After you set up an IMS, we're certain you'll be extremely happy with the results. Your life will be more organized, and you'll feel more focused, relaxed, and in control of your world.

The Integrated Management System consists of three separate systems, as shown in Figure 2-3:

- Collecting System
- Reference System
- Action System

A vision without a task is but a dream; a task without a vision is drudgery; a vision and a task together is the hope of the world.
—**From a church in Sussex, England**

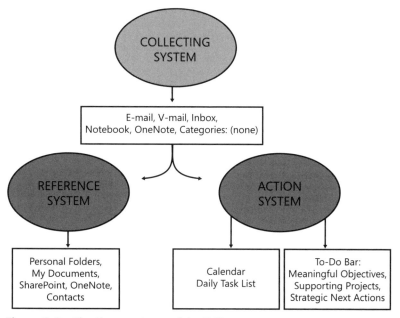

Figure 2-3   The three systems of the IMS.

Collecting System

A Collecting System is made up of a series of **approved Collecting Points** where you and others place your commitments and communications. Collecting Points are physical locations that you use to capture your actions and meeting notes, and where other people drop off Tasks or information for you. Typical approved Collecting Points are your e-mail program, voice mail, and a paper inbox. Sometime during the day, you must stop what you're doing to process the information in these Collecting Points and make deci-

Part One:
Laying the
Foundation for
Productivity—
Using an
Integrated
Management
System

Take Back Your Life!

sions about what to do with each item. You can throw the item in the trash can, store it in your Reference System, or store it in your Action System. You'll learn, in more detail, how to set up an effective Collecting System in Chapter 4.

The Reference System

The Reference System enables you to track information that *does not require action* but that you want to keep to access later. You store this type of reference information in Contacts, Microsoft Office OneNote, folders you create in the Folder List in Outlook, your Microsoft Windows Documents folder, or on a Windows SharePoint Services site. You'll learn how to set up an effective Reference System in Chapter 10.

The Action System

The Action System is made up of your Meaningful Objectives, Supporting Projects, 1:1 Meetings, and Strategic Next Actions. You track this type of information in the Outlook To-do List, Calendar, and preview pane list. You'll learn in more detail how to set up an effective Action System in Chapter 7.

Introducing ControlPanel

ControlPanel is a particular arrangement of panes that you create in the Outlook window, as shown in Figure 2-4. The ControlPanel gives you immediate access to your IMS. Most of our clients open Outlook to their Inbox. We suggest you open Outlook to the ControlPanel so that you can consistently monitor where you're going, ensuring you are headed directly toward your Meaningful Objectives.

Much like the instrument panel in the cockpit of a plane, which shows you all the parameters associated with flying, the ControlPanel in your IMS shows you the data you need to review to achieve your objectives effectively.

To set up the arrangement of windows we call the ControlPanel, first make sure the vertical Navigation Pane is open on the left side of the Outlook window. If it's not visible, click View on the standard toolbar, click on Navigation Pane, and select Normal. Then, click the Calendar icon in the lower left corner.

Chapter Two: **Defining Productivity**

Part One:
Laying the
Foundation for
Productivity—
Using an
Integrated
Management
System

To complete setting up the ControlPanel, follow these steps:

1. On the View menu, select To-Do Bar, and then select Normal.

2. On the View menu, select To-Do Bar, and then clear the Appointments option.

3. If the Daily Task List is not showing below the Calendar, on the View menu, select Daily Task List, and then select Normal.

4. On the View menu, select Week to see the calendar as shown in Figure 2-4.

5. The final step is to click the folder icon in the bottom left to display the Folder List.

Now your Outlook window should look just like the one shown in Figure 2-4.

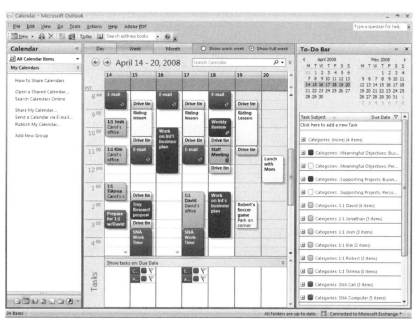

Figure 2-4 The ControlPanel shows your Integrated Management System.

On the far right of the ControlPanel is the To-Do Bar, in the middle is the Calendar, and below the Calendar is the Daily Task List. Together these views make up the Action System. In Figure 2-4, notice that Carol Philips, a sales manager from Lucerne Publishing, has grouped her tasks into multiple categories in the To-Do Bar: Meaningful Objectives, Supporting Projects, 1:1 Meetings, and Strategic Next Actions. On the left is Carol's Reference System, where she tracks all of her reference information.

Part One:
Laying the
Foundation for
Productivity—
Using an
Integrated
Management
System

Take Back Your Life!

The ControlPanel enables Carol to see her Action and Reference Systems simultaneously. This view gives her access in one place to the information she needs to do her job, which is extremely powerful.

Introducing the ControlPanel with the MPS Cycle of Productivity

In Figure 2-5, you can see Carol's IMS with the MPS Cycle of Productivity overlaid on top of it.

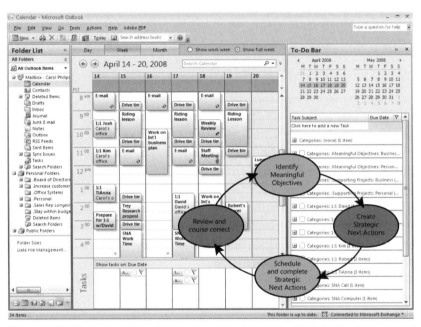

Figure 2-5 The ControlPanel helps you to maintain the MPS Cycle of Productivity.

Step one: Her Meaning Objectives are categorized at the top of her To-Do Bar, followed by her Supporting Projects. Step two: her Strategic Next Actions are categorized at the bottom of her To-Do Bar. Step Three: Carol can prioritize her Strategic Next Actions, and then schedule them onto her Calendar to complete them. Step four: Carol can review on-course/off-course feedback to ensure she is moving toward her objectives effectively. This ControlPanel enables Carol to maintain the MPS Cycle of Productivity, ensuring she successfully accomplishes her objectives.

Part One:
Laying the
Foundation for
Productivity—
Using an
Integrated
Management
System

Bringing It All Together

Part Three of this book guides you through setting up your IMS and shows you how to integrate the MPS Cycle of Productivity and the MPS Action Hierarchy Model. As you work in your IMS, you'll be pleasantly surprised at how much your productivity will improve, and as you "course-correct" when your objectives don't support balance, you'll discover how much the quality of your life can increase. The key to all of this is to take the time to set up an IMS and use it consistently. Like any change in your life, it requires focus and discipline, similar to what is required to go to the gym. You won't get fit in one workout. It takes an unfailing focus, week by week, to make that happen!

The unexpected benefit of an IMS is that when you turn it off, you get to turn off this part of your world, enabling you to really "be" in your life instead of just "doing" in your life. You can enjoy counting rain drops, watching the snow fall, and spending time with your family and friends. Remember, the purpose of an IMS is to help you create an environment in which you can increase productivity and move from the old model of coping and surviving to the new model of thriving, creating, and causing your dreams to come true.

Productivity: completing Strategic Next Actions that link directly to and drive your Meaningful Objectives.

We are what we repeatedly do. Excellence, then, is not an act, but a habit.
—**Aristotle**

Part One:
Laying the
Foundation for
Productivity—
Using an
Integrated
Management
System

Chapter Three

Creating an Integrated Management System

Part One:
Laying the
Foundation for
Productivity—
Using an
Integrated
Management
System

Setting up your Integrated Management System (IMS) consists of three distinct phases, which we refer to as the Three Phases for Creating an Integrated Management System:

- Phase 1: Collecting
- Phase 2: Processing and Organizing
- Phase 3: Prioritizing and Planning

In this chapter, we give you a brief overview of each phase so that you'll understand its purpose, what you can expect to learn, and how it will help you build your IMS. Don't be fooled by the seeming simplicity of these phases. We've spent thousands of hours in discussions, working one on one with clients, and monitoring and measuring results to create something that moves from the complexity of managing life to the simplicity of managing a system.

We will also discuss whether or not you want to integrate your personal life into your IMS or keep it separate. This is a question you'll want to answer sooner rather than later because it will impact how you develop your System.

We believe that by setting up and using an IMS you'll be able to make your life more cohesive and recapture valuable time, energy, and focus. Most important, you will be able to use your system to assist you in moving from the old model of coping and surviving to the new model of thriving, creating, and causing your dreams to come true.

Part One:
Laying the
Foundation for
Productivity—
Using an
Integrated
Management
System

Phase 1: Collecting

The purpose of the Collecting Phase is to assist you in developing a seamless **Collecting System** that will capture all of your communications, commitments, and agreements. This phase also helps you manage interruptions, assisting you in reducing the number and improving the quality of those you receive. And last, you'll complete an exercise called "clearing the mind" in which you transfer the actions from your head into the Categories: (none) section of your To-do List, assisting you in keeping more of your agreements and maintaining your integrity.

Setting Up a Collecting System

A Collecting System is made up of a number of approved **Collecting Points**. Collecting Points are physical locations where you gather actions, communications, meeting notes, and where colleagues or family members can drop off tasks and information for you. Typical approved Collecting Points are e-mail, voice mail, and paper inboxes both at home and at work. Sounds simple enough; however, it's not quite that straightforward in real life!

When we ask clients how many Collecting Points (buckets) they have on average, they say four to six. However, after closer scrutiny, we find that it's really more like 25 to 35—which is a big difference! Having this many buckets is a bit more complex and confusing. You may not realize it, but your car seat, the kitchen table, your pockets, and even the notes you scribble on the back of an envelope are all places where you're collecting information and to-do's. Discovering how many Collecting Points you actually have can be an eye-opener, not to mention a wee bit overwhelming! When you have a large number of Collecting Points, it's difficult to remember where you put things, and you can spend considerable time sorting through piles to find critical items.

By deciding which buckets are the most useful and practical, you can consolidate your 25 to 30 locations down to 5 to 10. The result is a Collecting System that will simplify your life and ensure that you're capturing all relevant communications, commitments, and reference information. This makes it easier for you to focus on keeping your agreements and moving toward your Meaningful Objectives.

Part One:
Laying the
Foundation for
Productivity—
Using an
Integrated
Management
System

Managing Interruptions

In this section, we create more awareness for you about interruptions and how to improve them successfully for yourself and for your team. We look at why you get so many and assess how to create an environment where you can reduce the number and improve the quality of the ones you do get.

We believe that interruptions are a necessary part of your personal and business life; however, how big a part do they need to play and are you aware of the impact they're having? Too many interruptions cause you and your team to work longer hours to get your work done, and over time the environment becomes reactive as you deal with last-minute issues when staff expect you to drop everything.

We all need to deal with interruptions; however, we recommend you work with your staff to handle them more effectively and, as a result, reduce the volume, create a more proactive environment, and get more focused work done during the day.

Clearing the Mind Exercise

Even as you're reading this book, you've probably wandered off into the recesses of your mind, thinking about actions you have to do. True? This indicates that you're collecting actions in your head—ah-ha!—another very popular, "unapproved" Collecting Point!

Most of our clients are completely unaware of how much they're tracking in their heads and the kind of impact this has on their effectiveness. When you're busy remembering to print handouts, download voice mail, and order Valentine's Day gifts, it's hard to focus on anything else. You're in your head recalling what you have to do! We hear clients mumbling to themselves, "Don't talk to me now; I'm trying to remember something!" That's a bit dramatic, but I think you understand the point. It's hard to be present when you're in your head focusing on your to-do lists.

In Chapter 6, you complete the "clearing the mind" exercise in which you download all the commitments you've got floating around in your brain and capture them in the Categories: (none) section of the To-Do List in Microsoft Office Outlook. Most clients experience a huge sense of relief when they get everything out of their minds and captured into a leak-proof Collection System. Some of our clients tell us they even sleep better at night.

Part One:
Laying the
Foundation for
Productivity—
Using an
Integrated
Management
System

The Collecting Phase is designed to help you set up a leak proof Collection System and to routinely and effectively transfer the contents of your Collecting Points into your Integrated Management System. This is a very empowering phase and ultimately makes it easier for you to manage your commitments and agreements while maintaining balance.

Phase 2: Processing and Organizing

The Processing and Organizing Phase has two purposes. The first is to set up your Action and Reference Systems to support you in effectively tracking your commitments and agreements. The second is to help you understand how to use the McGhee Productivity Solutions (MPS) Workflow Model to make rapid and effective decisions, empty your Collection Points, and effectively transfer data into your IMS.

By the end of this phase, you'll have completed building your IMS. Your system will contain all relevant Meaningful Objectives, Supporting Projects, Strategic Next Actions, reference materials, and your e-mail, voice mail, and paper inboxes will be empty. Picture that in your mind—a system that supports your objectives in which everything is empty and organized in one centralized system that you can access 24/7.

Setting Up Your Action and Reference Systems

It doesn't take a lot of difference to make a difference.
—**Sally McGhee**

In Chapters 7 and 9 we show you how to set up and use your Action System. This system enables you to centralize all your actions into the To-Do Bar using Planning and Action categories so you can easily begin to organize, and plan your tasks onto the calendar. Figure 3-1 shows you Carol Philips' To-Do List.

Chapter Three: Creating an Integrated Management System

Part One:
Laying the
Foundation for
Productivity—
Using an
Integrated
Management
System

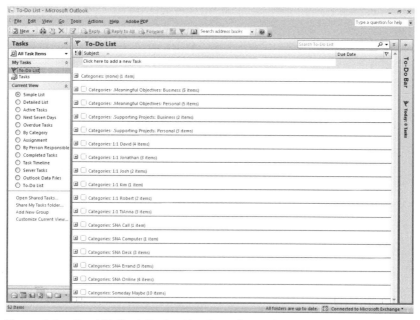

Figure 3-1   Carol Philips's To-Do List shows her tasks categorized.

In Chapter 10, we show you how to set up an effective Reference System that supports you in remaining focused on your objectives and how to clearly distinguish action material from reference material. With a more effective Reference System, our clients can reduce finding and filing time from 50 minutes a day to 10 minutes a day, which is a substantial time saving.

Introducing the MPS Workflow Model

The Workflow Model, shown in Figure 3-2, helps you to process and organize information from your Collecting Points into your Action and Reference Systems and supports you in making rapid decisions that drive toward your objectives.

The Processing and Organizing Phase consists of two individual parts: one, processing, and two, organizing. They are intrinsically linked but separate. Processing helps you decide what to do with items in your Collecting Points, and organizing helps you decide where to put the items in your Action or Reference System so that you can access them easily when needed.

Part One:
Laying the
Foundation for
Productivity—
Using an
Integrated
Management
System

Take Back Your Life!

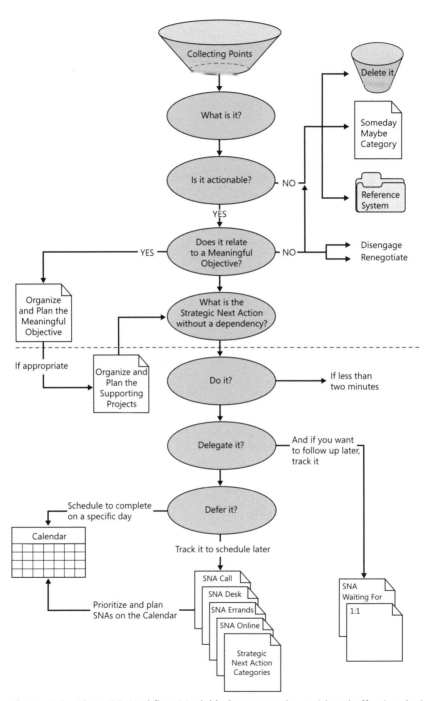

Figure 3-2 The MPS Workflow Model helps you make rapid and effective decisions, enabling you to empty your Collection Points regularly and stay focused on your Meaningful Objectives.

Part One:
Laying the
Foundation for
Productivity—
Using an
Integrated
Management
System

Let's look at an example to distinguish these two parts. When you open an e-mail message in your Inbox, you need to decide *what* to do with it; otherwise, it ends up staying in the Inbox. If you decide to write a proposal for Alpine Ski House, you then must decide *where* you're going to capture that task in your Action System so that you can complete it. Part one—deciding what to do with it—and part two—deciding where you're going to put it.

As you can see in Figure 3-2, processing is a series of questions represented by ovals. These questions help you decide what to do with the contents of your Collecting Points. Organizing is a series of files and categories, represented by rectangles, which help you decide where to store your information. The Workflow Model assists you to make immediate and meaningful decisions, enabling you to empty your Collecting Points and supporting the successful completion of all your objectives, both personal and work related.

Making decisions is a critical component of being productive, and the MPS Workflow Model is designed to help you make those decisions. In today's electronic world, with anywhere from 60 to 250 e-mail messages flooding your Inbox each day, you will find yourself confronted with lots of decisions. There is a contradiction here: you need to make rapid decisions, but you also need to pause to give yourself time to make effective decisions. We like to remind our clients that "you have to slow down to speed up." *We believe strongly that it's in these pauses that effective decisions are made.* When you allow the "noise" in your environment to drive you, what gets lost in the shuffle is effective decision making and, therefore, effective action.

The Processing and Organizing Phase is designed to assist you to process and organize information from your Collecting Points into your Action and Reference Systems so that you can stay focused on achieving your objectives and maintaining work-life balance.

Phase 3: Prioritizing and Planning

The purpose of the Prioritizing and Planning Phase is to prioritize and plan your tasks on the Calendar, enabling you to achieve your Meaningful Objectives and stay in balance. This phase has two parts: the first is learning how to use the Calendar as a prioritization tool, ensuring you're realistic about what you can and cannot do so you can maintain your integrity. The second is learning how to maintain your IMS so that it is continuously up-to-date and accurate. With an up-to-date IMS, you can effectively course correct to stay on track with your professional and personal objectives. Both of these parts are managed by an activity called the Weekly Review.

Part One:
Laying the
Foundation for
Productivity—
Using an
Integrated
Management
System

Take Back Your Life!

Prioritizing and Planning Activities onto the Calendar

In this chapter, we introduce the concept of using your Calendar as a valuable prioritization tool that can support you in keeping your agreements and maintaining integrity. When you put a task on the Calendar, it brings that task into reality and ensures you focus on it. Our statistics prove that **there's a 75 percent greater chance that you'll complete a task if it's on your Calendar rather than on your Task list.** Therefore, it's essential to use the Calendar to prioritize and plan all of your activities. To do this, you first learn how to create a Baseline Calendar that ensures you have the necessary routine appointments tracked to keep you moving toward your goals.

Introducing the Weekly Review

The Weekly Review helps you keep your IMS up-to-date and accurate.. When your system is up-to-date, you can review progress toward objectives and implement the appropriate course corrections to stay on track. As you may know, an airplane is technically on track only 25 percent of the time, the pilot has to course correct 75 percent of the time to ensure the plane reaches is destination. The Weekly Review is your time to course correct and ensure your objectives are accomplished, it is your time to be accountable for what you said you would do.

This sounds simple enough. Well, it is. And not only that; it's powerful and saves time and resources. However, making sure you do it every week so that it becomes a habit can be challenging for some. Our clients get so caught up in the day-to-day stuff, it's hard for them to pull themselves away from the keyboard to update their systems and look at the big picture.

We use an analogy here that might be helpful in understanding the Weekly Review and why it is so critical. For a moment, imagine an airport. The control tower gives you a 30,000-foot view; using the radar system you can see how many planes you have in the air at one time and how best to guide them to take off and land safely. The tarmac gives you the ground-level view: planes are being guided into gates, trucks are loading bags and transferring them to baggage claim, and customers are picking up their bags.

From the control tower, you manage your Meaningful Objectives and through course correction guide them to take off and land safely. The tarmac is where you are completing Strategic Next Actions and working on more tactical activities. When you are on the ground moving bags, it is often hard to pull yourself away to go to the control tower and manage the

Part One:
Laying the
Foundation for
Productivity—
Using an
Integrated
Management
System

30,000-foot view. When customers are complaining about missing suit-cases, their issues appear so urgent. However, when you compare a lost bag with a plane crash, the two are just not equal.

That about sums up the Weekly Review: with it, you can manage your objectives so that they land safely, and to do this you have to embrace the discipline of pulling yourself away from the baggage claim area to move to the control tower to make sure your objectives are on track so they can be completed successfully.

The most important system in the control tower is the radar equipment; it has to be accurate for you to guide your planes to safety. Your IMS is no different, it has to be up-to-date and accurate for you to guide your objectives to completion; otherwise, it could be equally as disastrous.

Completing a Weekly Review does take discipline and a conscious, consistent focus; however, after it becomes habit, you'll wonder how you ever operated without one. Our clients feel more focused, controlled, and motivated after completing a Weekly Review.

The ControlPanel, shown in Figure 3-3, is the view you'll use to complete a Weekly Review. It's much like the cockpit of an airplane, showing you all the dials to ensure you reach your destination safely. The Calendar and To-Do Bar on the right give you access to your Action System, showing your Meaningful Objectives, Supporting Projects, 1:1 Meetings, and Strategic Next Actions. The Folder List on the left gives you access to your Reference System, showing all of your e-mail and other folders. With this view, you can see everything you have to do in one place, which makes course correcting, prioritizing, and planning much easier.

Part One:
Laying the
Foundation for
Productivity—
Using an
Integrated
Management
System

Take Back Your Life!

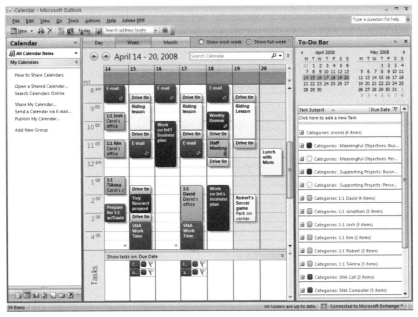

Figure 3-3   You conduct your Weekly Review in the ControlPanel view.

In Chapter 12, we talk in detail about prioritizing and planning. This is the last of the three phases for creating an Integrated Management System, and it helps you maintain an experience of control, focus, and balance.

Integrating Personal and Business into One System

We realize that for some of you this is a very sensitive topic. Many of our clients have successfully integrated their personal and business lives and now couldn't imagine it otherwise, while others are extremely uncomfortable about mixing the two. We respect both points of view.

Your IMS is built around whether you integrate personal and business, and therefore to move forward you must resolve this question before you start to set up your IMS, which you do in the next chapter.

Integrating Your Personal Life into Your System

We recommend that you do integrate your personal and business lives into one Integrated Management System because it will save you time and make work/life balance a lot easier to manage. Many of our clients have no con-

Chapter Three: **Creating an Integrated Management System**

Part One:
Laying the
Foundation for
Productivity—
Using an
Integrated
Management
System

cerns about mixing the two; however, some do and their concerns relate to personal beliefs, technology, and company policies.

Personal Beliefs

When Sally was in her early twenties, she was told repeatedly not to combine personal and business. It was drilled into her that it would be inappropriate and unprofessional. However, the working environment today is very, very different from the way it was 25 years ago. In those days, her wardrobe was also filled with suits and pantyhose, and now it's filled with jeans and socks! This took her a while to adjust to. Integrating personal and business is just another level of adjustment and may also take a little while.

Technology

Clients often get a bit stuck figuring out how to integrate the two digitally. With the introduction of Pocket PC and Smartphone devices that you can carry wherever you go, and that synchronize with Outlook, it starts to make more sense to combine personal and business information. For instance, with these devices, when you are out shopping, you have immediate access to your grocery list. At the video store, you have access to your DVD list. If you need to call a doctor while you are at work, the phone number is in your Contacts. If you need a baby-sitter, the phone number is also in your Contacts. Personal appointments and personal contacts can be marked as private so that others who view your Calendar and Contacts cannot see them.

There are so many ways to use Outlook to integrate personal and business and still keep your personal life separate and private. Let's face it, you're going to do personal activities at work—making doctor appointments, scheduling car services, and calling to clarify insurance claims—it's a lot easier to manage all this using one central system instead of having two systems. You'll find that your life will be simpler if you integrate personal and business. Life itself is integrated, and so having a system that reflects that is a blessing.

Company Policies

Making sure you feel comfortable integrating personal when you are at work is helpful. We've consulted with a variety of corporations and most of them allow employees to integrate personal data (personal e-mail messaging, personal contacts, personal calendar appointments, and personal folders), as long as the content is appropriate. Be sure to find out what your

Part One:
Laying the
Foundation for
Productivity—
Using an
Integrated
Management
System

company guidelines are. Knowing that your company supports you in combining the two helps make the decision a lot easier. Most of the time, our clients just need to know for sure they have permission to integrate their personal data, and after they have it, they are gung-ho to include it.

Keeping Your Personal Life Separate

In some situations, you may need to keep your personal data separate from your work data, causing you to have two systems. When company policies stipulate this and are serious about enforcing such a policy, then you have to cooperate. We recommend that if you have a desktop or laptop at home, you run Outlook on it and use it as your personal system exclusively. You can either print out the data that you need daily or purchase a Pocket PC and synchronize it with your personal system. You'll then use your work computer or laptop for business only and carry your Pocket PC for your personal life.

Some clients carry a portable paper management system for their personal information and keep their computer and Pocket PC for work use only. We recommend staying entirely electronic rather than working with paper because our daily lives are increasingly moving into our work world. Of course, over time you will discover which system works best for you.

The key with two systems is to keep them simple, keep the distinctions clear, and be disciplined about what goes where. We believe that in the future there will be increased security embedded in software that enables us to feel more comfortable including our personal lives in our IMS. Most companies support this now, and it may be only a matter of time before more of the corporate world does see the value of integrating personal and business because it does simplify part of the complexities of managing our lives in balance.

Small Things Make a Big Impact

Most of the changes we recommend in this book are small and aren't difficult to implement—but they create a big difference. For example, we're sure you've opened an e-mail message, decided you didn't want to deal with it, and closed it back in the Inbox. This is a small thing that takes seconds to do. If you repeat the same thing over and over, it doesn't take long before you have hundreds, or perhaps thousands, of e-mail messages in your Inbox. This is an example of how "small things done consistently in strategic places create major impact." Conversely, if every time you open an e-mail

Part One:
Laying the
Foundation for
Productivity—
Using an
Integrated
Management
System

message you make a decision about what to do with it and where to put it, you can immediately remove it from the Inbox and dramatically reduce your Inbox size. This is equally as powerful as the previous example, but with more positive results.

There's no way you can make all the changes we suggest in this book in one sitting. Modifying behaviors takes time for all of us. However, you can choose two or three changes that would make the biggest impact and focus on them first.

The remaining chapters are dedicated to assisting you in completing the Three Phases for Creating an Integrated Management System so that you can effectively set up your IMS. Creating the system is the most time-consuming part, but once it's set up and you've entered all of your Action and Reference information, you'll find that managing the system is actually quite simple and will quickly become a habit and an effective part of your life.

Small things done
consistently in
strategic places
create major
impact.
—**Unknown
author**

Tools You Need to Get Started

To get started on the Three Phases for Creating an Integrated Management System, make sure you have the following set up and available:

- We recommend using the latest version of Outlook, Microsoft Office Outlook 2007. However, Outlook 2003, Outlook 2002, Outlook 2000, and Outlook 98 will work just fine. The book's screen images show Outlook 2007, but you can still set up your IMS in an older version of Outlook. Some of the instructions will just be slightly different.

- Ensure that your e-mail is being downloaded directly into Outlook.

- We recommend that you use some type of personal digital assistant (PDA) or smartphone and ensure that you can synchronize your information on the device with Outlook and categorize your tasks. You may need to install third-party software such as Power Tasks from Developer One (*www.developerone.com*) to categorize your tasks on your PDA or smartphone. This book's examples use the Pocket PC or smartphone. (You can purchase an inexpensive PDA or smartphone that synchronizes with Outlook on eBay.)

Part One:
Laying the
Foundation for
Productivity—
Using an
Integrated
Management
System

Take Back Your Life!

■ Verify your corporate policies allow you to store personal and business information in Outlook. It is *essential* to know if you can incorporate your personal data into Outlook. We recommend that you integrate the two to make your life simpler and to help maintain work/life balance.

Part Two

Creating an Integrated Management System— The Collecting Phase

Part Two:
Creating an
Integrated
Management
System—The
Collecting Phase

Chapter Four
Setting Up Your Collecting System

Chapter Four: **Setting Up Your Collecting System**

Part Two:
Creating an
Integrated
Management
System—The
Collecting Phase

The first step in the Collecting Phase is developing a leak-proof Collecting System so that you can effortlessly capture all of your communications, commitments, and agreements. A Collecting System is made up of a series of approved Collecting Points. Collecting Points are physical locations where you gather your tasks, reminders, and meeting notes, and where colleagues or family members can drop off actions and information for you. Typical approved Collecting Points are e-mail, voice mail, paper notepads, and paper inboxes. The benefits of this phase are simplification, an increased sense of well-being, and a greater experience of personal control.

Identifying Your Current Collecting Points

To create an effective Collecting System, you first need to become aware of how many and what type of Collecting Points you're currently using, and then evaluate if your current system is really working for you.

Before we start, let us ask you a question: "If you were to guess how many Collecting Points you have, how many do you think it would be?" Most of our clients say four or five. However, we suspect you actually have a lot more than five; let's investigate this more closely.

In Figure 4-1, you'll see lots of empty collecting boxes. Each box represents a physical or electronic **Collecting Point**. Take a moment and mentally walk through your life, from home to work, and write down as many physical places as you can think of where you're collecting information, commitments, and communications. After you know where you are collecting, you can decide if those locations are working for you. But if you don't know where you're collecting, you cannot evaluate if your system is working.

Part Two:
Creating an
Integrated
Management
System—The
Collecting Phase

Take Back Your Life!

Figure 4-1 Where are you currently capturing your commitments and agreements?

Where Are You Currently Capturing Your Commitments and Agreements?

If you run out of steam, review the following questions. They'll help you think of additional locations. It's important to identify all of your Collecting Points so that you can assess their usefulness and streamline your system.

While you're at work:

- When you're in meetings, where do you record notes and actions?

- When you get stopped in the hallway for a "drive-by" interruption, where do you capture the action?

- When your boss sends you an e-mail message asking you to "Create a product strategy," where do you track it?

- Where do you collect your paper faxes?

- When you receive an overnight delivery package, where do you put it?

- When you're in your office, where do you put actions that result from face-to-face interruptions?

While you're on a business trip:

Part Two:
Creating an
Integrated
Management
System—The
Collecting Phase

- When a client gives you a business card and asks that you call him, where do you put it?

- Where do you collect hotel and car receipts?

- When you're in baggage claim and get a great idea, where do you record it?

While you're traveling home from work:

- Where do you put the dry cleaning receipts after you drop off your laundry?

- When you answer your cell phone and a colleague needs you to call a client about a contract issue, where do you track it?

- On the radio, you hear Bruce Springsteen is coming to town, and you want tickets. Where do you record that?

- When you get a slip for a free car wash, where do you put it?

While you're at home:

- When the phone rings, and it's a message for your daughter who's not at home, where do you put the message?

- Where do you record that you've run out of breakfast cereal and need to buy more?

- Where do you make a note that the gutter is broken and needs fixing?

- Where do you put the paper mail?

- Where do you track soccer practice for your son?

- When friends show up with tickets to a ball game in three weeks, where do you store them?

In general:

- How many e-mail boxes do you have?

- How many voice mailboxes do you have?

- How many notepads do you have?

- How many calendars do you have?

Part Two:
Creating an
Integrated
Management
System—The
Collecting Phase

Take Back Your Life!

Deciding to Consolidate Your Collecting Points

After you complete this exercise, you may be surprised by the number of buckets you've identified. Most of our clients are taken aback to find themselves with 20 to 25 Collecting Points as opposed to just the four or five they thought they had. Carol Philips, a sales manager for Lucerne Publishing, said it perfectly, "Wow! That's a whole lot of buckets. I have over 26!" When you have this many Collecting Points it becomes cumbersome to keep track of your commitments and locate information easily. Your Collecting Points become unorganized and overpopulated storage points, and, in some cases, they collect dust as well as actions.

If we were to ask you, "What are the specific priorities you must complete this week?" would you be able to answer this with integrity? To answer this question you'd need to go to each of your 20 to 25 Collecting Points to identify what you needed to do. Only then would you be able to prioritize your list. Hmmm, that sounds time consuming and somewhat complicated, which leads to the question, "Does having so many Collecting Points work for you?"

Carol Philips's response was, "I need to consolidate everything. It's all too overwhelming. No wonder I can't find anything!" After our clients become aware of how many Collecting Points they're using, the realization is always the same: "I need to minimize the number of Collecting Points I have!"

I am rather like a mosquito in a nudist camp; I know what I want to do, but I don't know where to begin.
—**Stephen Bayne**

Setting Up Your Approved Collecting Points

If our clients could consolidate everything into one bucket, they would; however, for most of us that's not possible given the complexity of our lives. Nevertheless, you can funnel your information into as little as five approved Collecting Points, as shown in Figure 4-2, which is a dramatic reduction from what you now have. You might end up with a few more than five because of the duplications required to support your personal as well as your business life, but it's still less than 20 to 25.

Chapter Four: Setting Up Your Collecting System

Part Two:
Creating an
Integrated
Management
System—The
Collecting Phase

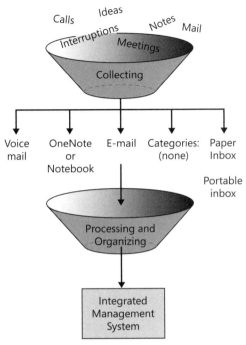

Figure 4-2 The Collecting System shows you how to funnel your information into five approved Collecting Points.

The five basic Collecting Points we suggest are the following:

1. A paper inbox and/or a portable paper inbox for road warriors

2. A digital notepad; Microsoft Office OneNote and/or a paper notepad

3. E-mail

4. The Microsoft Office Outlook To-Do List/Categories: (none)

5. Voice mail

1. Using a Paper Inbox and Portable Paper Inbox

Having a central paper inbox at work or at home is a simple concept, and it's a revelation for some of our clients.

Mary North a publishing client, loved her paper. Paper was her business, after all! She had papers on her desk, on the floor, and on her credenza. Wherever there was a flat surface, there were papers. She was having a hard time finding and filing papers with so many of them placed randomly about.

Part Two:
Creating an
Integrated
Management
System—The
Collecting Phase

Take Back Your Life!

We began our coaching by getting her a physical paper inbox a large one—labeling it clearly, and putting it on her desk. Then, we stacked all her papers in it. We took all the sticky notes off her computer monitor, removed the business cards from the window ledge, removed loose papers from her credenza, and put everything in her inbox. In 20 minutes, her office was surprisingly clean! Mary now had a pile of papers in her inbox that needed to be processed and organized into her Integrated Management System (IMS). That was her next challenge.

Mary also created two paper inboxes at home, one for herself and one for her husband. When she picked up the mail, she would distribute it either into her inbox, her husband's inbox, or the trash can. Her home inboxes weren't as professional-looking as the inboxes in her office. Mary used a Mary Stewart wicker basket with a raffia tie and a label indicating "Mary's Inbox." Mail went directly into these inboxes; it didn't go on the kitchen counter, the kitchen table, or the dining room table. Using a paper inbox is a simple process, and it makes finding papers much easier because they're in one spot rather than five different places. Mary now enjoys eating on the kitchen table without using this week's mail as a placemat!

When you first set up your physical paper inbox at home, gather up all the papers from the various locations you've been using and drop them into your inbox. This might be a bit overwhelming at first, but after you empty this Collecting Point a couple of times you'll start to trust it. Before long, using it will become second nature. The good news is that there'll be no more papers in the kitchen or on the dining room table. That's worth the price of an inbox right there!

At work, Mary put all of her paper faxes, overnight delivery envelopes, mail, and internal documents into her paper inbox on her desk, and made it was very clear where to put stuff. Many clients we work with don't have paper inboxes; they use their desk, credenza, and any flat surface they can lay their hands on. Staff members who want to drop off papers end up putting stuff on our clients' chairs or leaving sticky notes on their desks because it's the only way to call attention to these items. After clients start using a paper inbox, they need to let their staff know where it is and how to use it; otherwise, their chair and desk will continue to collect papers and sticky notes. Even though some of us are almost 100 percent digital, we're not 100 percent paper-free, and so for now, the paper inbox still has great value and helps keep a clean office.

Many times during the day Mary is not near her paper inbox, but still needs to collect bits of paper, receipts, meeting handouts, meetings notes, and

Chapter Four: **Setting Up Your Collecting System**

Part Two:
Creating an
Integrated
Management
System—The
Collecting Phase

business cards. To solve this problem, Mary created a portable paper inbox to carry with her. As you know, a quick trip to any office supply store can provide all kinds of wonderful, colorful file folders and expanding folders that you can use to create a portable inbox. Mary's portable paper inbox was an 8-by-11-inch expanding file, including four dividers, an 8 -by-11-inch notepad, and pockets for CDs, pens, and business cards. See Figure 4-3 for a diagram of Mary's portable paper inbox.

Meeting Agenda/Trip Notes   Outbox

Inbox | Receipts

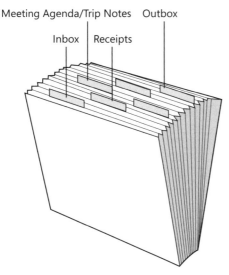

Figure 4-3   Example of Mary's portable paper inbox.

The four dividers in Mary's portable paper inbox are labeled as follows:

Inbox   Collects papers Mary receives while away from her office, business cards, meeting handouts, agendas

Meeting Agendas/Trip Notes   Stores printed handouts and agendas Mary needs to take on business trips

Receipts   Keeps all of Mary's travel receipts so that they're ready for reimbursement when she gets home

Outbox   Stores papers Mary is given that she needs to file or distribute when she gets back to her office or home

When Mary is on the road, she always carries her portable paper inbox, which she can use to capture receipts, business cards, and meeting handouts in one location. Without the portable inbox, these items would go into her wallet, her briefcase, or her back pocket, often never to be seen again! When she returns from the road or a local appointment, she simply empties

Part Two:
Creating an
Integrated
Management
System—The
Collecting Phase

Take Back Your Life!

her portable inbox into her paper inbox on her desk and distributes her outbox. Mary's portable paper inbox is then ready to take to her next meeting or on her next trip. This system ensures that all of Mary's paper items are centrally located, ready to be processed and organized into her IMS. If you don't travel much or not at all, a simple plastic file labeled "Work Inbox" stored in your briefcase helps collect papers that need to go back to your office inbox. You can also have one labeled "Personal Inbox" for your home inbox.

The paper inbox still has value today. It helps reduce alternative Collecting Points—a desk, credenza, kitchen counter—and centralizes your papers into one location. We highly recommend that you dust off your inbox or go purchase a new one. It's a simple concept that works.

2. Carrying a Paper Notebook and/or a Digital Notebook

Having one notebook, rather than multiple notebooks, is a way to instantly minimize the number of Collecting Points you have. It's also another great opportunity to visit the office supply store and pick out a very fun notepad. Nobody said you can't have fun getting organized! Microsoft OneNote users hold onto your horses, we'll be discussing OneNote in a moment!

One of our technology clients, Katie Jordan, had 12 notebooks. Yup! She had 12. No kidding! Each notebook tracked one of her 12 different projects. Note-taking worked well for Katie; however, she had one little problem. She often found herself in a project meeting with the wrong project notebook. Katie also kept track of her project tasks in her 12 notepads, and keeping her eye on them each day was becoming cumbersome. She wanted a simpler way to track notes and retrieve action steps.

We recommended that she used one notebook and take notes in chronological order. This way she'd always have the right notebook wherever she went. She'd have only one place to look up notes, and she'd have it organized by date. We also suggested that she track action steps on a separate page and use clear symbols, such as a square, to distinguish them from reference information. Then, when Katie looks back over her notes, she could easily identify the actions by their symbols and transfer them to her To-Do List. There are many ways to do this, the key is minimizing the number of notepads and creating a system to clearly distinguish reference data from actions.

Katie archived her old notebooks on her bookshelf and put elastic bands around them. She bought herself a spiral-bound notebook, and when she

Part Two:
Creating an
Integrated
Management
System—The
Collecting Phase

took notes she separated out her action items on a single page. When she returned to the office, she'd tear out the action page and, you guessed it, put it in her paper inbox. Now all her paper actions were stored in one central location ready to be processed into Outlook, leaving her notepad to track only reference information.

Sally: Noteebooks are a great place to have fun. Back in the old days, I used to have a round, bright red leather notepad and a red ink pen. I hasten to add, it was a pen that didn't leak on airplanes and it had an additional cartridge inside so that I never ran out of ink! I loved writing in a round notepad with a red ink pen.

Today many of our clients use a Tablet PC so that they can capture handwritten notes directly into OneNote. OneNote is software product that enables you to to take notes during meetings, either by writing on the screen with a pen or using your keyboard. We recommend using OneNote as part of your Reference System for several reasons; it enables you to sort information using a simple folder structure, and its search functions are incredibly powerful, making it easy to find handwritten or digital notes quickly. With the click of a button, you can transfer action items from OneNote directly into the To-Do List in Microsoft Outlook enabling you to centralize all your actions in on location in your Action System. You can also generate a Meeting Notes page in OneNote 2007 from an appointment dialog box in your calendar. These two items are linked so that you can jump from Outlook to the corresponding OneNote notes page or from the OneNote notes page to the linked Outlook appointment. This enables you to keep your notes in one location but also have them posted inside of appointments available for you to view during a meeting. These features alone make OneNote a very powerful Collection Point to add to your Collection System. We will show you the basics of OneNote in Chapter 10 Improving Your Reference System.

Clients often carry a Pocket PC that they can use to record handwritten notes. And some clients combine using a Tablet PC and a Pocket PC, eliminating the need for paper. This results in one less Collecting Point and one less item to carry around when you're traveling. I avoid working with paper, too; however, I do have small red leather Levenger notepad holder in my purse for when I need to take a quick note.

To ensure my system is seamless, when I take paper notes I drop them in my paper inbox and from there transfer them into Outlook. I have a Smart-

Part Two:
Creating an
Integrated
Management
System—The
Collecting Phase

phone, and making quick notes on the type of phone I have is not so quick. This is a choice I made when I picked out my phone; size was more important to me than getting one with a functional keypad. You need to be flexible about how you set up your system, ensuring it works for you. The key is to minimize Collecting Points and make sure you use the ones you have and empty them regularly into Outlook. This can take a little bit of customization on your part; your situations may be unique and may require individualized solutions.

Take a look at your notebooks and assess if it's possible to consolidate to one notepad and archive the rest. You could download OneNote as a way of taking digital instead of paper notes, or you could purchase a Smartphone so that you can synchronize with Outlook as well as take digital notes, or you could combine some of these solutions. Whatever your approach, make sure you customize it to work for your unique circumstances.

3. Using E-Mail

E-mail is now a mainstream Collecting Point and is a particularly effective one. It captures information for you on a continual basis, and captures the information in writing. Most of your family, friends, coworkers, and community use it, so it's a very familiar medium for all of us. The features in Microsoft Outlook that enable you to integrate e-mail messages with the To-Do List and Calendar make it especially productive. You'll learn more about using e-mail effectively in Chapter 11.

We recommend reducing your e-mail to one account rather than having multiple e-mail accounts. We've worked with clients who have as many as seven e-mail addresses; therefore, consolidating their e-mail accounts made a huge difference. If you can, the ideal situation is to combine all your accounts into one. This might not work if you're unable to integrate personal and business e-mail or if you feel uncomfortable about mixing the two. However, we think you'll be surprised to learn how many information workers now combine personal and business into one system! We're consistently taken aback by it ourselves. Company policies have relaxed on the topic of mixing personal and business items, and most companies we work with allow employees to receive "appropriate" e-mail in their Outlook Inboxes.

Sometimes having multiple Inboxes can actually support your productivity. There are always exceptions to the rule. David Simpson, a bookkeeper, has four clients. He visits them on four different days. David has an e-mail address and an Inbox for each client. David bills by the hour, and so he

Chapter Four: Setting Up Your Collecting System

Part Two:
Creating an
Integrated
Management
System—The
Collecting Phase

wants to work only on his clients' e-mail requests during the time he's working for them. On Tuesdays, he works with a health club and only wants to read and sort the club's e-mail on that day. In this instance, having separate e-mail addresses actually supports David's productivity. Another way to accomplish this would be to use Outlook Rules to set up a single "inbox" folder for each client and automatically route e-mail associated with each client into their corresponding "inbox" folders. There are always exceptions and Outlook 2007 caters nicely to many of these kinds of exceptions.

Take a look at your current e-mail accounts, and if you can consolidate them in some way—do it!

4. Using Categories: (none)

The Outlook To-Do List, and specifically the **Categories: (none)** category, is an ideal Collecting Point for capturing to-do's from your head and actions from conference calls, meetings, and voice mail. In Figure 4-4, you can see that Carol Philips has multiple categories in her To-Do List. Her first category is Categories: (none), which is the default category Carol uses as her primary digital Collecting Point. You'll set up this category later in the chapter.

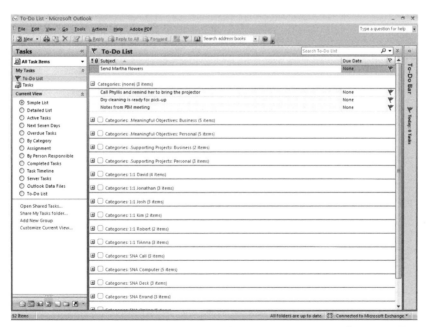

Figure 4-4 Categories: (none) in the Outlook To-Do List is an effective Collecting Point.

Carol has found that the Categories: (none) Collecting Point helps her stay more focused and assists her in capturing all of her action items instead of

Part Two:
Creating an
Integrated
Management
System—The
Collecting Phase

Take Back Your Life!

tracking them in her head. When Carol gets distracted by a mental "action reminder" while processing her e-mail, she simply types it into the To-Do List, where it's automatically placed in the Categories: (none) Collecting Point. Similarly, when her mind wanders off in meetings, she captures those thoughts in Categories: (none) as well, mentally bringing her mind back to being present.

Carol also uses a Pocket PC as well as a Tablet PC. Both of these devices run Microsoft Outlook and can be synchronized with each another. Carol captures actions into Categories: (none) using her Pocket PC just as easily as using her Tablet PC. This means that wherever Carol is, she has access to Categories: (none) and can transfer information into it. Whether you're at a hockey game or out to dinner with friends, using a Pocket PC to capture your reminders is pretty slick, not to mention practical. Whipping out your Tablet PC just isn't as handy and as cool as whipping out your Pocket PC!

We've also seen clients use Categories: (none) to assist them in emptying their voice mail. If they can't handle a message right away, they transfer the action item into their Categories: (none) Collecting Point and delete the message from their voice mailbox. This enables them to completely empty their voice mail and places the actions they can't do in the Categories: (none) Collecting Point, ready to be processed later. This helps them reduce the number of locations where they're storing action information, centralizing the collecting of actions in the To-Do List.

The mind is powerful. Left to its own devices, it can be a huge source of distraction, pulling you away from being present and taking you down the mental corridors of your thoughts. A great way to prevent this from happening is to keep emptying the to-do's from your head into Categories: (none) so that you can continue to be present in whatever you're doing.

You must configure three technical settings to set up the Categories: (none) Collecting Point properly in your To-Do List. To complete the default selections for the fields and to group by categories follow these steps:

1. Click the Tasks icon at the bottom of the Folder List.

2. Under My Tasks, click To-Do List to highlight it.

3. Right-click the Task Subject heading and select Customize Current View from the shortcut menu. Here you can choose the fields to view and group your actions by category. If you see Custom instead of Customize Current View, select Custom and be sure to follow the steps

Part Two:
Creating an
Integrated
Management
System—The
Collecting Phase

below in the section addressing Click Here to Add a New Task and showing Custom instead of Customize Current View.

4. In the Customize View dialog box, click Fields.

5. Under the heading Select Available Fields From, and choose All Task Fields from the drop-down menu.

6. In the Show These Fields In This Order area, select Priority, Attachment, and Due Date.

7. Under Select Available Fields From, choose All Mail Fields from the drop-down menu.

8. Select Task Subject and Flag Status, then add to the Show These Fields In This Order area. Rearrange your fields so they're listed in the order shown in Figure 4-5.

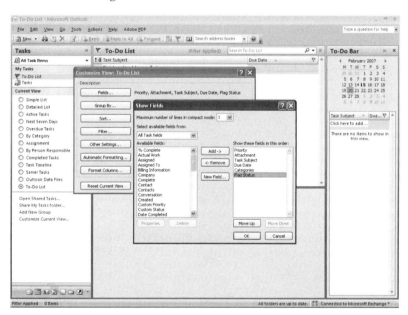

Figure 4-5   Selecting the To-Do List fields.

9. Click OK to return to the Customize View dialog box.

10. In the Customize View dialog box, click Group By.

11. Click the drop-down menu, and select Categories from the Group Items By section, and in the bottom right-hand corner in the Expand/Collapse Defaults list, select All Collapsed from the drop-down menu, as shown in Figure 4-6.

Part Two:
Creating an
Integrated
Management
System—The
Collecting Phase

Take Back Your Life!

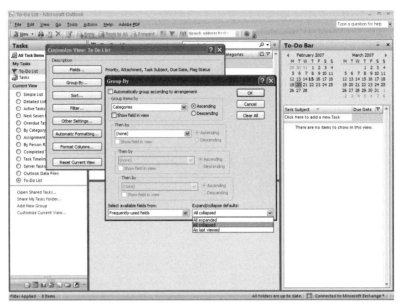

Figure 4-6   Grouping Tasks by categories

12.   Click OK.

13.   Click OK again.

To attach contacts to Tasks, follow these steps:

1.   On the toolbar, select Tools, and then click Options.

2.   Under the Contacts And Notes heading, click the Contact Options button.

3.   Under the Contact Linking heading, select Show Contact Linking On All Forms, as shown in Figure 4-7.

Chapter Four: Setting Up Your Collecting System

Part Two:
Creating an
Integrated
Management
System—The
Collecting Phase

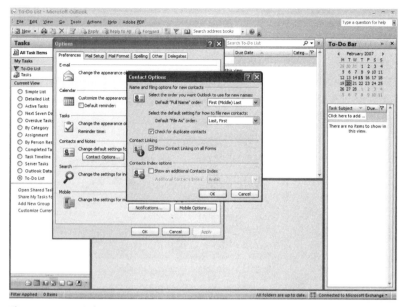

Figure 4-7   Linking contacts to your Tasks in the To-Do List

4.   Click OK.

5.   Click OK again.

At the top of the To-Do List you'll see a Task Subject heading, and under this heading is a field with the words Click Here To Add A New Task. If you don't see the words Click Here To Add A New Task or you see Custom instead of Customize Current View, follow these steps:

1.   Right-click the Task Subject column heading and select Custom or Customize Current View from the shortcut menu.

2.   Click the Other Settings button.

3.   In the Column Headings And Rows section, select the Show "New Item" Row option, as shown in Figure 4-8.

4.   If you get Custom instead of Customize Current view, be sure the "Always use single-line layout" is selected as show in Figure 4-8.

Part Two:
Creating an
Integrated
Management
System—The
Collecting Phase

Take Back Your Life!

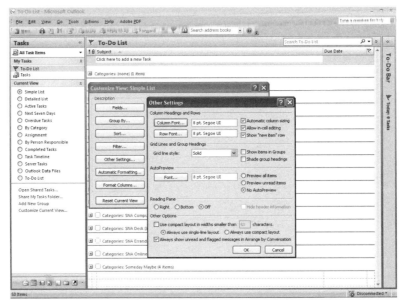

Figure 4-8 Showing "Click here to add a new Task"and "Customize Current View"

5. Click OK twice to return to the To-Do List.

Click the words Click Here To Add A New Task and type **IMPROVING PRODUCTIVITY**. Press the Enter key, and the Task will automatically show up under the Categories: (none) in the To-Do List, as shown in Figure 4-9. Notice it also automatically shows up in the To-Do Bar on the right.

Chapter Four: Setting Up Your Collecting System

Part Two:
Creating an
Integrated
Management
System—The
Collecting Phase

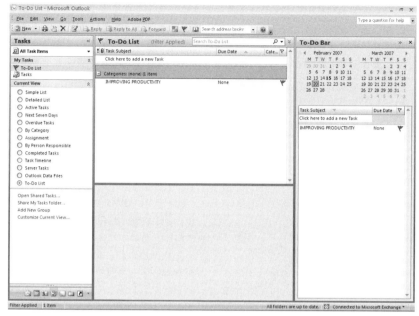

Figure 4-9　Creating an IMPROVING PRODUCTIVITY task in Categories: (none).

You will use the IMPROVING PRODUCTIVITY task later in this chapter, and so please keep it in the To-Do List for now.

After you have set up Categories: (none), you can start to use it as a Collecting Point right away. When you reach for a sticky note, put the pack out of reach and instead type in Categories: (none). When you are in a meeting with your PC and have a new idea, reach for Categories: (none); it's simple, quick, and easy.

5. Using Voice Mail

Voice mail is another wonderful, mainstream Collecting Point. Some of us have multiple voice mailboxes, and so there's a lot of opportunity to consolidate. Chris Cannon, one of our clients, had five voice mailboxes.

- A land line at home
- A land line at work
- A cell phone
- A pager
- A client land line on site

Part Two:
Creating an
Integrated
Management
System—The
Collecting Phase

Take Back Your Life!

Chris liked that his clients, family, and friends knew how to get hold of him. However, he was getting tired of downloading so many voice mailboxes. We discussed with Chris if he really needed five voice mailboxes and how we could consolidate them.

Chris realized that as long as his clients, family, and friends knew how to get hold of him, no one would mind using one number over another. He bit the bullet and consolidated to two voice mailboxes. He eliminated the client landline and the pager. He directed his work landline to his cell phone. (Redirecting a landline to a cell phone can also be a great way to eliminate one more Collecting Point.) He ended up with a personal land line and a cell phone voice mailbox.

You can also use voice mail not only to capture messages from others, but to capture your own to-do's. When you're in the car and remember you need to send Annie updated Microsoft Office PowerPoint slides, you can't safely write down a reminder or type it into your laptop, but you can call yourself and leave a message on your own voice mail system. This ensures that you get the information out of your head and put it into one of your approved Collecting Points to be processed later.

Some companies now have their voice mail transferred to their e-mail in a system called **unified messaging**. Unified messaging helps eliminate the land line at work, condensing two points into one. It takes your voice mail messages and directs them to your e-mail Inbox. When you open a specific e-mail message, you can hear your voice mail messages directly through your computer's speakers. Some clients use a headset for more private messages.

Consolidating voice mailboxes is another quick solution to reducing your overall list of approved Collecting Points. As you can tell, it is relatively easy to make a difference in this area, reducing your 20 to 25 buckets down to 10 or fewer.

You Are Not a Collecting Point

When you review the five key Collecting Points shown in Figure 4-2, you may notice that there isn't a Collecting Point with your name on it. Guess what? You're not an approved collecting bucket! Most people, however, spend a considerable amount of time during the day collecting information from various kinds of interruptions. In other words, they're using themselves as a "human Collecting Point."

Chapter Four: Setting Up Your Collecting System

Part Two:
Creating an
Integrated
Management
System—The
Collecting Phase

All of us get interrupted throughout the day, not only by people, but by technology—the ding of an e-mail message arriving in the Inbox, the ring of a cell phone, and the buzz of a pager. When we ask clients, "When do you do your best work?" most respond, "First thing in the morning and last thing at night." In other words, clients aren't getting their real work done in the office. Perhaps you've had the same experience. In Chapter 5, we address how you can successfully manage interruptions so that you can stop being a Collecting Point!

Implementing Your Collecting System

Carol Philips reduced her list of 26 buckets to 7 approved Collecting Points. She now uses her inbox at home, her inbox at work, her Categories: (none), OneNote, two voice mailboxes, and e-mail. She hopes to eliminate another voice mailbox soon and use only her cell phone for all her calls. That would drop her Collecting Points to six. It's a whole lot easier for Carol to manage six Collecting Points than the more than 26 she started with! The key to consolidating Collecting Points is to decide which ones you want to use, set them up, and consolidate all your other locations into these approved Collecting Points. Test them to make sure they work given your unique circumstances, empty them regularly into Outlook, and train people around you to use them.

After setting up her Collecting System, Carol commented, "My life is much simpler as a result. Gone are the days of collecting on my desk, fridge, dining room table, sticky notes, multiple notepads, my car dashboard, a white board, shelves, cupboards, floors, my briefcase, and in my head. From more than 26 to seven Collecting Points... what's not to like?"

To set up her approved Collecting Points, Carol purchased the following tools:

- Two physical paper inboxes: one for her desk at work and one for her desk at home
- A Pocket PC that synchronizes with Microsoft Outlook
- A travel Pocket PC cable so that she can synchronize her Pocket PC and her laptop while on the road
- A portable paper inbox

Carol then took a number of actions:

- Labeled the physical paper inboxes so others knew to use them

Part Two:
Creating an
Integrated
Management
System—The
Collecting Phase

Take Back Your Life!

- Learned how to use the Tablet PC's OneNote software
- Learned how to synchronize her Pocket PC with her laptop
- Labeled her portable paper inbox sections
- Cancelled a voice mailbox

And she changed a few habits:

- Downloaded reminders from her head to Categories: (none)
- Avoided using sticky notes or paper
- Put her mail in her inbox and not on her desk

After three months, Carol reported that using her Collecting System had now become a habit. She didn't even think about it and was relieved to have reduced her buckets to so few.

In this chapter, we discuss how to set up and minimize your Collecting Points to simplify your system, reduce clutter, eliminate chaos and confusion, and give you physical, mental, and emotional breathing room, not to mention a clean kitchen counter!

What Changes Are You Going Make?

Go to the To-Do List in Outlook, and open the Task you labeled IMPROVING PRODUCTIVITY. In the Notes section of this task, type three headings: Collecting Phase, Processing and Organizing Phase, and Prioritizing and Planning Phase, as shown in Figure 4-10.

Chapter Four: Setting Up Your Collecting System

Part Two:
Creating an
Integrated
Management
System—The
Collecting Phase

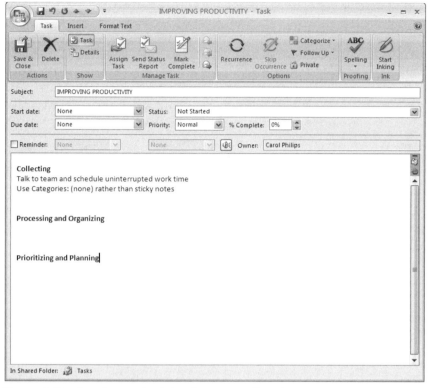

Figure 4-10   Keeping track of the changes you'll make.

As you go through the Three Phases for Creating an Integrated Management System and make decisions about the changes you want to make, we'd like you to come back to this task, open it, and record each of your decisions. These changes will enable you to "live the system" and ensure it works for you and becomes part of your life.

After you've created this task, please take a moment to record what you want to do differently to complete the setup of your Collecting System. Please type these actions under the heading "Collecting." It's very important to record the changes you want to make because this helps you clarify what you're going to do and reminds you to do it!

Here are a few examples from clients in the Collecting Phase:

- Use one paper notepad. Take all my additional paper notepads, put elastic bands around them, and archive them on my credenza—never to be used again!

Success is nothing more than a few simple disciplines, practiced every day.
— **Jim Rohn**

Part Two:
Creating an
Integrated
Management
System—The
Collecting Phase

Take Back Your Life!

■ Purchase OneNote software so that I can take meeting notes digitally and eliminate paper notepads

■ Set up a paper inbox on my desk at home and work. Put all the papers on my desk, floor, and credenza in the paper inbox.

■ Buy myself a Smartphone so that I can use Categories: (none) as a Collecting Point when traveling out and about and combine personal and business information.

■ Download voice mail messages when I am at my computer so that I can type appropriate actions into Categories: (none) instead of writing them on paper and then having to transfer them.

■ Eliminate my landline at home and use only my cell phone.

Elegant Edge of Productivity

As you'll learn throughout this book, you can use many different and fun tools to help you get and stay organized. Here are a couple of slick tools that work well for us. This list is just a sample of what we have on hand at the moment.

Fancy writing tools   Ink pens that are road-warrior proof and fun to write with: *www.writersedge.com*; *www.joonpens.com*

Cool notebooks   Great-looking leather Padfolios. Visit the Leather Tree Web site at *www.leathertree.com*. Or, for a notebook to fit your style, visit *www.moleskines.com*.

Tablet PCs   The Lenovo X60. You can read about it at the Lenovo Web site (www.lenovo.com). Search on "Notebook computers X60."

Slick inboxes   Leather or plastic inboxes. For more information, visit the Container Store. Shop by Category, select Home Office and check out Paper Storage. (*www.containerstore.com*).

Trendy Pocket PC cases   Cases customized to fit your personal digital assistant (PDA.) You'll find them at CasesOnline (*www.casesonline.com*).

High-tech portable inboxes   An expanding wallet, available at any office supply Web site.

Sexy cell phones   Smartphones that run Windows and synchronize with Outlook. You can search for them under your phone carrier by looking under "Smartphone." A few we suggest are: Dash (T-Mobile), Samsung Blackjack (ATT) and Motorola Q (Sprint/Verizon).

You can use this list as a guide for your own online shopping.

Part Two:
Creating an
Integrated
Management
System—The
Collecting Phase

Take Back Your Life!

Chapter Five

Successfully Managing Interruptions

Part Two:
Creating an
Integrated
Management
System—The
Collecting Phase

Many of our clients share with us that interruptions get in the way of them doing their work, commenting: "I have to come in at 6 AM; otherwise, I can't get any real work done," or, "My real job gets done in the evenings at home." As a result of being interrupted throughout the day, clients are compromising their time and focus. To solve these problems, they generously compensate by coming in early to work or working evenings at home. Unfortunately, after clients get used to working these additional hours it becomes the norm and a new pattern is created. Rather than addressing the real issue of managing interruptions, clients work longer hours and compromise their personal lives. Their intentions are honorable; however, long term, this strategy is not productive for themselves, their team, or their family.

The purpose of this chapter is to create more awareness for you about interruptions and how to improve them successfully for yourself and your team. We look at why you get so many and assess how to create an environment where you reduce the number and improve the quality of the ones you do get.

A balance needs be reached, and it has to do with how effectively you and your team are achieving your personal and business objectives. If you're achieving your objectives and experiencing balance, we would not look to change the number or quality of your interruptions. However, if you feel like your work is compromised, then we advise you to consider implementing a combination of solutions from this chapter. Your situation, of course, is unique, and therefore the solutions you implement must be tailored to fit the environment you work in and the objectives you're driving toward.

Now, for those of you interested in statistics, research at University of California–Irvine School of Information and Computer Science reports that office workers are interrupted every three minutes on average. And it can

Part Two:
Creating an
Integrated
Management
System—The
Collecting Phase

Take Back Your Life!

take 25 minutes to regain concentration after each interruption. Preliminary research from Hewlett-Packard Labs shows that in 41 percent of cases, we never return to our original activity. Definitely food for thought!

Are Interruptions Necessary?

We believe that interruptions are a necessary part of your personal and business lives; however, how big a part do they need to play and are you aware of the impact they're having? Following are a few questions to ponder.

- What percentage of your day is spent managing interruptions?
- What type of interruptions are you getting?
- What is the impact on your personal and business lives of these interruptions?
- Could the quality of your interruptions be improved?
- Are these interruptions moving your own and your team's objectives forward?
- Is the content of these interruptions reactive or proactive in nature?
- Could these interruptions be handled in some other way?

We've discovered that managing interruptions is a sensitive subject. Some of our clients get a little defensive, assuming that we're asking them to eliminate interruptions altogether. They make comments to defend their interruptions, stating how they increase their productivity.

We understand that being a hermit, camping out in your office, and never interacting with other people is not necessarily a good thing. Also, hiding behind technology, such as sending e-mail messages to coworkers who are literally in the next booth, is equally extreme. On the other hand, staying late at work because you can't get your job done during the day doesn't work either.

Of course, there are jobs where the primary function is managing interruptions, and these don't need fixing. Imagine for a moment that you're a receptionist, and when the phone rings, you pick up and politely say, "I'm sorry, I'm not taking calls for the next hour. Please call back at 2 o'clock and I'll help you then." This strategy is inappropriate because, in this example, your primary job is dealing with interruptions. However, for most of you, handling interruptions is almost certainly not your principal responsibility. A balance needs to be struck here, and your task is going to be finding that balance and customizing solutions that work for you and your team.

Part Two:
Creating an
Integrated
Management
System—The
Collecting Phase

Are You Training Your Staff to Interrupt You?

Interruptions come to us from multiple sources: people walking into our offices, instant messages, cell phones, landlines, e-mail alerts, and "drive bys" as you walk the corridors. If you're not careful, you can get a lot of interruptions throughout the day, and they can be quite distracting. If handling interruptions is not your primary job, why do you get so many of them? As Ted Bremer a client from a large telecommunications company once said to us, "Because I allow them!" We agree with him and think it really is that simple.

What underlies Ted's comment is that clients are actually unconsciously training their staff and coworkers to interrupt them and to leave things to the last minute. They don't realize they're doing this because it truly is unconscious. Let's look at this more closely. When you accept an interruption, you're sending a message that says, "It's OK to interrupt me." If you do this consistently, it becomes a habit and eventually it becomes the culture of your team. In other words, the behavior you accept from others is a form of training others, granted it is unconscious; however, it is still an effective form of education and is equally as efficient as teaching your staff consciously—that's the scary part!

After you become aware of this, you'll begin to see the impact that consistent interruptions can have. The short-term impact is that you and your team get distracted and end up working longer hours to get your real work done. The long-term effect is that your team becomes more reactive and less proactive; team members come to you with last-minute issues, expecting you to drop everything and address them. We all need to accept interruptions; however, we recommend that you consciously retrain your staff to handle interruptions more effectively and, as a result, reduce the volume.

When Ted's staff interrupted him, he always stopped what he was doing to help them. They felt respected and honored by this, but Ted wasn't getting his work done at work. He was working two hours every evening at home.

Ted had tried to change this pattern. One time when he got interrupted, he said, "I can't take this interruption right now. Can you come back later this afternoon?" The staff member replied, "But I need to have this data for a meeting in 30 minutes!" What choice did Ted have but to handle the interruption? Once again, he reinforced that he was available and the pattern continued. If you keep handling interruptions this way, you are training your staff that not only is it OK to interrupt you anytime, but coming to you with last-minute requests is also standard practice. Over time, this kind of

The average American worker has 50 interruptions a day, of which 70 percent have nothing to with work.
—**W. Edward Deming**

Part Two:
Creating an
Integrated
Management
System—The
Collecting Phase

Take Back Your Life!

behavior pattern creates a reactive culture in your team as opposed to a pro-active culture. Things are handled last minute because they can be because everyone is available to help out.

Scheduling Uninterrupted Work Time

We suggested to Ted that he first have a meeting with all of his staff to clearly communicate and reset their expectations so that he could get more work done during the day. He shared with his team that his work was intruding on his personal life and that he'd come to the conclusion that he was not managing his time as effectively as he could be. He decided he was going to book two hours of uninterrupted time a day so that he could get his work done at work. This time was scheduled on Ted's Calendar so that no one could book him for meetings and so that his team could see the reserved time and therefore respect it. Ted also clarified that if his team interrupted him during this time, he would ask them to come back later. Ted did a good job of reinforcing these boundaries, and therefore his team began to take him seriously and started to respect his two hours of uninter-rupted work time. This was a small change for Ted to make; however, it was effective and therefore lead to further changes.

Ted then asked his staff to consider alternative solutions to interrupting him: incorporating conversation points into 1:1 (1:1 meetings are face to face meetings involving one other person) or staff meeting agendas, send-ing e-mail messages with a 24-hour turnaround time, or mulling over how to handle the situation themselves.

Using 1:1 Agendas

Ted set up regular 1:1 meetings with his five direct reports. He scheduled them once a month for an hour for the full calendar year. He suggested to his directs that if they had an item they wanted to discuss with him, instead of interrupting him, they could add it to their 1:1 agenda. This way, they knew that once a month they'd have a face-to-face meeting and could dis-cuss the issue then. If it was an item that couldn't wait until the 1:1 meeting, they'd have to choose other forms of communicating with Ted. After Ted's directs got the hang of their monthly 1:1s and trusted they could count on them, it was easy for them to foresee discussion points and add them to this list instead of interrupting Ted.

Part Two:
Creating an
Integrated
Management
System—The
Collecting Phase

Using Staff Meetings

Ted did hold staff meetings; however, they were not at regular intervals, and so he implemented a routine weekly staff meeting to review objectives and relevant discussion points, and he asked his staff to plan agendas ahead of time. Ted's staff now had two forums—monthly 1:1s and weekly staff meetings—in which to discuss agendas instead of interrupting Ted directly.

Using E-Mail

After you get into the habit of physically interrupting someone in their office, you don't think twice about doing it, and it becomes standard practice. To change this habit in his staff, Ted informed them that he was going to add to his Calendar a one-hour e-mail appointment once a day in the mornings. During this time, he would not take interruptions so that he could respond to his e-mail messages within 24 hours. He asked his staff to defer physical interruptions as much as they could and use e-mail instead, promising he would respond within 24 hours. This created several benefits: his staff had to think 24 hours ahead of time, making them more proactive; his staff had to think through their points more clearly by writing them in an e-mail message instead of physically interrupting Ted; and it reduced Ted's physical interruptions.

Creating Solutions, Not Problems

Last, Ted asked his staff to help him handle walk-in interruptions a little differently. He asked them to prepare their points before they interrupted him and bring their proposed solutions instead asking him for solutions, therefore making the interaction more valuable. This request reduced interruptions because his staff realized they could answer some of their own questions. The quality of Ted's interruptions improved because they were forward-focused in nature, dealing with solutions and not problems.

As a result of all of these changes, Ted's team became more proactive, planning ahead rather than reacting and leaving things to the last minute. They reduced interruptions by using e-mail, weekly staff meetings, and monthly 1:1 meetings, and the quality of the interruptions improved because they were mostly necessary interruptions that were solution focused. Redefining expectations caused Ted's staff to think more proactively and to plan more effectively upfront instead of leaving things to the last minute, ultimately saving time and resources for everyone.

Part Two:
Creating an
Integrated
Management
System—The
Collecting Phase

Take Back Your Life!

Ted realized that if he took more time to train his team in this way, not only would he get more done, but his team would, too. His staff had relied on Ted without his realizing it. Now he wanted to help them help themselves and be more self-reliant. Ted was moving toward leading his team instead of a managing his team.

Ted's goal was not to eliminate interruptions entirely. He recognized that they were part of the rhythm of his day. However, he needed to approach them differently because the quantity was affecting the quality of his life. By resetting expectations and successfully reinforcing them with his team, he was able to create positive changes. From this, he began to realize other areas where his actions were unconscious and how to consciously reset and reclarify his boundaries. When you become more conscious of training your team, you begin to see how the lack of training is indeed training itself and so getting conscious about guiding your team is important. Training happens anyway, consciously or unconsciously, and so you might as well make is conscious.

As we often say to clients, be careful what you allow because what you allow becomes what you create. In other words, interruptions are a function of what you tolerate and what you consent to. Consenting is a successful form of training, but unfortunately it is not very conscious. After you become aware of this process, it then becomes a lot easier for you to contemplate changing it and being the cause in the matter. We've done studies in departments of 200 people or more where they've reduced interruptions by 20 percent as a result of setting and reinforcing clear boundaries. Some of our clients have even reduced interruptions by as much as 61 percent; anything is possible.

Are You Using Technology to Help or Hinder Your Focus?

Ted had successfully reduced his interruptions from staff members and reduced his hours working at home, both of which were big wins for him and his team. However, he began to notice another level of interruption that he hadn't recognized before: his cell phone, landline, instant messaging (IM), and e-mail alerts. These were constant sources of peripheral distractions for him. When he was doing his one hour of e-mail processing, he noticed that whenever his cell or landline rang, he stopped and glanced at his caller ID. When his instant messaging popped up, he stopped and responded. And every time a new e-mail message arrived, he glanced down

Part Two:
Creating an
Integrated
Management
System—The
Collecting Phase

to look at the notice. It was exciting and things were happening; however, it was definitely distracting his focus.

Ted recognized, similar to before, he was actually unconsciously training himself to be reactive and unfocused. He was also training his staff and vendors that he was available all day, and each time he responded he communicated, "I am available." Before long, they learned to expect a quick response, and when he didn't supply one, they got irritated. Ted realized that he was going to have to be really careful how quickly he responded to staff and vendors because over time it set a precedent and it may not be the most supportive precedent for him to be setting.

Ted realized by having all his devices and alerts ringing, beeping, and pinging, he was continually redirecting his focus from what he was doing. He was making it hard for himself to concentrate and get any real work done. Like physical interruptions, there is a time and place for alerts and notifications, and the key is figuring when to turn them on and off.

If you count the number of times your cell phone, landline, instant messages, and instant alerts grab your attention, you might be surprised, or even shocked. We worked with a very savvy financial broker who had lots of distractions, and she said, "Did I say I have a job other than dealing with all of these devices, because if I did, I am not sure when I am going to get it done!" This summary is extreme but nonetheless one we can all relate to.

After a while, being distracted by these devices became such a habit for Ted, he eventually found himself proactively checking his e-mail or cell phone before the device even alerted him, wondering why it was not pinging, dinging, or beeping. Now 'fess up, Ted is probably not the only person we've caught doing this—we're sure some of you have done this, too! This is an addictive behavior in the making! Try being alone for a day without your computer, cell phone, or landline and notice what happens. For some of us, it is a huge relief, and for others, something is seriously missing! Either way, it is an extreme that indicates a strong behavior pattern, or in other words a borderline addiction.

Once again, it is all about balance and what works and what does not work for you. If these behaviors serve you and your sense of balance and well-being, there's no need to fix what doesn't need fixing. However, if your e-mail is piled up, and you're working long hours, you might want to consider some changes. These are all habits we have created and we can just as easily create new ones.

Part Two:
Creating an
Integrated
Management
System—The
Collecting Phase

Take Back Your Life!

Turning Off E-Mail Alerts, Cell Phones, and Landlines During Work Appointments

Ted decided to create a few additional habits, during his one hour of e-mail-processing time and his two hours of work time, he turned off his e-mail alerts, cell phone, landline, and instant messaging system and concentrated on these appointments with 100 percent of his focus. As a result, he got so much e-mail completed he decided not to turn the e-mail alert on again. As long as he did an hour a day of focused e-mail time, his Inbox was manageable and he was getting responses out within 24 hours. The e-mail alerts served no purpose anymore. Ted still grazed through his e-mail during the day, and so for those of you having heart palpitations thinking you can check e-mail only once a day, relax and breath; remember, this is was what worked for Ted, and it might not work for you!

Ted's cell phone rang only two to four times a day, and so he kept that turned on continuously because the distractions were minimal. He asked his assistant to handle his landline completely and to e-mail messages to him with the items she could not deal with directly. That left instant messaging, and like his cell phone, he did not get profuse interruptions through IM, and so he kept it turned on.

Clarifying Response Times

Ted's last habit change was to inform his staff and vendors that he was moving to a 24-hour response time instead of an immediate response time. To do this he simply updated his signature line in his e-mail to the following:

Ted Bremer, Sales Manager, Consolidated Messenger
Phone: 555-0188 Web site: *www.consolidatedmessenger.com*
E-mail response w/in 24 hrs: ted@consolidatedmessenger.com
Cell phone response w/in 8 hrs: 555-0187
Landline response w/in 24 hrs: 555-0188

Ted used these as maximum response times, knowing he could respond quicker if he chose to. He discovered that as long as he was consistent with his response times customers did not have a problem with them. All they wanted were expectations they could rely on and trust.

Ted had now minimized people interruptions and device interruptions; he was working less hours and was more focused on his real job while maintaining balance. All the solutions Ted implemented were specific to his circumstances, team, and vendors; these solutions worked for him. Please bear

Part Two:
Creating an
Integrated
Management
System—The
Collecting Phase

in mind that these solutions may not work for you. You need to tailor your own solutions to meet your unique situation and circumstances.

Resetting Expectations and Holding People Accountable

If you don't create your own expectations, the world around you will create them for you, and you may not like what you get! Our clients often feel like they can't change expectations, and even that they're imprisoned by them. "You don't understand. That's the way it is around here. I can't change it!" Our clients can sometimes be resigned and cynical about the way things are.

Maybe they're right, and maybe they can't change the way things are. However, you can change what you personally do and how you personally manage or participate with your team. Take a look at the expectations you've created unconsciously—e-mail response times, drive-by interruptions, phone response times—and decide what changes you want to make. Then, meet with your team to clarify and align everyone to these new expectations. You don't have to wait for your boss to drive this action; you can drive it. Everyone is tired of incessant interruptions and will welcome the opportunity to talk about changing them.

After you've created new expectations, the next step is ensuring you hold yourself and your team accountable for making them happen. If you don't enforce accountability, nothing will change and you'll only teach your staff that these "change" conversations are meaningless and ineffective.

When you start to demonstrate new behaviors successfully, others will want to do the same. There's nothing like a little bit of authentic demonstration to spark the minds and hearts of those around you. People want to improve, and when they see others progressing, they're inspired to change themselves. Leadership by example is always more powerful than leadership by edict, and it doesn't have to come from the top. It can start anywhere someone decides to lead.

Ted successfully made changes. What he did was relatively simple. He added "dealing with interruptions" to his monthly staff meeting. During the meeting, he let his staff know that he planned to block out on his Calendar two hours exclusively for work and one hour for e-mail, and he described his purpose for doing so. He asked his staff to plan ahead what they'd need from him so that they could support his request for uninterrupted time. Ted made it very clear that he'd enforce this request, and if someone tried to

Part Two:
Creating an
Integrated
Management
System—The
Collecting Phase

Take Back Your Life!

interrupt him, he'd ask them to come back later, no matter what was going on (except for a real emergency, of course).

It's critical to set the stage before you set up new boundaries so that your environment can support you. Ted reset his expectations upfront so that his team would understand why he was behaving differently and could then support him. If he'd made these changes without discussing them with his team, his staff may have become confused and frustrated, saying, "He's not available and I don't know why!" Ted also was consistent with reinforcing these boundaries and asking staff to respect his requests—this can be the hard part of change for some of our clients. However, as mentioned earlier, if you don't reinforce the changes you request, your staff will not take you seriously. In other words, if you take your requests seriously, so will your staff. Ted's staff was most accommodating to his requests because they were all in the same boat—they weren't getting their work done either!

When Ted consistently kept his uninterrupted work time, his staff started to work in cooperation with him. There were fewer interruptions and his staff became more proactive. Ted modeled a purposeful change and supported his staff in doing the same.

Managing E-Mail Response Times

Another minefield of interruption bad habits is e-mail. E-mail isn't just a form of communication; it's an opportunity for huge productivity gains or huge productivity losses. If you don't train yourself and your staff to handle e-mail productively, watch it take over your lives, reduce your productivity, and become an endless cause of distraction, not only at work but also at home.

E-mail dominates the day-to-day operations of today's companies, and so it's time we all address it and stopped pretending that we don't have the time or resources to deal with it. Our company has client statistics that prove that educating staff regarding best practices for e-mail can cause an 81 percent drop in the total amount of e-mail in each employee's Inbox and a 26 percent reduction in the daily e-mail volume received by employees. These statistics are impressive, to say the least, and they demonstrate that education works. They confirm that employees are starved for knowledge, and when they get it—watch out!—because it makes a difference. For additional support managing e-mail, visit our Web site (*www.mcgheeproductivity.com*) and select Products to download our TBYL 101 E-mail Webinar Series. It focuses specifically on e-mail solutions mentioned in the book and is the perfect digital addition to your Take Back Your Life (TBYL) library.

Chapter Five: Successfully Managing Interruptions

Part Two:
Creating an
Integrated
Management
System—The
Collecting Phase

E-mail really isn't the problem. The problem is how we've allowed ourselves and our staff to approach it, and how little training we've provided. Much like handling interruptions, the training staff have received so far has been somewhat unconscious. When you process e-mail at 10 o'clock on Sunday night and during meetings, you send to others a message that it's fine to do that. However, when your team or colleagues see you in control—going home with an empty Inbox and taking your weekends off—they'll want to do the same. Who wouldn't? First, take the time to get your own house in order, and then you can train your staff and colleagues to do the same.

So, where do you start? By clarifying the new expectations, and holding yourself and others accountable.

FedEx is a good example of creating and reinforcing expectations. You can't send a FedEx package to arrive at its destination in less than three minutes. Delivery takes 12 hours, minimum. FedEx stands behind that boundary, and it's not negotiable. Also if you pay for 2-day service, your package is delivered in 2 days, not one, even if it arrives in the destination city in time for an "early delivery" – which it almost always does. FedEx is smart enough to know that if they ever compromised the expectations established by their pricing tiers, they'd encourage undesirable expectations.

When you call to set up your pickup with FedEx, you talk with a voice-activated service, not even a real person! However, FedEx works, and it's incredibly successful. Customers don't mind having to call 12 hours before they want a package to arrive, and they don't mind talking to a machine. Why? Because FedEx has established clear expectations and FedEx always delivers on these expectations. We can count on it. That's what makes FedEx the company it is today.

So, take another look at your internal and external customer expectations. It's better to have a 12-hour turnaround time and deliver 100 percent of the time, than it is to have a less-than-3-minute turnaround time and always miss deadlines, while feeling overwhelmed and out of balance. Also, you want to let your staff and customers know what your turnaround time is. One way to do that is to include it in your e-mail signature line as Ted Bremer did (see page 94).

Some jobs are designed to support short turnaround times. If you're a receptionist, a firefighter, an information technology specialist, or an emergency room doctor, your work requires an immediate response. This is not true of most other professions, though. Very few businesses and job descriptions can successfully support a less-than-3-minute turnaround

Part Two:
Creating an
Integrated
Management
System—The
Collecting Phase

Take Back Your Life!

time. Although with technology we can respond immediately, most of us have other work activities we need to complete that take longer than three minutes. You attend two-hour meetings, one-hour conference calls, write complex proposals, and create budgets, making it impossible to achieve three-minute response times. If you believe that you have to respond to everything immediately, you'll end up processing e-mail during meetings, conference calls, and the one-hour journey home, which means that you're never really present in any activity you're doing. Your e-mail is driving you and this can be frustrating and unsatisfying.

Ted noticed that his team was habitually responding to e-mails in less than three minutes. "They were addicted to the ding, compulsively checking mail on their Blackberries during meetings, on the way to meetings, and even in their cars while driving," Ted said. "Because everyone is e-mailing back and forth in less than three minutes, it's forcing the team to be super-reactive." His staff justified this behavior, saying, "If I don't reply quickly, decisions and discussions are held without my input, so I have to be on e-mail all day." Once again the belief justifies the pattern and the pattern justifies the belief. It is an endless circle and it is not productive

The three-minute response time drives environments to reactive and unproductive behaviors. Responding so quickly works occasionally, but maintaining that pace throughout the day is ineffective and unrealistic. Once it gets started, it's hard to stop unless you meet with your team, let them know you want to change expectations, clarify what you want the change to be, and reinforce them.

Ted held a staff meeting and, as a team, they came up with the following expectations: e-mail response times will be four hours. Less-than-two-minute interruptions will be sent by instant messaging. And the team will turn off the e-mail ding!

To support the four-hour response time, Ted asked his staff to be more proactive about communications. He tied e-mail effectiveness to performance reviews to let his staff know that he was serious about making changes. This approach caused his staff to become more proactive, thinking through their projects ahead of time rather than being reactive and shooting e-mail messages back and forth. His staff got more work done during the day because they did not have to check e-mail so often. The changes were very positive.

Carol Philips was telling us about her weekend e-mail experience: "My whole department does e-mail on Sunday evenings!" She sounded a tiny bit frustrated. With a little digging, we found out that when Carol was

Part Two:
Creating an
Integrated
Management
System—The
Collecting Phase

extremely overwhelmed with e-mail, she started processing it on Sunday nights to catch up. Her staff discovered she was online, and when they got immediate responses from her over the weekend, they began e-mailing one another, and this kept going until it became a "Sunday night habit." We suggested to Carol that she set up a staff meeting and discuss the Sunday e-mail culture. Interestingly enough, everyone wanted to be with family on Sunday night instead of doing e-mail, and so the team reset its expectations. E-mail sent over the weekend didn't have to be responded to until Monday, and any urgent decisions could be handled over the phone. This caused her team to be more proactive regarding e-mail and to protect the time they had at home with family. If people wanted to do e-mail, they could, but it was no longer a Sunday requirement.

E-mail is not the problem. The problem is how we approach it. If you change your approach, you can change your results. Whether you run a team or participate in one, you can lead these changes.

Managing Drive-By Interruptions

We bet you never think of yourself as a drive-by interrupter! **Drive-bys** are when colleagues interrupt you, in the office, in the corridor, or at breaks in meetings. Some of these interruptions are effective, but too many cause you to do your work at home, much like Ted was doing before he enforced boundaries. Imagine you're working on a financial worksheet when someone pops in and asks, "Got a minute?" Usually, that means "have you got 15?" If the same thing happens throughout the day, it's hard to get anything done.

We suggest talking with your team about how to decrease these types of drive-by interruptions, as Ted did. Common solutions are to e-mail requests instead of interrupting, add discussion points to meeting agendas, or capture action items in your Outlook To-Do List to be handled during 1:1 meetings. Whatever the solution, prepare the environment to expect change, communicate the change, and let everyone know how you'll reinforce it: "If you stop me in the corridor, I'll ask you to follow up with an e-mail to ensure that I act on it." This sets the stage and helps you reduce some of the discomfort you might experience redirecting these kinds of interruptions. It's not always easy to ask for what you want and change your behaviors. After you've addressed these issues with your team, you'll feel more comfortable making the changes.

You can successfully reduce drive-by interruptions with your team, but you need to be careful when considering people outside of your team. The best approach to effect change outside of your group is by personal demonstra-

Boundary setting is not about getting other people to change (even though at first, it may seem that way). It's really about deciding what you will and won't tolerate any longer in your life, and then communicating this firmly and consistently whenever you need to. Boundaries are essential to becoming a healthy adult and balancing your work and personal life effectively. They demonstrate your commitment to self-respect.
—Natalie Gahrmann

Part Two:
Creating an
Integrated
Management
System—The
Collecting Phase

Take Back Your Life!

tion. You may not think that by changing your own habits you can affect anyone else's, and it may seem like a small thing to do in comparison to changing a department, but it doesn't take much of a difference to make a difference. The little changes you make do make a difference and do positively affect the people around you.

Managing Cell Phones, Pagers, and Instant Messaging

If you always answer your phone and/or pager when it rings or beeps, people will always expect you to pick up when they call. If you always return messages within 24 hours, recipients will always expect a 24-hour response. Set realistic expectations, stick to them, and watch your internal and external customers get happy.

Phones and Pagers

It's important that response time expectations are indicated. With regard to voice mail, you can include something like this in your actual message: "Hi, you have reached Ted Bremer. Please leave a detailed message and I will respond within 24 hours." This allows people to know what to expect, and it reinforces the expectations of those you consistently interact with. No one said you have to answer your phone every time it rings; people just want to know what they can count on you for.

Our company has a four-hour response time on cell phones and pagers and eight hours on landline calls. As long as people stick to these response times, they can choose when they answer their phones and pagers and when they turn them off. The key is not that the phone is answered, but that people respond to their messages within the response time they've promised.

Instant Messaging and Text Messaging

The good news about instant messaging is that you can easily classify your status: busy, away, and online. Our company uses instant messaging for less-than-2-minute interruptions and minimizes the distribution list so that access is not granted to multiple users. We recommend keeping your distribution list limited to include your close team members and family members and creating exceptions for special vendor or client relationships. I must say that instant messaging is a joy for me and is not an interruption at all. I rarely am bothered, and if I am, the interaction is purposeful and brief. I have fun with winks and use them to cheer up my colleagues, celebrate wins, or just be silly. It lightens up the day! We are a virtual company, and so

Chapter Five: Successfully Managing Interruptions

Part Two:
Creating an
Integrated
Management
System—The
Collecting Phase

with instant messaging we can stay in touch with each other all over the world. We set clear expectations on how to use IM, the staff respects them, and the system is working and is fun.

Text messaging is another fun way to communicate with close team members, family members, and special vendors and clients. Again, clarify expectations on how you want to use text messaging and minimize distribution lists so that it does not get unwieldy.

Best approach with any communication device is to set clear expectations: clarify when and how to use it. Communicate expectations, identify distribution lists and keep them to a minimum, and outline how you're going to hold people accountable. This will improve your communication and reduce interruptions.

What Changes Are You Going to Make?

Go to the To-Do List in Outlook and open the Task you titled IMPROVING PRODUCTIVITY. In the Notes section of this Task, under the heading Collecting, type in some of the actions you are going to take to improve your boundaries, reduce interruptions, and clarify response times. We list a few examples from clients here:

- Turn off my e-mail alerts feature.
- Set up an agenda item in the next staff meeting to talk about e-mail and phone response times and drive-by interruptions.
- Book a two-hour recurring appointment on my Calendar to be in my office and work on my tasks and let staff know during that time I will not take interruptions.
- Change my e-mail signature line to state my official response times.
- Change my voice mail message to include response times.

In this chapter, we discuss how to create effective boundaries to reduce interruptions, making it easy to get more work done during the day and spend more quality time at home. Creating boundaries works, and if you reduce interruptions by only 40 percent, that alone makes it worthwhile!

Part Two:
Creating an
Integrated
Management
System—The
Collecting Phase

Take Back Your Life!

Chapter Six
Clearing the Mind

Part Two:
Creating an
Integrated
Management
System—The
Collecting Phase

This chapter completes the information you need to accomplish the Collecting Phase, which is the first of the Three Phases for Creating an Integrated Management System. The purpose of the Collecting Phase is to assist you in developing a leak-proof Collecting System, enabling you to effortlessly capture all of your communications, commitments, and agreements.

In this chapter, you complete an exercise called "clearing the mind" that allows you to transfer all the actions you've been carrying around in your head and move them into the Categories: (none) in the To-Do List in Microsoft Office Outlook. This process is extremely liberating and gives you a realistic view of how much you have to plan and to do.

You'll learn why it's essential to set up your Integrated Management System (IMS) so that it supports you in keeping your agreements, being accountable, and staying within your integrity. And you'll learn when to renegotiate and, in some cases, when to disengage from projects and how to gracefully say "no." This then concludes the Collecting Phase and prepares you to move to the next phase: Processing and Organizing.

Are You Using Your Mind As a Collecting Point?

Our company's experience proves that most of our clients underestimate how much they rely on their minds as a Collecting Point, and how dramatically this impacts their ability to be focused, to be present, and to realistically comprehend how much they have to do.

Part Two:
Creating an
Integrated
Management
System—The
Collecting Phase

Judy Lew, a sales executive for a retail company, shared with us how she feels like her mind is a constant source of distraction and how it literally interrupts her focus. "I was in a staff meeting and right in the middle of it I remembered I had to complete a School of Fine Art proposal. As I sat there, unable to do anything about it, I started to mentally figure it out and found myself taking notes on my notepad. My energy shifted from listening to working on my proposal. At the end of the meeting I had to ask a colleague what decisions were made because I completely missed some of the information during the meeting." Over time, these mental preoccupations affect the quality of your interactions and you end up spending more time catching up on information you missed because you weren't able to focus.

Worrying about what you have to do when you can't do anything about it is *not* a productive activity; in fact, it is really not a good use of your time and that is why we recommend you transfer this information from your head into your system where you can do something about it.

Imagine for a moment you're at home and in a conversation with your daughter. During the conversation, a voice in your head is reminding you to take your car to the dealership to have the oil changed. Some part of your daughter knows you're not really present with her–you're already driving your car to the dealership! Yet, if anyone asked you which experience was most meaningful to you, you'd answer "spending time with my daughter." Thinking about tasks when you're communicating with someone you care about compromises the relationship because you're just not present with that person. Effective communication requires you to be truly present and transforms the results you produce. Communication is the foundation of everything we do in our business and in our personal lives. Therefore, we strongly recommend transferring the information from your head into your system; by doing this, you can be more present in your communications.

When you track a lot of information in your head, not only does it affect your ability to focus and to be present, but it also impacts your ability to manage your commitments. It can be tough to get a realistic perspective on your priorities and how long they'll take to get done when you're organizing them in your head. Mental lists are harder to manage than written lists are because they can appear much bigger than they really are. Our clients often say, "I have more to do than I can do, and it's completely overwhelming!" However, we've discovered that this feeling is often disproportionate to the number of tasks they actually have to do! After they write down their commitments in a list the load appears to be quite manageable.

Only when your consciousness is totally focused on the moment you are in can you receive whatever gift, lesson, or delight that moment has to offer.
—**Barbara De Angelis**

Chapter Six: Clearing the Mind

Part Two:
Creating an
Integrated
Management
System—The
Collecting Phase

On the flip side, some clients completely underestimate what they have to do because their work is jumbled up in their heads with no organization, and after they write down their commitments they realize how many steps it will take to complete their commitments. Either way, mental lists do not support a realistic view of what you have to do and how long it will take. You cannot complete a commitment you cannot remember, and for some of us the mind is not a reliable reminder system anyway. These are just a few of the many good reasons to transfer information from your head into your Integrated Management System.

Understanding the Conscious and Unconscious Mind

When you understand the relationship between the conscious and unconscious mind, you'll begin to realize why it's critical to get the to-do's out of your head and into the Outlook To-Do List.

Your conscious mind has limited space and can track only small quantities of data at any given time; on average, 4 to 10 items. The unconscious mind, on the other hand, is unlimited and can track infinite quantities of data, as shown in Figure 6-1. It also has no idea of time, and it's not very organized, as you'll see in the following example.

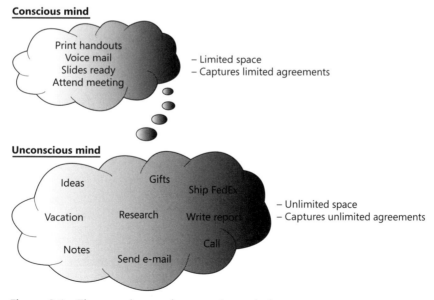

Figure 6-1   The conscious and unconscious mind.

Part Two:
Creating an
Integrated
Management
System—The
Collecting Phase

Take Back Your Life!

Molly is driving to work and reviewing her mental to-do list, which includes picking up a soy latte, checking e-mail, printing handouts for her 3 p.m. meeting, checking with Benny whether the room is set up, and calling Karen to sing "Happy Birthday."

As Molly arrives at work, Michael leaps out of his office and shouts, "Molly, just wanted to remind you to call Litware to make sure the presentation is set up!" Molly replies, "Of course. No problem." Molly's *conscious* mind, however, is completely occupied by her current to-do list, and there's no room for another item, and so it drops into her *unconscious* mind.

Molly then checks her e-mail, prints handouts, and walks over to her meeting. Her mental to-do list just got smaller, and so she now has space in her conscious mind. While Molly sits in the meeting, her mind wanders and she feels her unconscious trying to grab her attention. "Call Litware to make sure the presentation is set up." However, Molly's in a meeting right now and can't do anything about it, and so back it goes into her unconscious!

At the end of the meeting, Molly picks up additional action items and records them in her head. She goes back to her office where her e-mail is pinging and her phone is blinking. The next thing she knows, it's 6 p.m. and she's driving home, safely in the bubble of her car. She sighs and relaxes, her mind wanders off, and there it is again, "Call Litware to make sure the presentation is set up." Her cell phone battery has died and she doesn't have a charger in the car! Ah, well, it'll have to wait. Back it goes into the unconscious.

Molly gets home, feeds the dogs, takes a look at the mail, prepares dinner, and at 10:30 p.m., she finally relaxes in her easy chair and lets her mind wander off. There it is again! "Call Litware to make sure the presentation is set up." Too late for Molly to do anything about it right now, and so back it goes into her unconscious.

We're sure you can relate to this experience. When there's room in your conscious mind, the unconscious will remind you of incomplete tasks. It works like clockwork! You may have noticed, your unconscious jogs your memory at the most inopportune moments and in the most inconvenient places. It has no concept of time or priority.

Think of the times you've gotten into the shower only to remember that you need to buy shampoo. Of course, the next time you're in the drug store, you'll forget to buy it, only to remember it again when you take your next shower. Because you cannot buy shampoo in the shower this is a futile exercise. Not only is this frustrating, but it doesn't support you in getting things done.

Chapter Six: **Clearing the Mind**

Part Two:
Creating an
Integrated
Management
System—The
Collecting Phase

Are You Carrying a Heavy Load?

Carrying lists of incomplete tasks in your mind can create enormous mental, as well as physical, stress. Everything that's incomplete in your life, no matter how old, gets recorded in your unconscious or conscious mind. Fix the gutter, change the light bulb, repay Terry the $60 I borrowed, and finish reading that book. You get the idea. Each incomplete item that you carry around is allocated a certain amount of your mind's attention, ensuring that you don't forget about it. The more "incompletes" you have, the more attention you're locking up in your mind. For some of you, this is stressful and can be overwhelming.

Imagine, for a moment, that each incomplete in your head weighs 1 pound, and you have 100 of them. Picture yourself dragging a 100-pound load wherever you go, 24 hours a day, 7 days a week, even in your sleep! How would you feel trying to get things done while dragging this weight around?

Maybe you've grown strong and no longer realize how heavy your load is. The scary part of that is that you've gotten so used to the load that it's become normal. Just to be clear, it's not normal. You'll be amazed by how much lighter you feel when you let go of your mental incompletes and transfer them into your IMS.

Categories: (none) is the perfect Collecting Point because it's centrally located and designed to carry heavy loads. The To-Do List will remind you when and where actions need to be done so that you remember to buy shampoo when you're at the store as opposed to in the shower. You'll also remember to make your calls when you're near a phone and not in a meeting.

Why use your head and pay the price of lugging around a heavy load when you can use the To-Do List to carry it for you? It's time to unshackle the mind and give it some peace. You won't believe how much lighter you'll feel when you let go of all these incompletes. We'll have to scrape some of you off the ceiling!

Clearing the Mind and Lightening the Load

The purpose of the "clearing the mind" exercise is to empty your mind of all the to-do's you've been harboring in your head. To do this, you need to be ruthless, capturing every incomplete that you can possibly think of. Don't underestimate the mind! It's tricky, and it'll keep hold of your incomplete actions, and then wake you up in the middle of the night, reminding you to do them. We're sure you've had that experience before!

Part Two:
Creating an
Integrated
Management
System—The
Collecting Phase

This exercise is an opportunity to let go of everything that you've been carrying around in your head. Let Outlook manage your lists for you so that you can use your mind for more important activities, such as planning and strategizing and simply being present.

Doing the "Clearing the Mind" Exercise

You'll be using Categories: (none) as your Collecting Point for the "clearing the mind" exercise.

The palest ink is better than the best memory.
—**Chinese Proverb**

To ensure that you capture as many items as possible, from all areas of your life, I'd like you to allow yourself to think randomly—from work to home, from small to large, and from important to irrelevant. Just allow anything in your mind to surface, in any order it appears. Your job is simple: capture each thought, and type it in as a new Task. Even if some of the tasks you come up with are connected, please enter them as individual tasks. If you currently use categories to organize your lists, please ignore them for now and only enter items into the Categories: (none) Collecting Point. This is a free-flowing exercise, and you'll organize this list later, in Chapter 7.

Your system is only as good as your mind. If it's on your mind, it's not in your system.
—**David Allen**

Prior to beginning the exercise, we want you to change one default in Outlook 2007. Outlook's standard behavior is automatically to assign today as the due date for any new task you create. For the purpose of this exercise (and your peace of mind) we are going to change the setting so that when you create a new task, the default is no due date. To do this, follow these steps:

1. Go to the To-Do List and right-click the red flag on your IMPROVING PRODUCTIVITY task (or any other task), and then click Set Quick Click, which opens the Set Quick Click dialog box.

2. In the drop-down menu, select No Date, as shown in Figure 6-2.

3. Click OK.

Chapter Six: Clearing the Mind

Part Two:
Creating an
Integrated
Management
System—The
Collecting Phase

Figure 6-2 Changing the Outlook 2007 default due date to No Date.

Now you're ready to begin the exercise. Go to the To-Do List, and click the words Click Here To Add A New Task to enter a task, such as "Create a draft budget for 2005." Type your item in the Subject line, press Enter, and watch it instantly show up in Categories: (none). If you are an experienced user, this is normal. However, if you are learning how to use the To-Do List, this is a pretty cool feature. Now, enter the next item that comes to mind, such as "Buy dog food," and press Enter. Then, add the next item, such as "Set up United Airlines travel for Minnesota trip." As you can see, these items are unrelated, random, and a mix of both personal and business. That's OK. This is how clearing the mind works. Allow your mind to flow in the order it wants. Just go with it, and try not to hinder it by organizing it any particular way.

Spend at least 15 minutes clearing the mind, and then, read through the personal and professional triggers listed in Listings 6-1 and 6-2. These lists are designed to prompt you to remember items that you may have forgotten. If you get to the end of your mind sweep and haven't read these trigger lists, review them carefully to make sure that you've captured everything you can possibly think of. You want to get this "stuff" out of your head and into your system. As a reference point, clients usually enter anywhere from 20 to 45 incompletes at a time. Not everything you enter will end up being a task you have to complete, but sometimes you need to get it out of your head so that

Part Two:
Creating an
Integrated
Management
System—The
Collecting Phase

Take Back Your Life!

you can evaluate it and decide not to do it—the key is getting it out of your head.

You'll be building your IMS around the list you've created, and so it's critical that you complete this exercise *before* continuing on with the next chapter of this book. Please don't skip this process because it's very important for the integrity of the system. You'll also feel better after you've done it.

Listing 6-1   Professional triggers

- Projects started, not completed
- Projects to be started
- Commitments/promises to
    - Others
    - Bosses/partners
    - Colleagues, subordinates
    - Other people in organization
    - Outside people
    - Customers
    - Other organizations
    - Professionals
- Communications to make/get
- Initiate or respond to
    - Phone calls
    - Voice mail
    - E-mail, pages, faxes
    - Letters, memos
- Other writing to finish/submit
    - Reports
    - Evaluations/reviews
    - Proposals
    - Articles
    - Promotional materials
    - Manuals, instructions

Part Two:
Creating an
Integrated
Management
System—The
Collecting Phase

- ❑ Rewrites and edits
- ■ Meetings that need to be set/requested
- ■ Who needs to know about what decisions?
- ■ Planning/organizing
  - ❑ Formal planning (goals, targets)
  - ❑ Current projects (next stages)
  - ❑ Upcoming projects
  - ❑ Business/marketing plans
  - ❑ Organizational initiatives
  - ❑ Upcoming events
  - ❑ Meetings
  - ❑ Presentations
  - ❑ Organizational structuring
  - ❑ Changes in facilities
  - ❑ Installation of new systems
  - ❑ Travel
- ■ Financial
  - ❑ Online banking
  - ❑ Cash flow
  - ❑ Statistics and budgets
  - ❑ Forecasts and projections
  - ❑ P and Ls
  - ❑ Balance sheet
  - ❑ Credit line
  - ❑ Banks
  - ❑ Receivables
  - ❑ Payables
  - ❑ Petty cash
- ■ Administration

Part Two:
Creating an
Integrated
Management
System—The
Collecting Phase

Take Back Your Life!

- ❏ Legal issues
- ❏ Insurance
- ❏ Personnel
- ❏ Policies and procedures
- ■ Customers
  - ❏ Internal
  - ❏ External
- ■ Marketing, promotion, sales
- ■ Customer service
- ■ Systems
  - ❏ Phones, computers, equipment
- ■ Inventories
- ■ Supplies
- ■ Office/site
  - ❏ Office organization
  - ❏ Furniture/decorations
- ■ Waiting for...
  - ❏ Information
  - ❏ Delegated tasks/projects
  - ❏ Replies to...
    - ● E-mail
    - ● Calls
    - ● Proposals
    - ● Requisitions
  - ❏ Reimbursements
    - ● Petty cash
    - ● Insurance
  - ❏ Ordered items
  - ❏ Items being repaired
  - ❏ Tickets

Chapter Six: **Clearing the Mind**

Part Two:
Creating an
Integrated
Management
System—The
Collecting Phase

- ❏ Decisions of others
- ■ Professional development
  - ❏ Training/seminars
  - ❏ Things to learn/look up
  - ❏ Skills to practice/learn
  - ❏ Computer training
- ■ Research/need to find out about
- ■ Professional wardrobe
- ■ Projects started, not completed
- ■ Projects to be started

Listing 6-2 Personal triggers
- ■ Commitments/promises to
  - ❏ Spouse
  - ❏ Children
  - ❏ Family
  - ❏ Friends
  - ❏ Professionals
  - ❏ Borrowed items
- ■ Projects: other organizations
  - ❏ Service
  - ❏ Church
  - ❏ Volunteer
- ■ Communications to make/get
  - ❏ Family
  - ❏ Friends
  - ❏ Professional
- ■ Initiate/respond to
  - ❏ Phone calls
  - ❏ Letters

Part Two:
Creating an
Integrated
Management
System—The
Collecting Phase

Take Back Your Life!

- ❑ Cards
- ■ Upcoming events
  - ❑ Special occasions
  - ❑ Birthdays
  - ❑ Anniversary
  - ❑ Weddings
  - ❑ Graduations
  - ❑ Holidays
  - ❑ Travel/vacation
  - ❑ Social events
  - ❑ Cultural events
  - ❑ Sporting events
- ■ Research
  - ❑ Things to do
  - ❑ Places to go
  - ❑ People to meet/invite
  - ❑ Local attractions
- ■ Administration
  - ❑ Financial
  - ❑ Bills
  - ❑ Banking
  - ❑ Investments
  - ❑ Loans
  - ❑ Taxes
  - ❑ Legal affairs
  - ❑ Will
- ■ Filing
- ■ Waiting for . . .
  - ❑ Mail order
  - ❑ Repair

Part Two:
**Creating an
Integrated
Management
System—The
Collecting Phase**

- ❏ Reimbursements
- ❏ Loaned items
- ❏ Medical data
- ❏ RSVPs
- ■ Home/household
  - ❏ Landlord
  - ❏ Property ownership
  - ❏ Legal
  - ❏ Real estate
  - ❏ Zoning
  - ❏ Taxes
  - ❏ Building/contractors
  - ❏ Heating/air conditioning
  - ❏ Plumbing
  - ❏ Electrical
  - ❏ Roofing
  - ❏ Landscaping
  - ❏ Driveway
  - ❏ Walls/floors/ceilings
  - ❏ Decoration
  - ❏ Furniture
  - ❏ Utilities
  - ❏ Appliances
  - ❏ Light bulbs/wiring
  - ❏ Kitchen things
  - ❏ Washer/dryers/vacuum
  - ❏ Areas to organize
  - ❏ Garage
- ■ Vehicle repair/maintenance
- ■ Pets

Part Two:
Creating an
Integrated
Management
System—The
Collecting Phase

Take Back Your Life!

- Health care
- Hobbies
- Books, records, CDs, DVDs
- Errands
  - Hardware store
  - Drug store
  - Supermarket
  - Bank
  - Cleaners
  - Stationers
- Community
  - Neighborhood
  - School
  - Local government

Awarenesses

To help you learn more about yourself and build a system that works for you, consider some of the awarenesses that our clients have observed while doing the "clearing the mind" exercise.

- I had a lot more personal items than I ever expected.
- My mind was random. I'd remember small things, big things, personal things, business things, important and unimportant things.
- I feel totally overwhelmed looking at this list!
- I like having it all written down in one place.
- The list is much bigger than I ever thought it would be.
- I feel guilty looking at what I haven't done that I need to do.
- I was storing more in my head than I realized.
- I feel much lighter getting all this stuff out of my head. It's a relief!
- I just got started and I have a lot more to go!
- I noticed a lot of little things that have been nagging at me.
- I remembered items that I had completely forgotten about.

As a result of completing this exercise, you probably are feeling much lighter and relieved. You just freed up a whole bunch of "attention" units and cen-

Chapter Six: **Clearing the Mind**

Part Two:
Creating an
Integrated
Management
System—The
Collecting Phase

tralized your list! However, you might also be feeling overwhelmed and wondering to yourself, "How will I ever get all of this done? I'm more stressed out now than before I started this exercise!" Don't be surprised. This is a common reaction!

Interestingly enough, you didn't create more to do. You may feel that way, but these items were already in your head *before* you started the exercise. By writing them down, you became more conscious of them, and it was a bit of a shock. Before, all your to-do items were unconscious and, as my mother used to say, "Ignorance is bliss!" Yup, ignorance *is* bliss. But the trouble with bliss is that you forget agreements, you can't buy shampoo in the shower, and you can't call Litware when you're in a meeting!

When you start being conscious of what you have to do, consistently recording your commitments in Outlook, your lists will get longer. You may not have been aware of how much you had to do because you tracked your tasks in your head. An important element in being organized is getting comfortable having longer lists. This can take a little while to get used to, but the benefit of tracking your commitments in Outlook far outweighs the value of tracking them in your head.

After you successfully have transferred all your commitments and agreements into your system, the system helps you remember what you need to do and when you need to do it. The value of having a system like this soon overshadows your concerns about having longer lists. You'll end up feeling lighter, being more focused, and having the right data you need to prioritize and plan your schedule effectively.

Using Categories: (none) as a Collecting Point

Most of our clients adopt Categories: (none) as one of their main Collecting Points. They use it throughout the day to capture random ideas that pop into their heads, action items from meetings, and any other tasks that their mind is hanging onto. Our client Molly told us that Categories: (none) was her favorite Collecting Point. She shared with us, "I have access to it both on my smartphone and my Tablet PC. Therefore, no matter where I am, I can capture information in my system instead of in my head. This gives me a central Collecting Point that I can easily access. It sure feels good to get actions out of my head, and use my system to do the organizing for me. Whenever I am feeling snowed under, I complete a mini 'mind sweep' and I instantly feel better and it clears my head."

Part Two:
Creating an
Integrated
Management
System—The
Collecting Phase

We've noticed that that our clients have a harder time making effective decisions when their minds are trying to get their attention. We recommend to all of our clients that they do mini "mind sweeps" every week to ensure that they're not unconsciously carrying around communications, commitments, or agreements in their heads. Categories: (none) really is a great location to capture this data, and if you have a smartphone, it becomes even more valuable because 24/7 you can use this Collecting Point, allowing you to be really present both at work and at home.

Keeping Your Agreements and Maintaining Your Integrity

After you've completed the "clearing the mind" exercise, you may notice that some of your tasks have been on your list for quite some time. A number of them might be items you promised to complete, and yet they're still not done. The good news is that you have them written down, and so they're on your radar screen; the bad news is that you either broke an agreement with yourself or with someone else. Most of us are not aware of the number of agreements we make and the number we break. And we are also not sensitive to the impact this can have on our lives and the lives of those around us.

We often hear clients say such things as the following: "We all procrastinate and over commit; that's just part of life." "I'll never get it all done; I just do the best I can." "Clearly, there's more to do than I can do." If you really listen to these statements and where they're coming from, you'll realize that there is a note of resignation and cynicism present. Our clients have resigned themselves to the fact that "this is just the way it is, and I have to come to terms with it." And that is exactly what our clients have done—they've "come to terms with it" and in most cases they don't even register that they're breaking agreements anymore because they've become unconscious and numb to the fact.

Some clients are better at keeping agreements with others than they are at keeping agreements with themselves. They seem to abandon their own personal commitments, making others their priority. How many of you put appointments on your calendar either to process your e-mail or go to the gym, and then don't honor them, booking over them with business meetings? That's a broken agreement with yourself and one you're likely to repeat over and over. However, some part of you does not consciously register this, and blowing off the appointment enables you to justify repeating the pattern.

Part Two:
Creating an
Integrated
Management
System—The
Collecting Phase

How many of you tell colleagues, "Yup, I'll get that back to you on Friday"? You don't make it a habit to track it in your system and consequently forget about it until someone else reminds you. There are so many areas where we go unconscious related to agreements. It's not a bad thing, and we don't want you to go into any judgment about it; however, it does have an impact and therefore we want to bring that to your attention so that you can decide if you want to change your behavior.

We completed some consulting with Molly around this area, and she said, "I couldn't believe how many promises I made that I didn't keep. I thought if I kept the big ones, the little ones wouldn't matter, and you know what, they do matter. I discovered that keeping my word does make a difference." When you break agreements, people lose trust in you, and, more important, you erode personal trust in yourself. Imagine how you would judge others if they were consistently breaking agreements. Well, that's how you're judging yourself when you break agreements you've made with yourself—how scary is that!

Others are also affected when you don't do what you said you would do; for example, when Molly agreed to do the Litware proposal and promised it by Friday and didn't get it done. The account manager had to call the client to renegotiate, but because it was Friday and rather late in the day, the client had already gone home. This affected the account manager, the client, and Molly, and it slowed down the sales cycle and ultimately it affected an objective.

We're sure you've noticed that when you keep your agreements it builds your self-confidence and your sense of self-worth. Over time, your word becomes who you are, and it becomes your integrity. It inspires trust and respect from others. Your friends may even refer to you as a woman or man of your word, and this in many ways is the ultimate compliment because at the end of the day, your word is really all you have. It is powerful when you can say, "Such and such is going to happen," and it does happen, simply because you said it would. Living in this type of integrity is commanding. Most of us are not living at this level; however, you can be, and it all starts with doing what you said you would do, right down to keeping your e-mail appointment or an exercise appointment with yourself.

If you want to be the cause related to your Meaningful Objectives, you have to live a life in which you do what you say you will do, a life where your word is vital and important, and where your word defines who you are. This takes you out of resigned and cynical and puts you smack bang in the driver's seat of being cause in the matter. This is the new model of productivity: doing what you say you will do over and over again, completing actions that link to

Part Two:
Creating an
Integrated
Management
System—The
Collecting Phase

Take Back Your Life!

and drive your Meaningful Objectives. This is the cycle of productivity in action; this is personal integrity.

Being Discerning

After you start tracking your agreements more consciously you'll find yourself wanting to be more discriminating when making agreements. Discernment will become a skill you use to identify what you can and cannot agree to. That is where your IMS comes in handy. Your IMS allows you to view all your agreements in one place on the To-Do Bar. When this list is up-to-date, it is relatively easy to prioritize and then plan the top priorities onto your Calendar, ensuring you have time to complete them.

This sounds simple, and it is, except sometimes there's no space on your Calendar to add another appointment. When this occurs, you need to prioritize what you wanted to schedule against what is already there. This leads either to renegotiating or disengaging from existing appointments, or talking to your boss about potentially hiring more resources. In other words, your Calendar becomes your reality, it is your guide to how much you can and cannot do. Your IMS supports you with information, causing you to be more discerning about what you agree to do.

Over time, this process becomes natural, and as you're offered new projects you will find yourself automatically reaching for your IMS to check out if you can realistically accept them. At that point, you know the system is working and you are operating within your integrity as it relates to time and your agreements. Your IMS then becomes like a mirror reflecting back to you when you have too much to do and when your integrity is out. As longs as you keep your system current, it will mirror back to you how you are doing. Sometimes the reflection ain't pretty; however, if you take responsibility for what you created, you can fix it so that it comes back into balance.

Managing your life this way takes courage because you have to be extremely responsible. Over time, it becomes a way of life and a natural part of who you are. You come to rely on your IMS because it will help you be more discerning and help you stay in your integrity.

Figure 6-3 shows the ControlPanel. On the right are all of Carol's agreements in her To-Do Bar, and on the left is her Calendar showing what time she has available. The ControlPanel enables Carol to see whether she has time to complete her priority tasks. It gives her the information she needs to make tough decisions about which agreements she'll keep, which agreements she needs to renegotiate, and which agreements she needs to disen-

Chapter Six: **Clearing the Mind**

Part Two:
Creating an
Integrated
Management
System—The
Collecting Phase

gage from. Carol is the only one who can support herself in making these decisions, no one else can do it for her, it is up to her to decide.

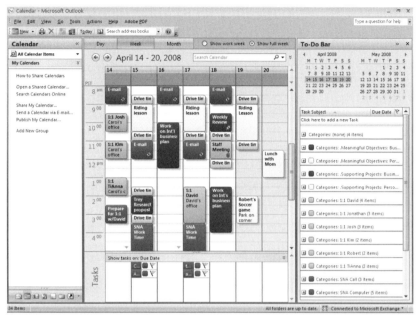

Figure 6-3 The ControlPanel provides a central location for all of your commitments and agreements.

Keeping Agreements with Yourself First

Remember, *nothing will lower your self-esteem more rapidly than breaking agreements*. We're highlighting this statement because, later in the book, you'll look at how you process and organize your e-mail, and we suggest that you book a one-hour meeting with yourself each day to work through your messages. When you put this daily, concentrated, and uninterrupted time on your calendar, it's a commitment that you're making with yourself. You need to be clear that this is a commitment, and even though no one else will be meeting with you, your agreement is just as important as if someone were. If you decide to schedule time on your calendar for exercise, that appointment is also as important as any other meeting in your day. When you get to the section on planning your calendar, you will see that this level of personal commitment is essential to maintaining balance and making sure you get your work done at work.

Some of our clients have a hard time keeping agreements with themselves. We've noticed that these clients are working with an unconscious belief—"I

He who controls
others may be
powerful, but he
who has mastered
himself is mightier.
—**Lao Tsu**

Part Two:
Creating an
Integrated
Management
System—The
Collecting Phase

Take Back Your Life!

am not as important as others." This belief is not easy to recognize and clients often resist accepting and owning it. At this point we ask them, "Do you make appointments with yourself and cancel those appointments to meet with other people or complete actions to support other people?" In almost all cases the answer is, "Yes." The next question is, "How often do you do this?" Clearly, these clients are making others more important than themselves.

To be more productive, you must have a healthy level of self-esteem so you can keep agreements not only with others, but with yourself. Therefore, it's important to change the belief, "I am not as important as others" so that you can complete the work that will keep you on track with your objectives *and* experience work-life balance. Once you're honoring and protecting your own e-mail and planning appointments, you'll know you have changed this belief and you'll experience greater freedom, productivity, and balance.

Keeping your word with yourself creates personal integrity, and it really is the cornerstone of who you are. Without it, true productivity and work-life balance is almost impossible to achieve.

Renegotiating Agreements

After you have all of your commitments tracked in your system, your e-mail Inbox has been emptied, you've gotten through all of your voice mail, and your head is "clear," you'll have a very complete to-do list represented by the To-Do Bar. When you review this list against your Calendar, you'll be able to see if you can, in fact, complete all of your agreements on time. It's incredibly empowering to have this information at your fingertips. You might come to the conclusion that you can't get everything done, and so something has to give. This is where **renegotiating** comes in.

Renegotiating involves proactive, honest communication. It's important to renegotiate an agreement as soon as you know you will be unable to keep it. If you must renegotiate a commitment, offer potential solutions to move the agreement forward. The solutions could take multiple forms, such as changing a deadline, hiring more people, disengaging from alternative agreements, or changing the scope of a project. The key is that when you determine, ahead of time, that you won't be able to keep your agreements, you let people know as soon as possible so that they have the opportunity to do something about it

The situation we all dread is finding out at the last minute that a project won't get done. When this happens repeatedly, we lose respect for people. Renegotiation, however, allows you to maintain your credibility, integrity,

Chapter Six: **Clearing the Mind**

Part Two:
Creating an
Integrated
Management
System—The
Collecting Phase

and responsibility. When you let someone know, with enough warning, that you can't do what you said you'd do, you give that person the chance to evaluate the impact of the change and the time to go with alternative solutions. If you break an agreement without any advance warning, the person has no way to evaluate and reduce the impact of your change.

We really appreciate people who renegotiate with us. This lets us know that they care about their agreements, that they are sensitive to the impact they may have, and that they are being responsible. We'd prefer to know ahead of time, no matter how uncomfortable it is to hear the news!

Disengaging from Agreements

After you learn discernment as a skill you will rarely take on projects you cannot handle; however, when you first start to set up your IMS you may come to the uncomfortable realization that you have agreed to do more than you can actually do given the available time on your calendar. Some of these projects you can renegotiate; however, there may be some you actually have to disengage from completely.

A good question to ask to find out if disengagement is the appropriate strategy is, "Does this directly relate to one of my objectives?" If it does not, this is a good indication that you need to disengage. As with renegotiation, communication is the key here and particularly learning to tell the truth fast.

When disengaging, you first want to identify who the involved parties are and let them know that you wish to disconnect from the project and why. You want to find out what the impact will be and how best to reduce it. These are not always easy conversations to have; however, if you truly do not believe you should be working on a project, it is outside of your integrity not to communicate this to the parties involved.

We're always delighted to have these conversations because we know that our staff and colleagues have deliberated long and hard and we respect that their motivation is achieving their objectives. The key is being honest, putting yourself in the other person's shoes to really understand what the impact will be, and perhaps apologizing for having agreed to do it in the first place. After you begin the conversation, which is the hardest leap to take, you'll be pleasantly surprised by the solutions that come forward and how cooperative people are. Telling the truth and telling it fast is a skill just like discernment, and it's another one to add to your tool box and the process of using an IMS.

Part Two:
Creating an
Integrated
Management
System—The
Collecting Phase

Take Back Your Life!

Learning to Say "No" to Agreements

You are probably realizing that to keep your word, stay balanced, and keep on track with your objectives, you're going to need to say "no" to some of the new opportunities that don't support your current objectives. This is a paradigm shift—the more you say "no" to activities that don't move your objectives forward, the more you can say "yes" to activities that do. We've learned that there is tremendous power in saying, "I will not be able to do that" because it enables you to maintain your focus on your objectives and lets people know that they can rely on you to give straight, honest, and clear feedback. Remember, you have more to do than you can do, and so you need to start saying "no" more frequently, if only to protect the current objectives you have.

As in renegotiation, a key to saying "no" is having the right information available in a central location to support your decisions. It's very hard to decline when you don't know what you've already agreed to.

Using the ControlPanel gives you very strong data to back up your decisions. You can say "no" with conviction because you have evidence that declining is necessary for you to be successful with your current objectives. When you truly acknowledge that by taking on more, you jeopardize what you've already agreed to do, it's a whole lot simpler to say "no" with confidence. You can give the "thumbs down" knowing you are operating from your integrity and doing what is best for your objectives and the objectives of the team.

Sally: I'm passionate about my objectives because they're meaningful to me; I truly want them to happen. I am equally passionate about protecting my time so that I can accomplish my objectives. This makes it easier for me to stay focused and decline new incoming opportunities that are less critical. I take my time evaluating whether saying "no" is the correct course of action, and if I decide that it is, I'm very clear about it. No one wants to be left in limbo; they want to know if you can do something or not. You're better off saying "no" than letting yourself and others down.

When we're asked to take on a new project or objective, we always go to our system first to see what the impact will be on our current work and home lives. Here's how you can do the same: when your boss asks you to create a new proposal, you can say that you'll respond by the end of the day after you've reviewed your workload. At the end of the day, you can respond by saying, "I can do this by the end of February; however, I'll need to put off the

Chapter Six: **Clearing the Mind**

Part Two:
Creating an
Integrated
Management
System—The
Collecting Phase

telecommunications proposal deadline until the first week of March. Is that OK with you?" This enables you to keep all of your agreements instead of burning yourself out to get everything done or missing other deadlines. It also allows for a positive discussion with your boss about priorities so that you can renegotiate what's on your plate and ensure that you're working on the most important activities.

We admire and respect our teammembers when we ask them to do something and they respond by saying, "I can't complete that unless I renegotiate my current timelines." We know they're taking care of themselves and that they'll do what they say they'll do. We also know that by saying "no," they are really saying, "I believe my objectives are important for me to focus on and they won't get done if I take on this project." It's hard to argue with that approach.

Saying "No" Without Justifying

Don't fall into the trap of feeling that you can't decline without sufficiently justifying why you're doing so. Our clients often feel that they have to justify their "no's" and even apologize for them. Most of the time, people just want a "yes" or "no" so that they can go about their day. If they want reasons, they'll ask for them. We often hear clients go into all kinds of justifications and stories, wanting the other person to know why they need to say "no," as though declining was a bad thing!

Saying "no" is a strategy that supports you in achieving your objectives on time, within budget, and at the appropriate level of quality. We know that in some companies, saying "no" is seen as uncooperative. Within the context of achieving your objectives, saying "no" can be a good thing no matter what the corporate culture is.

Our clients have taught us that saying "no" in the appropriate circumstances keeps you focused on completing important objectives. In fact, in many instances, you must say "no"; otherwise, you'll never get meaningful work done. If you don't say "no," you'll be really, really busy. But really, really busy doesn't mean that you're working on your most important goals! You're back into the belief, "I've got to get it all done." Remember: productivity is not about doing more; it's about getting the right things done.

Part Two:
Creating an
Integrated
Management
System—The
Collecting Phase

Take Back Your Life!

John: When I first started to say "no" without justifications, I'd leave the conversation feeling guilty that I'd gotten away with something! After a while, though, it began to feel very good. I was standing up for myself and being true to myself and my priorities. Of course, people will sometimes ask for reasons and they deserve an explanation. But after you establish a pattern of accountability, you won't have to justify the decisions you've made. I soon discovered that people respected my word, and when I said "no," that was enough for them. I realized that I didn't trust myself as much as others trusted me and *that* was a great revelation!

By having an IMS that reflects all of your agreements, you can start to see what you can and can't do. This enables you to renegotiate or disengage in a very proactive way. It's extremely powerful; so, take care of yourself and get your tasks out of your head and into your system. That way you can manage your commitments and create greater balance and integrity in your life.

What Changes Will You Make?

Take a moment to contemplate the changes that you want to make as a result of reading this chapter: tracking your commitments and agreements in your To-Do List instead of your head, coming to grips with the reality that you'll always have more to do than you can do, keeping your agreements, and renegotiating or disengaging from them when appropriate.

In the To-Do List in Outlook, open the IMPROVING PRODUCTIVITY task that you created in Chapter 4. Under the heading "Collecting," enter the specific tasks that you want to do differently to support the completion of the Collecting Phase. It's very important to record the changes you want to make because this helps clarify what you're going to do.

Keeping Track of the Changes You're Going to Make

For inspiration, here are some comments that our clients have written:

- Get tasks out of my head and type them into Categories: (none)

- When I am driving my car and I think of to-do's, call my voice mail and leave a message for myself

- Buy a personal digital assistant (PDA) so that I can type in actions when I am not at my computer

- Review my list against my calendar to see if I can get it all done

126

Part Two:
Creating an
Integrated
Management
System—The
Collecting Phase

- Renegotiate agreements that I made that I know I can no longer do

- Disengage from agreements that I can't complete

After you've entered the changes you want to make in the task labeled "IMPROVING PRODUCTIVITY," please close it into Categories: (none). You'll be referring to it again at the end of each of the Three Phases for Creating an Integrated Management System. Eventually, you will transfer it into your list of personal objectives.

Success Factors for the Collecting Phase

Congratulations! You're one-third of the way through setting up your Integrated Management System. Before you move on to the Processing and Organizing Phase, here's a summary of the key takeaways from these last three chapters.

- Be aware of the number of physical locations that you're using to collect your commitments and agreements. For most of us, this is quite an eye-opener, and it demonstrates how overwhelming it can be to have multiple Collecting Points.

- Define the approved Collecting Points that you'll use, and eliminate the rest. By minimizing your Collecting Points to between five and eight, you'll find it easier to seamlessly capture data, find it quickly, and process it easily into your IMS.

- Use only approved Collecting Points to collect your information. This means that you have to identify specific behavior changes to ensure you keep using these points and not others.

- Manage interruptions to reduce volume and increase quality. By communicating with your team and creating boundaries, you can easily shift the culture of interruptions and reduce them dramatically.

- Make keeping your agreements a way of life and put yourself first in that list. By transferring your agreements to your To-Do Bar, you are able to prioritize them weekly and transfer prioritized items onto your Calendar to complete them.

- Use Categories: (none) as a Collecting Point. This is a quick and easy location that enables you to capture voice mail, ideas, and actions from meetings. It synchronizes with your Pocket PC, which enables it to be portable.

> You seldom get what you go after unless you know in advance what you want.
> —**Maurice Switzer**

Part Two:
Creating an
Integrated
Management
System—The
Collecting Phase

Take Back Your Life!

■ Consistently "clear the mind" by tracking your agreements in your IMS. This will enable you to manage your agreements more carefully, be more present with others, and lighten up!

■ Review the interruptions you've been unconsciously allowing. Set up an agenda with your team to reset expectations so that you can reduce interruptions and get more of your real work done.

■ Set up your IMS to support you in keeping your agreements and renegotiating and declining them where appropriate.

You have now completed the Collecting Phase, the first of the Three Phases for Creating an Integrated Management System. As a result of reading this chapter, we hope that you truly recognize that you will always have more to do than you can do and that you will never ever get it all done. Therefore, the game is not figuring out how to do it all. Instead, the game is choosing the most strategic activities you can do with the time you have, while maintaining balance.

The next phase is the Processing and Organizing Phase, in which you'll learn how to organize your mind sweep list into the Planning and Action Categories. This will give you a better idea of exactly what you have to do. The third phase, Prioritizing and Planning, will assist you in moving your actions successfully onto the Calendar, giving you a better idea of exactly when you have to do it. This will be a reality check in which you'll discover if you can do what you said you would do, and do it in balance. Keep in mind that this is a process that will transform your effectiveness and give you peace of mind.

Moving right along...

Part Three

Creating an Integrated Management System— The Processing and Organizing Phase

Part Three:
Creating an
Integrated
Management
System—The
Processing and
Organizing
Phase

Take Back Your Life!

Chapter Seven
Setting Up Your Action System

Chapter Seven: **Setting Up Your Action System**

Part Three:
Creating an
Integrated
Management
System—The
Processing and
Organizing
Phase

Now that you've completed the Collecting Phase, the next step toward implementing your Integrated Management System (IMS) is setting up your Action System and the relevant Planning and Action Categories.

Your Action System is where you track and manage all of your commitments, agreements, and communications; you do this using the Microsoft Office Outlook Calendar, To-Do List, and Daily Preview list as shown in Figure 7-1. We call this view the ControlPanel because it enables you to see what you have to do and when you have to do it.

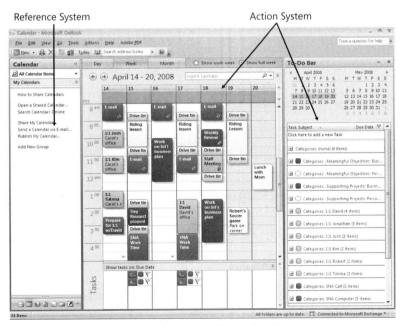

Figure 7-1   The ControlPanel showing the Action System.

Part Three:
Creating an
Integrated
Management
System—The
Processing and
Organizing
Phase

Take Back Your Life!

The Planning and Action Categories are a set of specific buckets that help you organize your To-Do List, making it easier to stay focused on your objectives and complete strategic activities to move them forward. This chapter is dedicated to setting up your Action and Planning Categories. Later in Chapter 9 and Chapter 11, you'll process and organize the contents of your Collecting Points into these Categories. Imagine all your Collecting Points empty and all your actions items categorized in the To-Do List. Everything is in one place making it easy to prioritize what you have to do and schedule when you have to do it—now that's organization!

Introducing the Planning and Action Categories

As you may have discovered from your mind sweep, you have anywhere from 30 to 250 tasks tracked in your Categories: (none) list. This type of linear list can be overwhelming to manage, as you can see in Figure 7-2.

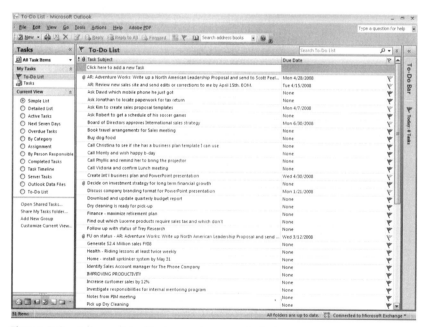

Figure 7-2 A linear list of tasks can be overwhelming.

Now, if you take that list and apply Planning and Action Categories to it, the list instantly becomes more manageable. See Figure 7-3.

Chapter Seven: Setting Up Your Action System

Part Three:
Creating an
Integrated
Management
System—The
Processing and
Organizing
Phase

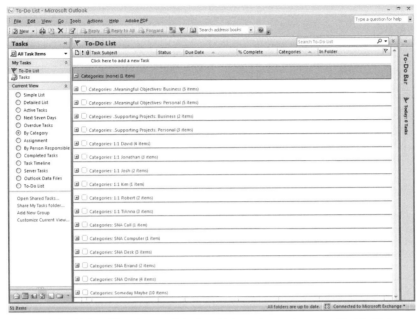

Figure 7-3 Using Planning and Action Categories makes your To-Do List manageable.

The Planning and Action Categories are designed to help you organize all of your actions into one central location so that you can easily manage and complete your objectives and maintain work-life balance. See Carol's Planning and Action Categories in Figure 7-3.

The Planning and Action Categories are also designed to integrate with the McGhee Productivity Solutions (MPS) Cycle of Productivity—*Consistently completing Strategic Next Actions that link to and drive Meaningful Objectives*, as shown in Figure 7-4. The first step in the cycle is "Identify Your Meaningful Objectives," and the second step is "Create Strategic Next Actions." These categories are shown on the To-Do Bar. The third step is "Schedule and complete Strategic Next Actions," and the fourth step is "Review and course correct." These steps take place as appointments on the calendar. The MPS Cycle of Productivity is the foundation of your IMS and integrates with the Planning and Action Categories.

Part Three:
Creating an
Integrated
Management
System—The
Processing and
Organizing
Phase

Take Back Your Life!

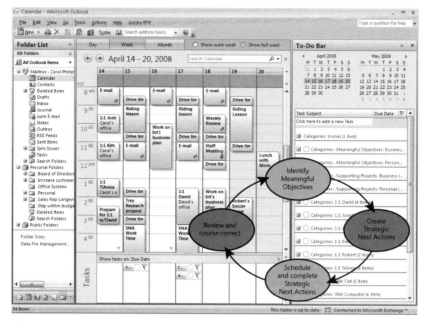

Figure 7-4 Cycle of Productivity integrates with your Action System.

Defining Planning and Action Categories

The Planning and Action Categories are critical to the success of your IMS. For now, we'd like you to use these specific categories exactly as they're presented in this chapter. Later in the book, you'll learn to customize them to your individual situation and circumstance.

The *Planning Categories,* listed as follows, assist you to refocus continually on your Meaningful Objectives and update, review, and reprioritize their associated Support Projects to ensure you complete them successfully.

Planning Categories:

- .Meaningful Objectives: Business

- .Meaningful Objectives: Personal

- .Supporting Projects: Business

- .Supporting Projects: Personal

- 1:1 Meetings

The *Action Categories*, listed as follows, assist you to capture Strategic Next Actions (SNAs). These actions can be completed immediately and have no

Chapter Seven: **Setting Up Your Action System**

Part Three:
Creating an
Integrated
Management
System—The
Processing and
Organizing
Phase

dependencies. These categories draw your attention to the most important actions you need to complete to move toward your Meaningful Objectives. These categories are essentially the "work" you are doing to complete your plans.

Action Categories:

- SNA Call
- SNA Computer
- SNA Desk
- SNA Errand
- SNA Home
- SNA Online
- SNA Waiting For
- Someday Maybe

Before we set up these Categories in your Action System, we're going to discuss each Category individually so you can understand why we created it and how to use it effectively.

Meaningful Objectives

- .Meaningful Objectives: Business
- .Meaningful Objectives: Personal

Meaningful Objectives, both business and personal, appear at the top of the list because all of your decisions are driven by these objectives. They are your North Star and guiding light. This business category tracks business objectives that you're accountable for and relates directly to your Unifying Goal and performance review. Your Personal Meaningful Objectives category tracks your personal objectives that you're accountable for and relates to your personal vision and maintaining work-life balance. Carol Philips, an account manager for Lucerne Publishing, loves this category because it inspires her to keep focused on both her business and personal objectives, enabling her to really keep her eye on the ball and maintain balance at work and home.

135

Part Three:
Creating an
Integrated
Management
System—The
Processing and
Organizing
Phase

Take Back Your Life!

Supporting Projects

- .Supporting Projects: Business

- .Supporting Projects: Personal

A complex objective is easier to manage and track when you break it down into Supporting Projects. Supporting Projects can be a component of your Meaningful Objectives; they're projects that support the objective in being accomplished. For example, the Meaningful Objective "Publish a productivity book" could be split into a number of Supporting Projects such as follows:

- Complete a book proposal

- Select a literary agent

- Complete a vendor agreement

- Complete a book contract

- Write the book

- Edit the book

- Approve screen shots, quotes, and diagrams

- Approve cover, inside and out

The Supporting Projects category enables you to track specific projects and their related execution plans. This makes it easier for you to see each Supporting Project with its related Tasks and Subtasks in one place because the Tasks and Subtasks are stored in the Notes section of the Outlook Task. There are exceptions where objectives may not be complex or large enough to warrant Supporting Projects, and we discuss this more in Chapter 9.

1:1 Meetings

This category enables you to track key relationships and the relevant communications you need to initiate or complete. If you delegate to key staff members, you probably have weekly or monthly one-on-one meetings with them. This category enables you to track and monitor their objectives, follow up on action items you've delegated, and list any important discussion points to address during the 1:1 meeting.

You can also use this category for one-on-one meetings with your manager or boss to review how you're progressing with your objectives. This includes questions, coaching, escalations, and possibilities.

Chapter Seven: Setting Up Your Action System

Part Three:
Creating an
Integrated
Management
System—The
Processing and
Organizing
Phase

Here's an example of how Carol Philips uses her 1:1 categories at work and at home. She has six 1:1 categories altogether. Three organize her direct reports—Kim, Josh, and TiAnna—one is for her boss, David, and two help her organize her personal life—Jonathan, her husband, and Robert, her 17-year-old son. Figure 7-5 shows some of these 1:1 categories.

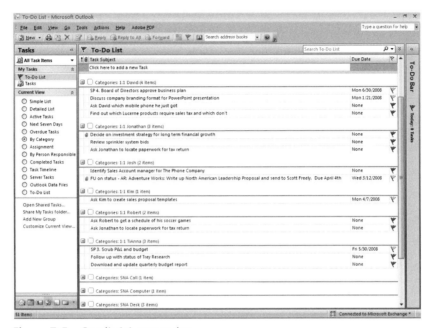

Figure 7-5   Carol's 1:1 categories.

Carol's 1:1 categories are set up as follows:

- 1:1 David
- 1:1 Jonathan
- 1:1 Josh
- 1:1 Kim
- 1:1 Robert
- 1:1 TiAnna

In each 1:1 category, you can use individual Tasks to track the following:

- Agenda items that you want to cover at the next 1:1 meeting
- Delegated tasks that you want to follow up on
- Status of Meaningful Objectives that a person is accountable for

Part Three:
Creating an
Integrated
Management
System—The
Processing and
Organizing
Phase

Take Back Your Life!

You can also use this category for anyone you have routine conversations with, such as outside vendors, clients, or cross functional team members, simply by adding a category for them.

It may sound clinical to include your spouse in your 1:1 category list; however, many of your personal objectives hinge on conversations with your spouse. How often do you talk to your partner about to-do's (kids, dogs, errands, garden, shopping, honey do's) and personal objectives? Sometimes your spouse doesn't remember what you said, and you don't remember what he or she said. Sound familiar?

Carol has a category for Jonathan, her husband, which she uses when she goes to breakfast with him on Sunday mornings. This is a great way for her to discuss all of their personal to-do's at one time. By the end of breakfast, they know who's going to do what for the week, and they can enjoy the rest of their time together. By being organized, you can spend more quality time with the people you love!

You can also use the 1:1 category in several areas of your personal life. If you're involved in a community project, you probably have a point person you deal with. In this case, you could create a specific category for that person so that all the items you want to discuss, delegate, or follow up on are recorded in one place. There are no limits as to how you can use this category.

Earlier, you created a category named 1:1 Meetings. Go ahead and delete this category, and set up the specific 1:1 categories that you want in the Color Categories list, following the instructions given earlier. As a reminder, create categories for direct reports, your boss/manager, vendors, spouse, and any other person you are in communication with on a regular basis. As we mentioned earlier, until you categorize a task under a 1:1 category, it won't show up in your To-Do List.

Strategic Next Actions

- SNA Call
- SNA Computer
- SNA Desk
- SNA Errand
- SNA Home
- SNA Online
- SNA Waiting For

Part Three:
Creating an
Integrated
Management
System—The
Processing and
Organizing
Phase

Each category records Strategic Next Actions that have no dependencies and can be completed immediately to move an objective forward. Notice that these categories are organized around particular locations where you need to be to accomplish the specific tasks.

SNA Call tracks actions that require you to use your phone, for example, "Call Helen and set up a staff meeting." If a phone is not handy, these actions can't happen.

SNA Computer tracks actions that require you to be at your computer, but don't require you to be online. For example, if you have a task "Edit the annual budget" and the budget document is in your My Documents folder in Microsoft Windows, you don't need to be connected to the Internet to edit this document. You can edit it while you're on a plane, in a hotel room, or wherever your computer is handy.

SNA Desk tracks actions that require you to be at your desk, such as "Read stock option plan," a paper document filed in your "Pending Read" folder. Or "Complete credit card application," a paper form filed in your "Pending Action" folder. You must be at your desk to complete both of these actions.

SNA Errand tracks actions that require you to go somewhere to complete them, such as "Go to store to buy a new Pocket PC" or "Go to cleaners to pick up dry cleaning." You need to be in your car to go do these errands.

SNA Home tracks actions that you can only do at home, such as "Put up bike hooks in storage room." If you already have the bike hooks and a drill, all you have to do is be at home to install the hooks.

SNA Online tracks actions that require you to be online, such as, "Complete online performance review" or "Go to Amazon.com to buy a book for Dad's birthday." These actions can't be accomplished unless you are online.

SNA Waiting For tracks actions that someone else must complete before you can move forward. In other words, you're waiting for another person or party to complete the action. For example, if you ordered a book from Amazon.com for your father's birthday, you have to wait for it to arrive before you can sign it and wrap it. To ensure it comes, you could track this in your Waiting For category and use the confirmation notice from Amazon as the Waiting For information in the Task. If it does not come, you have the data you need to follow up. Or perhaps you're waiting for a vendor to get back to you with a price quote. There are many items you can track in this category; in fact, most of our clients never used to track Waiting For's until learning about this list, and they find it extremely valuable.

Part Three:
Creating an
Integrated
Management
System—The
Processing and
Organizing
Phase

Someday Maybe

After you start planning and prioritizing agreements from your To-Do List onto the Calendar, you'll quickly see if you have time to complete them and, if not, if you'll need to renegotiate or disengage from them. This category enables you to track those items you need to disengage from but don't want to lose track of, such as "Sign up for Women's Business forum" or "Buy new smartphone." It's also useful for actions you're excited about doing, but don't have the time to do, such as "Spend three weeks in Italy" or "Read the Robert Jordan book series." The best part about the Someday Maybe category is that it unclogs your system from items you can't do now, but it keeps track of them, in case you have the time to do them later.

As you can see, Planning Categories (Meaningful Objectives, Supporting Projects, and 1:1 Meetings) track high-level thinking and planning. All of your Strategic Next Actions categories track specific actions you need to get done to support your Planning Categories.

The Planning Categories assist to you to review and reprioritize your plans. Action categories assist you to complete specific actions related to those plans. A phrase we use with clients is, "You don't 'do' objectives; you plan and strategize objectives. You only 'do' Strategic Next Actions." In other words, you cannot do a Meaningful Objective or a Supporting Project, but you can plan it, review the status, reprioritize the plans, and meet about it; there is nothing you can *do* because all the plans related to it, the Task and Subtasks, have dependencies. You can only do Strategic Next Actions because they're the only actions that do not have dependencies. You do Strategic Next Actions; you plan and review Meaningful Objectives and Supporting Projects.

If the categories you've set up so far in this chapter don't make complete sense, don't be concerned. You work with them in much more detail in Chapter 9, and you'll have plenty of time to customize them to your unique situation and circumstance.

Setting Up the Planning and Action Categories

You will be using the Color Categories list in Outlook to set up your Planning and Action Categories. With this list, you can access your categories from your To-Do List, the To-Do Bar, your Contacts list, and your Calendar.

Chapter Seven: Setting Up Your Action System

Part Three:
Creating an
Integrated
Management
System—The
Processing and
Organizing
Phase

To open the Color Categories list so that you can enter Planning and Action Categories, follow these steps:

1. Go to the To-Do List by clicking the Tasks icon or by clicking the Go menu and selecting Tasks.

2. If necessary, click the plus sign to the left of Categories: (none) to expand the category and view its Tasks.

3. Right-click the subject line of any Task.

4. On the shortcut menu, click Categorize, and then select All Categories. You'll see a list of default color categories, as shown in Figure 7-6.

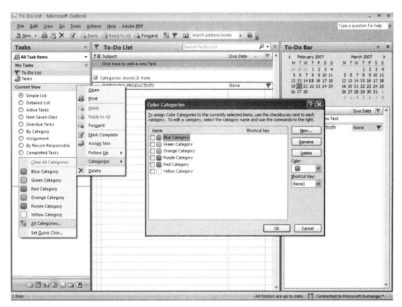

Figure 7-6 Accessing the Color Categories list.

Before you add the Planning and Action Categories to your Color Categories list, delete any of the default categories that you don't already use. (To do this, simply click on the name of the category and press the Delete button. Be sure not to put a check mark in the box.) If you're using categories you've already created, be sure to keep them. (If they have a color associated with them, click the name of the category, and in the Color drop-down list, select None.) For those of you who are reticent about deleting the default categories that you don't use, this will give you a little practice deleting items before you get to the e-mail section. Ha!

Part Three:
Creating an
Integrated
Management
System—The
Processing and
Organizing
Phase

Take Back Your Life!

In Microsoft Outlook 2007, categories are associated with colors. We discuss the best way to use colors in Chapter 12. For now, you can set up your Planning and Action Categories using no colors. To do this, follow these steps:

1. In the Color Categories list, click the New button to open the Add New Category dialog box.

2. In the Name field, enter the category **.Meaningful Objectives: Business**

3. Select None from the Color drop-down list.

4. Ensure (None) is selected in the Shortcut Key drop-down list.

5. Click OK.

6. The category you just added should appear in the list. If a checkmark appears to the left of the category, clear it.

Repeat steps 1 through 6 until you have entered the thirteen Planning and Action Categories in your Color Categories list, as shown in Figure 7-7. Type these categories exactly as you see them in the list. The first category is .Meaningful Objectives: Business. Notice that the category name includes a period in front of the words *Meaningful Objectives*. Be sure to include the period when you type the category name. Categories are listed alphabetically in your To-Do List, and the period brings this category to the top of the list. Meaningful Objectives are at the top because you want your objectives to drive everything you do.

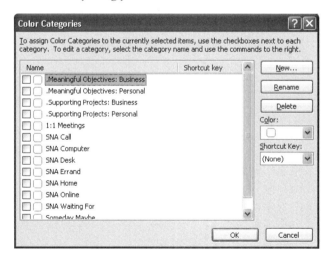

Figure 7-7   Entering the thirteen Planning and Action Categories.

Note that at first you won't see the changes you've made in the To-Do List because you must attach a category to a task before it will show up.

Part Three:
Creating an
Integrated
Management
System—The
Processing and
Organizing
Phase

Congratulations! You have now completed the first step in setting up your Action System. In Chapter 9 you will be using these categories as you start to process and organize your Collecting Points into your To-Do List.

Onward and upward...

Part Three:
Creating an
Integrated
Management
System—The
Processing and
Organizing
Phase

Chapter Eight

Creating Meaningful Objectives

Part Three:
Creating an
Integrated
Management
System—The
Processing and
Organizing
Phase

All of us have been impacted by the information age. With multiple channels of communication, increased volumes of data, and 24/7 connectivity, being able to focus on what's important, maintain boundaries, and hold true to our values has proved extremely challenging. Therefore, having clearly stated professional and personal objectives is now more important than ever before.

In this chapter, you have the opportunity to create both your professional and personal objectives. You learn how to create them in alignment with your company's and family goals, how to ensure you're accountable for them, and how to maintain work-life balance.

Objectives are a critical element to productivity and to your Integrated Management System (IMS). In Figure 8-1, you can see the McGhee Productivity Solutions (MPS) Cycle of Productivity. The first step in this model is "Identify Meaningful Objectives," and without this step the cycle cannot begin or end. Objectives are a reference point for making decisions, monitoring progress, and increasing effectiveness. We often say to clients, "Your productivity is only as good as your objectives." We have seen that without objectives our clients are frequently distracted, pulled in multiple directions, and unable to generate and cause their success.

Part Three:
Creating an
Integrated
Management
System—The
Processing and
Organizing
Phase

Take Back Your LIfe!

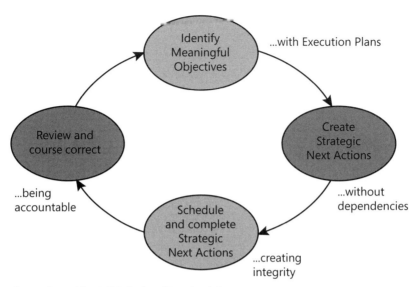

Figure 8-1   The MPS Cycle of Productivity.

Objectives are your North Star and serve as an essential reference point for meaningful direction, alignment, accountability, and decision making. This is why it is so important to track and manage both your personal and business objectives in your IMS.

Five Steps to Creating Personal and Professional Objectives

We recommend completing the following five steps to assist you in creating your Meaningful Objectives:

1. Integrating professional and personal–creating balance

2. Creating alignment and accountability–The MPS Action Hierarchy Model

3. Establishing your professional and personal Meaningful Objectives

    ❏ Are your Meaningful Objectives outcome related and meaningful?

    ❏ Are your Meaningful Objectives specific, measurable, and realistic?

4. Being in alignment and accountable

5. Organizing your Meaningful Objectives in your IMS

Part Three:
Creating an
Integrated
Management
System—The
Processing and
Organizing
Phase

1. Integrating Professional and Personal—Creating Balance

Tracking both personal and business objectives in your IMS not only increases your productivity, it assists you to create and maintain work-life balance. Remember, "You go where you focus." If you have only business goals tracked in your system, you'll migrate to a purely business focus. Your personal life will be without clear direction and your results will reflect that lack of attention, as we're sure some of you have experienced.

Most of the companies we work with today have specific systems and tools to manage their business goal setting process. However, employees are not using these systems and tools to manage their personal goal setting. Clients hardly ever track all their personal actions in their systems let alone their personal goals! They're overwhelmed, spending most of their time at work, neglecting their priorities at home, and feeling like they don't have a personal life.

When clients do track personal activities, more than likely, it's happening in their heads and not in their systems. This causes them to feel overwhelmed or to underestimate the time it takes to complete personal activities. We've noticed that if clients don't use their IMS to manage their personal lives, it's easy to overlook them and default to a business focus, putting their private lives at the bottom of the list. For some of you, your personal lives don't even make the list! That's exactly why we suggest you use your IMS as a tool to track and manage your personal objectives just as you would your business ones. With both recorded in one central system you can begin to improve your sense of balance and ensure your true values and priorities are being achieved.

For example, Lola, one of our clients, is a vice president at a retail company. She had a personal objective this year to learn how to jump horses, which involved taking jumping lessons three times a week: Tuesday, Thursday, and Saturday mornings. She also had an objective to launch a new product line in a four-month time period, which was an aggressive time frame. Riding was a fun activity that enabled her to more easily spend long hours ensuring the launch was successful. These two objectives complemented one another; Lola had a lot of fun and was also highly productive. Having clear personal and business goals that promote your well-being and self-expression is not only possible, it's actually more productive.

Part Three:
Creating an
Integrated
Management
System—The
Processing and
Organizing
Phase

Take Back Your LIfe!

2. Creating Alignment and Accountability—The Action Hierarchy Model

When you create business objectives, it's important that they align with your department's overall Mission, Vision, Values, and Unifying Goals. This kind of alignment ensures everyone in the company is focusing in the same direction, working toward department goals that ultimately roll up to the company goals.

In Figure 8-2, the MPS Action Hierarchy Model, you can see five levels of planning and action starting with Mission, Vision, Values, moving down through Unifying Goals to Strategic Next Actions. This model combined with the MPS Cycle of Productivity demonstrates how to create an environment in which alignment and accountability thrive. These two models are powerful and provide a simple way to improve productivity not only for you, but for your team and your organization.

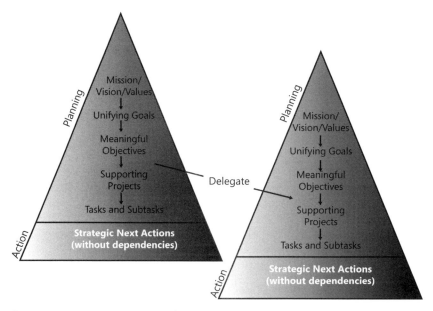

Figure 8-2   MPS Action Hierarchy Model demonstrating alignment.

Alignment

One of the key elements we're highlighting with the Action Hierarchy Model is aligning your Meaningful Objectives with your division's Unifying Goal. A Unifying Goal spans a year and is the most important goal a division can achieve. Senior management is accountable for it, and all Meaningful

Chapter Eight: **Creating Meaningful Objectives**

Part Three:
Creating an
Integrated
Management
System—The
Processing and
Organizing
Phase

Objectives in the division directly support and roll up to it. This kind of alignment ensures that all individual contributions and actions directly impact the Unifying Goal. It is a critical factor. Without it, you and your staff can easily end up focusing in different and opposing directions, creating lots of activity but not moving toward any meaningful result. Figure 8-3 demonstrates nonalignment versus alignment: the first arrow shows particles moving in the same direction and the second arrow shows particles moving in opposing directions. As you can tell, it is more productive if all the particles are moving in the same direction!

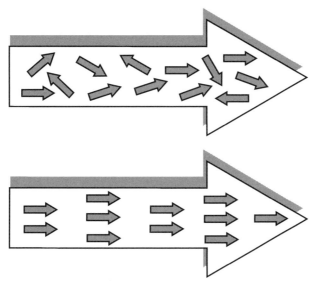

Figure 8-3   Nonalignment versus alignment.

Accountability

The next key element we highlight is accountability, and this relates to the Cycle of Productivity. Imagine if everyone in your company had clear Meaningful Objectives and routinely focused on completing Strategic Next Actions. Each time they'd complete a Strategic Next Action, they'd unlock a dependency that was keeping one of their Subtasks inactive. As they continued the Cycle of Productivity, consistently completing Strategic Next Actions, they'd eventually unlock their Subtasks completely, and then their Tasks, and then their Supporting Projects, and then their Meaningful Objectives, and eventually the Unifying Goals and Mission of their division. Finally, the Unifying Goals and Mission of the company would be achieved. Obviously, reaching the Mission requires completing many cycles of action, which is why we recommend tracking your objectives in your Integrated

Part Three:
Creating an
Integrated
Management
System—The
Processing and
Organizing
Phase

Take Back Your LIfe!

Management System. By having them tracked in your To-Do List, you're able to review them, create appropriate Strategic Next Actions, and maintain the Cycle of Productivity.

Not only is it important to have objectives that align with your Unifying Goal, it's also important to be accountable to routinely complete the actions necessary to achieve your objectives. None of this is new information; however, implementing it into our daily lives takes a conscious effort and discipline. A church in Sussex, England, dating from 1720, displays this quote: "A vision without a task is but a dream. A task without a vision is drudgery. A task and a vision together is the hope of the world." This sums up this section beautifully; it takes both vision and action to cause something to happen. Another way of saying this is: consistently completing Strategic Next Actions that link to and drive Meaningful Objectives—not as poetic, but definitely in alignment.

When you combine the Cycle of Productivity with the Action Hierarchy Model you begin to create an environment where alignment and accountability become commonplace. Individuals want to contribute to a higher purpose and they want to know that what they do does make a difference. This kind of environment ensures that individuals are taking actions that link to Meaningful Objectives and contribute to the overall goals and mission of the company.

3. Establishing Your Meaningful Objectives

Business Objectives

Before you start to create your business objectives, we suggest you first meet with your boss to find out what your department's Mission, Vision, Values, and Unifying Goals are. This information gives you a reference point to align with when developing your individual objectives.

When we ask our clients to share their corporate Mission, Vision, Values, and Unifying Goals, many of them stare at us like deer in a headlight! Creating this level of clarity can be a tiny bit intimidating even for the most successful executive. Often this information is stored in their minds and is not documented, or if it is documented, it can be unclear, hidden in digital folders, and rarely viewed.

Do not expect your boss to have this information prepared and be using it as we suggest in this book. If he or she does, this is great news and it'll make your life easier. However, in the absence of such clarity this process can still

Part Three:
Creating an
Integrated
Management
System—The
Processing and
Organizing
Phase

be completed. Simply start to think about your own objectives based on what you perceive the Mission, Vision, and Values of your department to be and what you think the Unifying Goal would be. The Unifying Goal is the most critical piece for you to identify because your Meaningful Objectives roll up to this goal.

Unifying Goal   A Unifying Goal is a department or company goal that spans a year or more. It is the most important goal. Not all staff are accountable for it, only the senior management team is; however, all the staff's Meaningful Objectives link to and align behind it.

Examples of some of our clients Unifying Goals are as follows:

- Grow revenues by 20 percent and profit by 5 percent by December 31
- Generate 1,200 qualified leads to support product revenue goal of $2.5 million by December 31

After you have an idea of what the Unifying Goal would be for your department, write it down in Exercise 8-1, titled "Identifying the Unifying Goal and Areas of Focus," which follows. When this is done, you can then transition from the Unifying Goal to creating your Areas of Focus and finally your Meaningful Objectives.

Areas of Focus   To simplify the process of creating Meaningful Objectives, we're going to introduce what we call Areas of Focus or Roles. **Focus** means to concentrate, to spotlight, or to be a focal point for. **Role** relates to specific functions you perform or parts you play. These Areas of Focus and Roles are specific to a one-year time period, and you'll likely end up with three to six of them. They are unique to your industry, your role, and your Unifying Goal. More simply said, Areas of Focus and Roles are the primary areas you have to pay attention to in order to support the department Unifying Goal.

We suggest you limit these Areas of Focus to a minimal number, four to six, and prioritize them relative to the impact you want to have and the amount of attention and/or resources you want to give them. Having too many Areas of Focus dilutes your time, attention, energy, and financial resources, causing you to become reactive and distracted.

Following are a few examples of Unifying Goals and Areas of Focus from our clients that might help bring more clarity to this process for you.

Susan Burk and Jeff Ford run a small CPA firm in Denver where they have five staff members. They're both excited to grow their business, understand-

Part Three:
Creating an
Integrated
Management
System—The
Processing and
Organizing
Phase

Take Back Your Life!

ing they'll need to do additional marketing and business development to expand it At the same time, they want to continue servicing existing clients and running the day-to-day operations. Susan and Jeff created the following Unifying Goal and Areas of Focus for their business:

Unifying Goal

■ Grow revenues by 20 percent and increase profit by 5 percent by December 31

Areas of Focus

1. Marketing

2. Business development

3. Services

4. Operations

Linda Contreras, another client who is a product marketing manager, created the following Unifying Goal and Areas of Focus:

Unifying Goal

■ Generate 1,200 qualified leads to support product revenue goal of $2.5 million by December 31

Areas of Focus

1. Advertising and promotions

2. Sales tools

3. Trade shows and events

4. Revenue

5. Web site

As you can tell, Susan and Jeff's and Linda's Areas of Focus are quite different because their industries, roles, and Unifying Goals are different. Your Unifying Goal and Areas of Focus will also be unique to your industry, department, and situation.

To assist you in drafting your Areas of Focus, ask yourself the following question: "What areas or roles do I need to focus on to achieve my Unifying Goal?" List these areas or roles below in Exercise 8-1, in the column titled "Draft Areas of Focus."

After you have them written down, review them and ask the question, "Which areas will impact the Unifying Goal the most?" Rewrite your list in

Chapter Eight: **Creating Meaningful Objectives**

Part Three:
Creating an
Integrated
Management
System—The
Processing and
Organizing
Phase

priority order according to the impact each would have on the Unifying Goal. List these under the section titled "Prioritized Areas of Focus."

Exercise 8-1   Identifying the Unifying Goal and Areas of Focus

Unifying Goal:	
Draft Areas of Focus	**Prioritized Areas of Focus**
	1.
	2.
	3.
	4.
	5.
	6.

Meaningful Objectives   After you've clarified your Unifying Goal and Areas of Focus, you can start the process of drafting your Meaningful Objectives. A Meaningful Objective is a long-term significant result that directly supports the accomplishment of a Mission and Unifying Goal statement. A Meaningful Objective is something that you're personally accountable for achieving as opposed to a shared goal, such as a Unifying Goal.

All of us have objectives; however, they may not all be documented or clearly identified. This section assists you in clarifying and recording them.

Following are the five characteristics of a Meaningful Objective:

- Rolls up to a corporate Mission and Unifying Goal statement
- Involves multiple Supporting Projects and resources
- Is written from an outcome perspective
- Takes place over time and has specific due dates
- Includes metrics to measure progress and completion

It's important to understand the distinctions between Unifying Goals, Meaningful Objectives, and Supporting Projects because this will support you in creating Meaningful Objectives that are indeed Meaningful Objectives.

A Unifying Goal is expansive and broad, it relates to your department as a whole and not to your specific individual role. You are not personally

Part Three:
Creating an
Integrated
Management
System—The
Processing and
Organizing
Phase

Take Back Your LIfe!

accountable for achieving the Unifying Goal; you support it, align with it, and are directed by it.

Meaningful Objectives are large and complex, they involve multiple resources and affect multiple stakeholders. You're individually accountable for them, they normally take a year to complete and they directly support the Unifying Goal.

Objectives are then broken down into multiple Supporting Projects. Supporting Projects make it easier to plan and manage your Meaningful Objectives and help reduce the complexity into simplicity and give you an idea of how detailed and large the objective really is.

Susan's Meaningful Objectives roll up to her Areas of Focus and Unifying Goal:

1. **Unifying Goal**

   ❑ Grow revenues by 20 percent and increase profit by 5 percent by December 31

2. **Area of Focus: Marketing**

   ❑ Meaningful Objective 1: Local paper publishes business article about our company and services–April 27

   ❑ Meaningful Objective 2: Distribute 12 monthly digital newsletters that add value for readers

3. **Area of Focus: Business Development**

   ❑ Meaningful Objective 3: Create 15 new "small to medium" business clients

4. **Area of Focus: Services**

   ❑ Meaningful Objective 4: Deliver $200,000 in billable services

5. **Area of Focus: Operations**

   ❑ Meaningful Objective 5: Hire vendor to implement new customer relationship management (CRM) system, centralizing tracking of client information, within budget

In Exercise 8-2, "Creating Professional Meaningful Objectives," rewrite your Unifying Goal and your Areas of Focus. Then create your Meaningful Objectives, picking the ones you think will contribute most to each Area of Focus and the Unifying Goal(s). We suggest that you have no more than 10 objectives total; this causes you to be more strategic and focused about the objectives you create and makes it easier to manage and complete them. Don't be concerned about writing them perfectly the first time around. The idea is to

Chapter Eight: Creating Meaningful Objectives

Part Three:
Creating an
Integrated
Management
System—The
Processing and
Organizing
Phase

take an initial stab at them; you'll be reviewing and fine-tuning them several times in this chapter before you complete them to ensure they are meaningful, outcome focused, specific, measurable, and realistic. You use the five characteristics of a Meaningful Objective mentioned earlier as a reference point for confirming that your objectives are indeed objectives.

Imagine yourself celebrating with your colleagues on December 31. You're sitting in a snowy vacation resort at dinner toasting your teammates and acknowledging each other for what you've accomplished this year. What objectives did you accomplish that supported the Unifying Goal? What were you most proud of that you created and completed? What was most meaningful to you?"

Exercise 8-2 Creating professional Meaningful Objectives

Unifying Goal:
Area of Focus 1:
Meaningful Objective:
Meaningful Objective:
Area of Focus 2:
Meaningful Objective:
Meaningful Objective:
Area of Focus 3:
Meaningful Objective:
Meaningful Objective:
Area of Focus 4:
Meaningful Objective:
Meaningful Objective:
Area of Focus 5:
Meaningful Objective:
Meaningful Objective:
Area of Focus 6:
Meaningful Objective:
Meaningful Objective:

Part Three:
Creating an
Integrated
Management
System—The
Processing and
Organizing
Phase

Take Back Your LIfe!

Personal Objectives

The process of creating personal goals is slightly different from creating business goals. Companies have more structure and purpose around goal setting because more people are involved and the mission is paramount; therefore, goal-setting frameworks are hierarchical. Families don't require the same hierarchy; their processes are more independent and more organic. Some of our clients have created their own personal Mission, Visions, and Values and create joint Unifying Goals with their partners; however, it's not required to complete personal objectives successfully.

Vision   We suggest that you start by creating a one-year vision for yourself and from that vision create your Areas of Focus or roles. A vision is a specific written image of how you would like the future to be. This will be a one-year vision that represents how you want to contribute and express yourself. How you want to support your purpose and values. It relates to what brings you joy, enthusiasm, and happiness.

Susan's personal vision is the following:

> "Grow my business easily and gracefully, working in cooperation with my partner Jeff. Celebrate getting married to Henry in October with all my family and friends present. Take an awesome honeymoon with Henry in Africa and lose 15 pounds so I can look my best at the wedding and improve my general health. Increase my net worth by 20 percent in line with my long-term financial goals. Attend the Mile High Church at least one Sunday a month and continue monthly service work at the food bank. Enjoy spending time with family and friends in our newly renovated house. Complete the sprinkler system so I don't have to hand water the yard!"

To assist you in creating your own personal vision, imagine yourself at year-end sitting by a toasty, warm fire celebrating. "What happened that was most meaningful to you last year? What were you most grateful for?" We recommend you write your draft vision in Exercise 8-3 titled " Personal One-Year Vision," which follows.

Areas of Focus   Unlike professional Areas of Focus, which are incredibly diverse given the many different industries and jobs, your personal Areas of Focus are simpler and tend to be more standard. As is the case with your professional Areas of Focus we suggest you limit the number you have to a minimum and prioritize them relative to the impact you want them to have.

Part Three:
Creating an
Integrated
Management
System—The
Processing and
Organizing
Phase

Here is an example of Susan's Prioritized Areas of Focus:

1. Career
2. Family and friends
3. Finance
4. Health and well-being
5. Spiritual and community service
6. Home

Take a moment and create the Areas of Focus or roles you need to work in to impact your personal vision. Write down those Areas of Focus in Exercise 8-3 in the section titled "Draft Areas of Focus." Next, establish the priority order you would want them to be in to best support your vision, and list those in the section titled "Prioritized Areas of Focus."

Exercise 8-3 Creating One Year Vision

Personal vision:	
Draft Areas of Focus:	**Prioritized Areas of Focus:**
	1.
	2.
	3.
	4.
	5.
	6.

Part Three:
Creating an
Integrated
Management
System—The
Processing and
Organizing
Phase

Take Back Your LIfe!

Meaningful Objectives   Now that you've created your Areas of Focus, the next step is drafting your one year Meaningful Objectives for each of these areas. These objectives directly support your vision in happening, they are meaningful and specific, and you are accountable to make them happen.

Susan's personal objectives are the following:

1. **Area of Focus: Career**

    ❑ Meaningful Objective 1: Work in cooperation with Jeff to achieve our professional Unifying Goal

2. **Area of Focus: Family and friends**

    ❑ Meaningful Objective 2: Get married on October 9 with family and friends present

3. **Area of Focus: Finance**

    ❑ Meaningful Objective 3: Increase net worth by 20 percent

4. **Area of Focus: Health and well-being**

    ❑ Meaningful Objective 4: Lose 15 pounds by October 9

    ❑ Meaningful Objective 5: Complete dream honeymoon with Henry in Africa on October 23

5. **Area of Focus: Spiritual and community service**

    ❑ Meaningful Objective 6: Create two group work parties at the Food Bank

6. **Area of Focus: Home**

    ❑ Meaningful Objective 7: Set up new sprinkler system and have it working by May 1

Take a moment to draft your Meaningful Objectives in Exercise 8-4, "Creating Personal Meaningful Objectives," which follows. Remember, they do not have to be perfect because we will be revisiting them several times in this chapter to ensure they are meaningful, outcome related, specific, measurable, and realistic. (If you need more room, use a separate sheet of paper.)

Part Three:
Creating an
Integrated
Management
System—The
Processing and
Organizing
Phase

Exercise 8-4   Creating Personal Meaningful Objectives

Area of Focus 1:
Meaningful Objective:
Meaningful Objective:
Area of Focus 2:
Meaningful Objective:
Meaningful Objective:
Area of Focus 3:
Meaningful Objective:
Meaningful Objective:
Area of Focus 4:
Meaningful Objective:
Meaningful Objective:
Area of Focus 5:
Meaningful Objective:
Meaningful Objective:
Area of Focus 6:
Meaningful Objective:
Meaningful Objective:

Part Three:
Creating an
Integrated
Management
System—The
Processing and
Organizing
Phase

Take Back Your LIfe!

Are Your Objectives Outcome Related and Meaningful?

As you review your draft objectives, it's important to ensure they're outcome related and meaningful; they will be a lot more effective and inspiring.

Are your objectives outcome related?   We use the word **outcome** to remind clients to focus on the end result of their objectives, to make certain they're valuable . Sometimes our clients get so caught up in doing and achieving, they forget to ponder why they're doing what they're doing and what their desired outcomes are.

Outcomes define in more detail what you want to accomplish with your objective. They describe the **end result**, stating specifically what it'll look and feel like, and when it needs to be done, and they take into account the expectations of other interested parties who are affected by the objective.

When we reviewed Susan's professional objectives, we checked to see if she had considered the outcomes. We asked Susan what her number one objective was.

She said, "That's easy; I want to expand my business."

We asked her, "How would you know if you had completed this?"

She responded, "I would have more clients."

We asked, "How many more?" and she said, "Ten more."

"Hmmm," we wondered. "Now what if you had 10 more clients but your revenue and profit did not increase. Is that the outcome you want?"

She said, "Well, no. I want our business to make more money and profit so that we can grow."

We said, "Great. Then you need to state that in your objective because you could easily get more clients and not increase revenue or profit." We asked, "How much of an increase do you want to see with regard to profit and revenue?"

Susan replied, "Now you're really pinning me down!"

We responded, "That's exactly right. You want to pin yourself down so that the end result is perfectly clear. This way, you ensure you'refocusing on the objective that is most important to you.

One of our clients, Kelly Rollin, had a personal objective to go on vacation to Hawaii. Kelly and her husband were fairly new to their marriage and still learning about each other. After they finished different consulting engage-

Crystallize your
goals. Make a plan
for achieving them,
and set yourself a
deadline. Then,
with supreme con-
fidence, determina-
tion and disregard
for obstacles and
other people's criti-
cisms carry out
your plan.
—**Paul Meyer**

Chapter Eight: **Creating Meaningful Objectives**

Part Three:
Creating an
Integrated
Management
System—The
Processing and
Organizing
Phase

ments, Kelly arrived in Hawaii from the East Coast, and her husband, Russell, arrived from the Midwest. As Russell unpacked his luggage, Kelly noticed tennis rackets, golf clubs, and scuba gear and became a little nervous about the kind of vacation her husband had planned! She unpacked a couple of bathing suits, three books, earplugs, and her iPod. Kelly later told me, "We didn't discuss our outcomes for the vacation! It seems as though he planned to be 'outdoor action man.' Chase it, hit it, stab it, and whack it! I came to relax, sleep, read, watch movies, and be a sloth by the pool!"

What they missed was a brief conversation about the kind of vacation they each envisioned. They hadn't talked about what it would look and feel like, and how they'd know if the vacation was successful. Their objective was not outcome related.

Based on this information, we'd like you to buy a large 5 foot by 3 foot whiteboard and hang it in the kitchen so that you can brainstorm with your partner in your home. Only kidding! Going out to coffee and chatting about your objectives and what the end results would be, what they would look and feel like, and how you'd know they are successful is a good thing. After you've answered these questions, you'll have a better idea of what to expect and how to write outcome-related objectives that are both meaningful and inspiring.

When writing Meaningful Objectives, it's important to distinguish between objectives that are "end result" oriented versus objectives that are "how to" oriented. Stan, a program manager for a software company, had an objective to launch a new product by October 28.

We asked him, "If you successfully launch this product, what will happen?"

He replied, "Customers would buy it, find it useful, and refer friends."

We questioned, "Is the end result launching the product, or is the end result customers are buying the product?"

He groaned, "Well, if we don't launch it, customers won't buy it!"

We grinned. "That's true; however, what's the end result you're after, a product launch or product sales? A product launch may not give you product sales; it depends on the launch!"

He got the point. Launching the product was a "how to" statement not an "end result" statement. The outcome was more along the lines of "30,000 customers purchase XRT product in the first three months and customer feedback is high." Now of course the launch was part of the objective likely

Part Three:
Creating an
Integrated
Management
System—The
Processing and
Organizing
Phase

Take Back Your LIfe!

a Supporting Project and had to happen; however, the end result was that customers bought the product, loved it, and referred friends. Remember, "You go where you focus" and therefore it's important to review your objectives and establish "end result" statements. It's so easy to be lazy and state objectives in the form of "how to" instead of outcomes. Meaningful Objectives with end result statements take some thought and disciplined thinking.

The key with outcomes is to be specific and to think through the various ways you can measure the objective. These measurements will be the guiding light for team members as they walk through the many decisions they'll have to make related to the objective. Clear outcomes help people make clear decisions.

Take a few moments and review the Meaningful Objectives in Exercises 8-2 and 8-4. Ask these questions:

- What's the end result I'm truly after?

- When this objective is complete, what specifically will have happened that demonstrates I've been successful?

- Am I focusing on an *end result* statement or a *how to* statement?

Making your objectives outcome related will ensure you produce the results you truly want.

Some of our clients have clear objectives that are textbook perfect; however, they're not compelling or meaningful to them. You can't make an objective meaningful to you if it isn't. Meaningful Objectives are designed to support you in moving toward a vision that's compelling and motivational. If you're in a situation where the vision isn't inspiring to you, we suggest you pause and give this some thought. It could be a perfectly good vision, but for some reason you're not in alignment with it and it does not speak to you. At this point you may seriously want to consider your options and review transitioning to a department that has a vision that is compelling and really 'calls' to you. Ultimately, this will be better for both you and the company. There is nothing wrong with this—it's purely data for you to consider as you make choices about what you want to do and how you want to express yourself. Working with a vision and objectives that are motivating and meaningful are really important.

Remember the old model: surviving, coping, resigned, and cynical. Many individuals live in this condition on a routine basis; you have to decide if that is what you want. To transition to the new model of thriving, causing,

Chapter Eight: **Creating Meaningful Objectives**

Part Three:
Creating an
Integrated
Management
System—The
Processing and
Organizing
Phase

and generating your dreams to come true, you need to be discerning and courageous about your choices and about the objectives you want for yourself. The key here is remembering you do have a choice—a choice to have your dreams come true.

Creating Meaningful Objectives is a process. Give yourself time to check that your objectives align with a vision that calls to you and that they're compelling and inspiring to you personally.

When Susan reviewed her objectives, she felt clear she was in alignment, motivated, and inspired by them. She was thrilled to be growing her business with Jeff, getting married to Henry, going to Africa, and losing weight. All these objectives brought her joy and encouraged her to express herself fully. Even the sprinkler system was exciting to Susan because it meant she no longer had to water with a hose every other day!

Remember that simple things also make a huge difference. Objectives do not have to be loaded with significance to be meaningful to you. Sometimes they can be quite ordinary, and it's in the ordinariness we often find our greatest personal meaning. Be careful not to get too significant with your objectives; focus on the simple things and keep your eye on having fun—it's more inspiring that way.

Take a few moments now and review the Meaningful Objectives in Exercises 8-2 and 8-4 and ask these questions:

■ What is it about this objective that is meaningful and inspiring to me?

■ Am I motivated by these objectives?

Being clear on end result statements ensures all the little things go in the right direction. It also creates greater alignment not just for you but for your team and the people you interact with in different departments. Making sure your objectives are meaningful creates personal motivation and inspiration. Take the time to make sure your objectives reflect those outcomes and are personally meaningful to you.

Are Your Objectives Specific, Measurable, and Realistic?

To be accountable for your objectives you'll want to make them specific, measurable, and realistic. This enables you to evaluate progress, monitor on-course/off-course feedback, and determine if you have successfully completed them.

Part Three:
Creating an
Integrated
Management
System—The
Processing and
Organizing
Phase

Take Back Your LIfe!

Are your objectives Specific and Measurable?   When we reviewed each of Susan's objectives, we asked her, "How will you measure this? How will you know when this has been successfully achieved? When will this be completed?" These three questions cause you to be specific and ensure you have a way to measure progress and completion. Susan's only hiccup was around her newsletter objective: "Distribute 12 monthly digital newsletters that add value for readers." Susan knew that measuring if 12 newsletters were sent out was simple; however, measuring value to customers was going to take some thought.

After pondering, Susan decided to create a pre survey asking clients what they considered valuable and building the newsletter around the feedback. Then, she'd create a post survey, with an incentive to respond, asking if the newsletter was valuable. She planned to do this early in the year so that she could make the appropriate course corrections. Jeff and Susan also talked about monitoring the unsubscribe numbers, assuming that some level of value was being received if these numbers were few. This plan gave Susan and Jeff confidence that they would have some way to measure this objective; it was not as finite as "numbers of newsletter written and sent"; however, it was a lot better than no measurement at all.

When you start to look at measuring your Meaningful Objectives often you find that this process will cause you to change the objective because it had been written in such a way as to be unmeasurable. For example, Susan's original objective was "grow the business." Because this did not stipulate a specific amount, it was impossible for Susan to plan and manage this objective because there were no reference points for progress or completion. For example, did "grow the business" mean grow it by $100,000 or by $1 million? If it was $100,000, Susan would need to engage in $100,000 planning and managing. If it was $1 million, Susan would need to do $1 million planning and managing. These two scenarios are completely different!

"Grow the business" was not a useful objective because it was not specific or measurable. It didn't communicate the outcome that Susan and Jeff wanted. When we asked, "How will you measure this?" and "How will you know when this objective is successfully achieved?" Susan quantified the objective and changed it to "Grow revenue by 20 percent and profit by 5 percent by December 31." This level of specificity made planning and monitoring progress much easier. It also stipulated a very clear end point so that there would be no questions as to whether they achieved the objective or not. In the absence of specifics, planning and managing become quite meaningless.

Chapter Eight: **Creating Meaningful Objectives**

Part Three:
Creating an
Integrated
Management
System—The
Processing and
Organizing
Phase

It is easy to avoid being specific. It can be scary to put a limit on things—it boxes us in, eliminates the alternatives, and pins us down. It creates a clear milestone measuring if we did or did not make it. Specific goals put our butts firmly on the line and can create pressure; however, if they're meaningful, it's likely a pressure you'll welcome and be inspired to meet. Meaningful Objectives call you to account, they call you to take action, to get out of bed in the morning and keep completing cycles of action until the objective's done. In other words, specific objectives inspire you to move to the new model of causing and generating your success.

Are your objectives realistic?   Last, we're going to talk about your Meaningful Objectives being realistic. When you commit to a result and fall short, it doesn't always feel good. Frankly, it can feel pretty yucky, and we're sure you can think of more appropriate terms to use! We recommend you set yourself up from the beginning to achieve your goals and make them realistic from the get go. We suggest you get practical, pragmatic, and ask tough questions that get you to the brutal facts: "What did we do last year? What plans are currently in place to make this objective happen? Have we done this before? What resources do we have available to support this?" Realistic does not necessarily mean comfortable and is doesn't mean you've done it before; it means there's a level of reality involved: past history, available resources, and future projections that support the result.

Don't agree to an objective blindly. Make sure you have clear execution plans and some past history; otherwise, you could unwittingly be setting yourself up for failure. After you commit to an objective, you're accountable for it and it's important to honor your commitments, not just for yourself but for your team and your colleagues. Ask the tough questions, get to the brutal facts, don't be embarrassed to do that, and take the time that's required to get all of the information you need. Only when you know what is involved can you then decide if you can commit to it and be accountable for the result. When you don't make a goal, it's easy to look back and say, "If only I had done this" or "If only we had done that" or "If only I thought this through more carefully in the beginning." Do your thinking on the front end, not on the back end, and set yourself up to be successful—measure twice, and cut once!

Take a moment to review your objectives and make sure they're realistic, specific, and measurable and that you can be 100 percent accountable for them. Ensure you created objectives you can achieve or exceed, and make that a conscious practice; it will do wonders for your confidence, leadership, and credibility.

Part Three:
Creating an
Integrated
Management
System—The
Processing and
Organizing
Phase

Take Back Your LIfe!

4. Being in Alignment and Being Accountable

Business Focus

After you've created your professional objectives we suggest you book a meeting with your boss to discuss if the objectives are in alignment with the Unifying Goal and if you have your boss's support in achieving them. Your performance review is likely to be measured by these objectives; therefore, getting your boss's involvement and agreement is critical and will enable you to be 100 percent accountable.

Be prepared to fine-tune your objectives based on your boss's feedback. Some companies don't have clear Mission statements and Unifying Goals. In these cases, it's even more important for you to share your objectives with your boss to gain your boss's personal support and alignment. It's not easy to be accountable for objectives if your boss is not behind you 100 percent. You want your boss to be committed to you and your objectives.

After you've gained your boss's support, we recommend you review your objectives to see who else you're depending on, and then meet with these people to gain their support and cooperation. You might also want to consider who is affected by your objectives to see if you need to collaborate with that person or those people as well. What you're doing here is being accountable: lining up all the people you need to make sure you're going to meet your goals ahead of time, which will make your life easier and more fun.

Our clients who are managers have told us how empowering it is to have their staff come to them to discuss Unifying Goals, Areas of Focus, and Meaningful Objectives. Discussing the Unifying Goal lets your boss know that you're thinking of what's best for the department and for you. Sharing Areas of Focus and objectives lets your boss know you've taken time to strategize what will make the biggest impact for the Unifying Goal, where your time is best used, and what you're willing to be accountable for. Our clients have told us, "This type of conversation is proactive, solution-oriented, and inspiring. I want all my staff to be figuring this stuff out because it makes my job a lot easier." This type of conversation takes place in the new model of causing and generating your success. It is powerful and has a great deal of integrity.

Part Three:
Creating an
Integrated
Management
System—The
Processing and
Organizing
Phase

Personal Focus

Much like your business objectives, it makes a difference to gain the appropriate buy-in ahead of time with regard to achieving your personal objectives. Some objectives you can achieve independently without support; however, others directly involve your family, and so you'll want family members' encouragement and alignment. For example, Susan was not getting married without Henry agreeing and neither was she going to Africa without his support. These types of joint objectives cannot be created in a vacuum. Susan needed to communicate with Henry to gain his full agreement before moving forward. For Susan to be accountable for these objectives, she was dependent on Henry.

Susan also wanted to lose weight, and although she could manage this independently, she knew it would be a lot easier if Henry supported her food program while eating meals at home. Most of our objectives involve other people or at least their support and encouragement. We recommend that you get into communication with family members who are affected by your objectives and, when appropriate, co-create objectives with them or gain their alignment, support, and encouragement. As a result, you'll not be alone in your vision; you'll have partners working with you to support you in making your year more meaningful, easier, and a whole lot more fun.

Susan had completed writing her personal and business objectives, and she felt they were complementary and supported her work-life balance. She didn't mind working hard knowing she had a two-week honeymoon in Africa with her husband coming up. Also, her house was newly renovated and all that was left to do was install the new sprinkler system. This ensured that when Susan and Henry were at home, there was nothing for them to do but enjoy themselves, their family, and friends. Her professional and personal objectives now complemented each other and created work-life balance.

Assuming your objectives are now complete, we recommend you review them one by one from the top of your list to the bottom. Consider the time and energy it will take to achieve them, imagine the road blocks you might encounter and what you need to do to overcome them. Ask yourself, "Can I achieve all of these objectives and remain in balance? Do these objectives support and complement each other? Can I be accountable for each and every one of these?" You want to be able to achieve all of them and accomplish them with a sense of well-being and balance.

Also, you can check them against the five characteristics of an objective listed in the section titled "Meaningful Objectives" earlier in this chapter to

Part Three:
Creating an
Integrated
Management
System—The
Processing and
Organizing
Phase

Take Back Your Life!

ensure they're Meaningful Objectives as opposed to Supporting Projects or Unifying Goals. We describe all of the characteristics in this chapter except for the last one, "Including metrics to measure progress and completion," which we cover in Chapter 9.

Professional and personal objectives are critical elements to your productivity and work-life balance, they are essential for your Integrated Management System to work effectively. They're reference points for motivation, making decisions, monitoring progress, and course correcting. Your productivity and work-life balance are truly dependent on them. Take the time to make sure you complete them before you move ahead; it'll be one of the best investments you ever made in yourself and your system.

5. Organizing Your Meaningful Objectives in Your IMS

Now, you're going to enter your Meaningful Objectives into your Microsoft Office Outlook To-Do List and categorize them in either your .Meaningful Objectives: Business or .Meaningful Objectives: Personal category.

To do this, follow these steps:

1. Go to the To-Do List either by clicking the Tasks icon or by clicking the Go menu and selecting Tasks.

2. Double-click the words Click Here To Add A New Task.

3. Type your Meaningful Objective title in the Subject text box.

4. Click the Categorize button and select either .Meaningful Objective: Business or .Meaningful Objective: Personal, as appropriate (see Figure 8-4). If you do not see either of these choices, select All Categories, select the appropriate category from the Color Categories list by putting a check mark in the box to the left of the category name, and then click OK. Across the top of the Task you should see the name of the category you selected.

5. In the Task, press Save and Close, and watch it instantly show up in the category you selected.

Chapter Eight: **Creating Meaningful Objectives**

Part Three:
Creating an
Integrated
Management
System—The
Processing and
Organizing
Phase

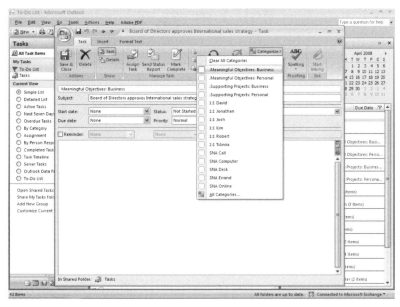

Figure 8-4   Categorizing your objectives in the To-Do List.

Some of you may want to include your professional Unifying Goal in your Integrated Management System as well, to do this you can either create a new Category called: ..Unifying Goal: Business or you can include it with your Meaningful Objectives: Business category and clearly label the subject line as a Unifying Goal. In terms of your personal vision, you can either create a new category or label it as a task under Meaningful Objectives: Personal.

Congratulations! It's time to celebrate! You just took another step toward setting up your Integrated Management System, increasing your productivity, and creating work-life balance.

Now it's very important that you do not move ahead to the next chapter until you have completed creating your Meaningful Objectives and entering them into your Integrated Management System. You will be significantly more effective at processing and organizing Categories: (none) with these already typed into your To-Do List.

If you would like assistance in creating your Meaningful Objectives either individually or with your team, we recommend you hire a McGhee Productivity Solutions (MPS) consultant to coach you through this process (send a message to info@mcgheeproductivity.com). If you want additional reading materials related to creating objectives, we recommend the book *Your Best Year Yet: Ten Questions for Making the Next Twelve Months Your Most Successful Ever* by Jinny Ditzler (Warner Books, 2000).

Part Three:
Creating an
Integrated
Management
System—The
Processing and
Organizing
Phase

Take Back Your LIfe!

What Changes Will You Make?

Take a moment to contemplate the changes that you want to make as a result of reading this chapter: creating personal and business objectives and categorizing them into the objectives section of your To-Do List.

In the To-Do List in Outlook, open the IMPROVING PRODUCTIVITY task that you created in Chapter 4. Under the heading "Processing and Organizing," enter the specific tasks that you want to complete to support the successful creation of your personal and business objectives. For example, Carol's processing and organizing tasks are shown in Figure 8-5.

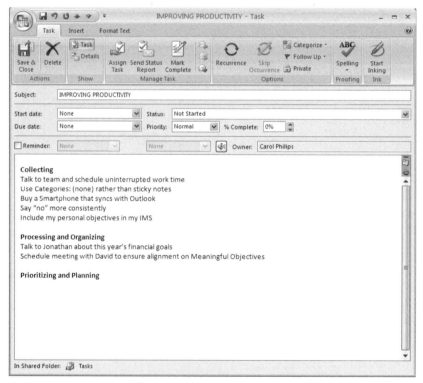

Figure 8-5   Keeping track of the changes you're going to make.

For inspiration, here are some comments that our clients have written:

- Talk to my family about our vision for next year
- Talk to my boss about the Mission, Vision, Values, and Unifying Goal for the department

Part Three:
Creating an
Integrated
Management
System—The
Processing and
Organizing
Phase

■ Book two hours on my Calendar to complete creating my personal and business objectives and entering them into my To-Do List

■ Create plans for the objectives I am not sure about to determine if they are realistic

■ Buy Jinny Ditzler's book *Your Best Year Yet*

After you've entered the changes you want to make in the Task labeled IMPROVING PRODUCTIVITY, please close it and keep it in Categories: (none). You'll be referring to it again at the end of each of the Three Phases for Creating an Integrated Management System, and eventually you will incorporate it into your list of personal objectives.

You seldom get what you go after unless you know in advance what you want.
—**Maurice Switzer**

Part Three:
Creating an
Integrated
Management
System—The
Processing and
Organizing
Phase

Take Back Your LIfe!

Chapter Nine

Processing and Organizing Categories: (none)

Part Three:
Creating an
Integrated
Management
System—The
Processing and
Organizing
Phase

Technology has dramatically increased the volume of information we receive. Some of us get as many as 250 e-mail messages a day! As you know, if you don't process and organize this information effectively, it piles up, and, before you know it, you've got 3,000 e-mail messages in your Inbox. It is so important to learn how to process this information effectively and productively so that you can put your attention on more important things.

In this chapter, you learn how to process and organize your Categories: (none) Collecting Point into your Planning and Action Categories using the McGhee Productivity Solutions (MPS) Workflow Model. The result is an empty Collecting Point and an extremely well-organized To-Do List in Microsoft Office Outlook. Most clients feel more relaxed, in control, and energized after completing this process. The skills you learn to process and organize Categories: (none) are the same skills you need to process any Collecting Point.

Introducing the MPS Workflow Model

You may find that learning how to use the MPS Workflow Model (shown in Figure 9-1) is a bit like learning how to ski or learning any skill for the first time. The ski school gives you skis, poles, boots, bindings, goggles, and a hat, and you're not sure what to do with them all, and you feel clumsy and awkward using them at first. However, with enough practice, everything comes together, and the next thing you know, you're skiing down the mountain with a big smile on your face and a lot of hooting and hollering! The same will be true of using the MPS Workflow Model. It might seem a little awkward at first, but with consistent focus, it will all come together to increase your productivity and quality of life. We might even catch you doing a little hooting and hollering when you're done!

Part Three:
Creating an
Integrated
Management
System—The
Processing and
Organizing
Phase

Take Back Your Life!

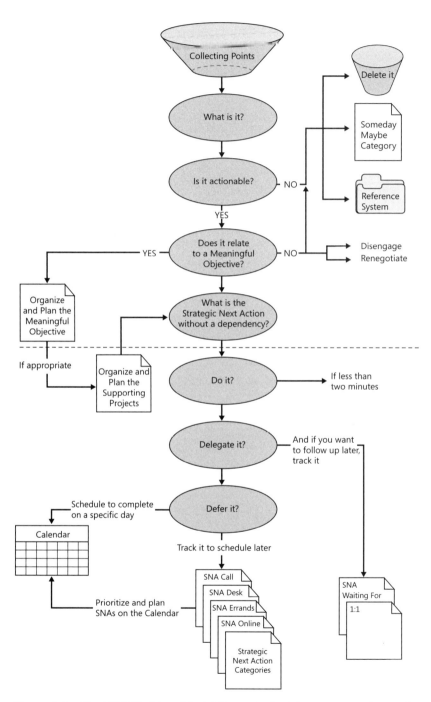

Figure 9-1 The MPS Workflow Model illustrates how to process and organize your Collecting Points into your Action and Reference Systems.

Chapter Nine: **Processing and Organizing Categories: (none)**

Part Three:
Creating an
Integrated
Management
System—The
Processing and
Organizing
Phase

The MPS Workflow Model, as shown in Figure 9-1, illustrates how to process and organize information from your Collecting Points into your Action and Reference Systems and supports you in making rapid decisions that drive toward your objectives and assist you in emptying your Collection Points.

The Processing and Organizing Phase consists of two individual parts: one, processing, and two, organizing. They're intrinsically linked but separate. Processing helps you *decide what* to do with items in your Collecting Points, and organizing helps you *decide where* to put the items in your Action or Reference System so that you can access them easily. In Figure 9-1, processing is shown as a series of seven questions, represented by ovals, and organizing is a series of files and categories, represented by rectangles, Part one—deciding what to do with it, and part two—deciding where you're going to organize it.

Let's look at these two parts in more detail: part one: processing. When you open an e-mail message in your Inbox, you need to *decide what to do with it*; otherwise, it ends up staying in your Inbox. As you know, it's all too easy to open an e-mail message, and then close it while saying, "Not sure what to do with it, it's too complicated, I don't have time right now, and I'll deal with it later!" Nothing happens except your Inbox eventually gets more full. You're procrastinating! It may not feel like it, but you are. No decisions were made to move this action forward, and it stayed right where you found it. The seven processing questions are designed to help you make tough decisions and assist you in moving your tasks forward. These questions are simple but incredibly powerful, as you'll see.

Part two: organizing. After you open an e-mail message and, for instance, decide to write a proposal for Alpine Ski House, you'll then want to *decide where to organize* it in your Action System to ensure it gets completed. This is where the Planning and Action Categories come in handy because they help you classify your actions so that you can find them easily. These categories help you organize and break down actions from Meaningful Objectives to Supporting Projects, from Supporting Projects to Tasks and Subtasks, and from Tasks and Subtasks to Strategic Next Actions. These Planning and Action Categories are extremely powerful and can change the way you approach your work and life, making it easier for you to stay focused on your objectives and on the activities that truly matter to you and your family.

Using the MPS Workflow Model

When you start to use the MPS Workflow Model, the first initial hour or two will involve placing all of your Meaningful Objectives and Supporting

Part Three:
Creating an
Integrated
Management
System—The
Processing and
Organizing
Phase

Take Back Your Life!

Projects into your tasks and categories. After this is done, you do not have to repeat this process and the model is considerably easier and quicker to use. Please be patient with yourself during this initial organizing and planning phase.

To begin using the Workflow Model, go to your Categories: (none) list and highlight the first item at the top of your list. No need to pick out a special item, just start at the top. You'll be using this item as you walk through the Workflow Model so that you can experience how the model flows while setting up and planning your Meaningful Objectives and Supporting Projects.

What Is It?

"What is it?" seems like a simple enough question, and it is, but it's also a revealing question! Sometimes what shows up in your Collecting Points is unclear, and so you need to stop for a second and review it. We're sure you've received e-mail messages and asked yourself, "What is this?!"

This first question is designed to help you pause and evaluate what's shown up. Is it reference or action material, personal or business, complex or simple? What the heck is it?

Clients often capture actions in Categories: (none), and then two days later when they start to process them, find the actions either are not clear, need more thinking, or turn out to be much bigger projects than they'd realized. Asking, "What is it?" helps evaluate what you're dealing with so that you can decide how best to move it forward. Don't be hasty answering this question. Take a moment to reflect. The value's in the pausing. This takes only a few seconds on the front end, but can save you hours on the back end.

Exercise 9-1   Take the item you highlighted in Categories: (none) and ask "What is it? Is it personal or business? Is it big or small? Am I clear what it is?" When you've clarified what it is, move forward to the second question in the Workflow Model, *"Is it actionable?"*

Example Carol was in a meeting with her boss David when he asked her to take on a special project of opening up the United Kingdom as new territory, which would be the first international region for Lucerne Publishing. Carol asked for some time to consider this. She captured the action in Categories: (none) and told David she'd get back to him by the end of the week. Later, when she came across this item as she was processing her Categories: (none) Collecting Point, she asked herself the question, "What is it?" On deeper thought, she realized that to open up the United Kingdom as a brand-new territory, she really needed to create an international sales strategy first and get approval on this strategy. This was going to take some research and thought to do. The question, "What is it?" got Carol thinking more realistically about what she was really dealing with.

Is It Actionable?

We all want to please other people by saying, "Yes, I'll do that." We're sure you've experienced that it can be much easier to say "yes" than to say "no." Right now, because your actions are scattered throughout Collecting Points instead of tracked in a central list, it's not as easy to make realistic decisions about what you can and can't do. Often, without clear data, a "yes" is easier to say than a "no." When your commitments are tracked in a central location, next to your calendar, it supports you in realistically assessing whether you can take on new agreements. This makes it easier to say "yes" and "no" with a lot more information and integrity.

Imagine for a moment, you've completed processing and organizing all of your Collecting Points so that they're empty. Your agreements are centrally located in your To-Do List in the Planning and Action Categories. Now, the question "Is it actionable?" has a lot more meaning because you can see all of your agreements in one location. This enables you to make well-informed decisions about accepting or declining new commitments.

Tasks in Categories: (none) are either actionable or not. When you come across a task that is not actionable, you'll have three choices, all of which assist you in removing it from Categories: (none), as shown in Figure 9-1:

1. You can delete it altogether.

2. If it's an action you're excited about doing, but can't do in the foreseeable future because of current commitments, you can categorize it into the Someday Maybe category. (We show you how to do this in Exercise 9-2, which follows.)

Part Three:
Creating an
Integrated
Management
System—The
Processing and
Organizing
Phase

Take Back Your Life!

3. If it is reference information and relates to an objective or company policy, you can drag it to your Reference System. (More about this topic in Chapter 10, "Improving Your Reference System.")

Someday Maybe Category

If we are realistic, all of us have more to do than we can do, and many of our clients use the Someday Maybe category for this very reason. It helps them lighten their load and keeps them honest and realistic about what they can and cannot do. And for those of you who over create, Someday Maybe can be a lifeline! It enables you to disengage from actions and let them go, knowing you can retrieve them if you wish. An example of this might be "Go on an African safari," or "Learn how to speak Spanish," or "Catch up on reading all my trade magazines." Your current workload may be such that you can't realistically complete these activities and you have no room to plan them in your calendar, and so Someday Maybe becomes a great category to put them in.

The Someday Maybe category doesn't work for everyone. Some of our clients want to eliminate a commitment entirely after they've decided to disengage from it. Storing it in a category simply doesn't work for them; they want it out of their system. However, for others, it's easier to disengage from commitments knowing that they can find them in their Someday Maybe category. You need to decide what will work best for you. There's nothing wrong with trying it on for size and observing whether you use it or not. ("The proof is in the pudding," as my mother used to say. She did make excellent English pudding, but that's another topic!—Sally McGhee)

Exercise 9-2 If the answer to the question *"Is it actionable?"* is *"No,"* do one of the following things:

- Delete it.

- Categorize it in the Someday Maybe category. To do this, open the Task you highlighted, click the Categorize button, and select Someday Maybe. If you do not see this choice in the list, select All Categories, select Someday Maybe, and then click OK. Across the top of the task you should see the Someday Maybe category you selected.

- Drag it into a reference folder in your Reference System.

Go back to Categories: (none) and pick the next item at the top of the list and start the Workflow Model over again. When you come across an item that is actionable, move to question 3, *"Does it relate to a Meaningful Objective?"*

Part Three:
Creating an
Integrated
Management
System—The
Processing and
Organizing
Phase

If the answer to the question *"Is it actionable?"* is *"Yes,"* go directly to the third question, *"Does it relate to a Meaningful Objective?"*

Example   Carol realized that her task "Create an international sales strategy" was actionable because she knew it was important to the company and to her boss. However, she was going to have to do some comprehensive planning to make this work given everything else on her plate.

Does It Relate to a Meaningful Objective?

We all have a natural desire to "do" and we've trained ourselves to get things done; but are we spending our time doing the right things, or are we just getting things done?

The purpose of asking, "Does it relate to a Meaningful Objective?" is to increase your awareness, enabling you to make well-informed decisions as to what you choose to focus your time and energy on. This question keeps you on your toes and ensures that, as much as possible, every action you take links to one of your Meaningful Objectives.

In Chapter 8, you created and organized your objectives into your . Meaningful Objectives Categories. These objectives become your reference point for answering this question. Now this doesn't mean you cannot add other objectives or rearrange the ones you have to include a more important one. The idea here is that you have a clear focus as to what is important so you can make decisions quickly.

As you ask this question consistently you will become aware of all the activities you are doing outside of your Meaningful Objectives. Our clients are always surprised to realize how much they do that doesn't relate to their objectives. It can be quite an eye-opener and leads to developing new skills around disengaging and renegotiating.

In Figure 9-1, the question "Does it relate to a Meaningful Objective?" leads to both a "yes" and "no" option. If the answer is "no," we suggest you first look to *disengage* from the commitment altogether. This involves contacting the respective stakeholder to let that person know you are disengaging and creating ways of doing this with integrity.

In some cases, you may not be able to disengage from the action because it is too far along the process and you have to complete it. At this point you can consider *renegotiation*: finding out if the task can be completed later, or changing the scope to make it easier to complete along with your other

Part Three:
Creating an
Integrated
Management
System—The
Processing and
Organizing
Phase

Take Back Your Life!

objectives. It can be uncomfortable to back out of an agreement you've already made; however, if you ask this question *before* you make agreements, you can ensure that you only involve yourself in commitments that link to one of your Meaningful Objectives. The key here is asking this question up-front so that you can let people know right away if you can assist them or not.

By disengaging from commitments that don't focus on your objectives, you free your time and energy, making it easier to stay focused on the objectives you have already agreed to accomplish.

No matter who we work with, from the CEO on down, we find that asking, "Does it relate to a Meaningful Objective?" is a powerful filter that enables individuals and teams to get present to what they are working on that does and does not link to their objectives. This information then allows them to create appropriate disengagement or renegotiation strategies. You'd be surprised how much of what you do does not relate to your objectives, and removing this level of distraction creates space for you to focus more of your attention on achieving your objectives. In other words, saying "no" actually supports you in saying "yes" to what's most important.

In Figure 9-1, if the answer to the question "Does it relate to a Meaningful Objectives?" is "yes," move to next part of the model, "Organizing and planning your Meaningful Objectives." In this section, you track and plan your Meaningful Objectives.

Exercise 9-3 If the answer to the question *"Does it relate to a Meaningful Objective?"* is *"No,"* do one of the following things:

- Delete the item.

- Open the Task and categorize it into the Someday Maybe category.

- Open the Task, in the subject line type the Strategic Next Action you need to take to disengage from it, and then categorize the Task into one of your SNA categories.

- Open the Task, in the subject line type the Strategic Next Action you need to renegotiate the item, and then categorize the Task into one of your SNA categories.

Go back to Categories: (none) and pick the next item on the top of the list and start the process over.

If the answer to the question *"Does it relate to a Meaningful Objective?"* is *"Yes,"* move to the next section, *"Organizing and planning your Meaningful Objectives."*

Example   The Task "Create international sales strategy" did not relate to one of Carol's current objectives. However, she decided that it was the right thing for her to do for the company and decided to talk to her boss about adding it as a Meaningful Objective.

Organizing and Planning Your Meaningful Objectives

In the Workflow Model shown in Figure 9-1, the question "Does it relates to a Meaningful Objective?" leads to two organizing and planning sections: Meaningful Objectives and Supporting Projects. In these two sections, you set up and plan your Meaningful Objectives and Supporting Projects. Be patient with this part of the process because it takes some time to complete. It's an important investment because it assists you in building your Integrated Management System (IMS) and supports you in focusing on your objectives and Supporting Projects, enabling you to achieve them successfully. The good news is once this is done, it is done, and you won't have to do it again for another year. After setting up and planning your objectives and Supporting Projects, using the Workflow Model gets a lot easier.

Exercise 9-4   In Exercise 9-3, if you decided that the task you were working with does relate to a Meaningful Objective and you do not currently have that Meaningful Objective tracked in your **.Meaningful Objective Category**, you'll want to track it now. Follow these steps to add the new objective:

1. In your To-Do List, double-click the words Click Here To Add A New Task.

2. Type your Meaningful Objective title in the Subject text box. Make sure it is outcome related, compelling, specific, and measurable.

3. Click the Categorize button, and select either .Meaningful Objective: Business or .Meaningful Objective: Personal. If you do not see either of these choices, select All Categories, select the appropriate category

Part Three:
Creating an
Integrated
Management
System—The
Processing and
Organizing
Phase

Take Back Your Life!

from the Color Categories list by putting a check mark to the left of the category name, and then click OK. Across the top of the Task you should see the category name you selected.

4. When you return to the Task, click Save and Close, and watch it instantly show up in Categories: (none).

Now we are going to assist you to organize and plan your objective. To do that follow these steps:

1. Open the objective you picked from the .Meaningful Objective category.

2. In the Notes section of your objective, enter two headings, all in capital letters: **SUPPORTING PROJECTS** and **METRICS**, as shown in Figure 9-2.

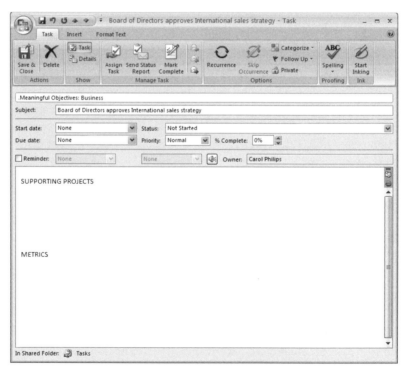

Figure 9-2   Organizing Supporting Projects and Metrics for your Meaningful Objective.

3. Minimize this Task. (We will be working with these headings in the following sections.)

Part Three:
Creating an
Integrated
Management
System—The
Processing and
Organizing
Phase

Example   Carol talked to her boss about adding "Create international sales strategy" to her Meaningful Objectives and he agreed. They edited the Meaningful objective to ensure it was end-result oriented: "Board of Directors approves international sales strategy." Carol then added this new objective to her .Meaningful Objective: Business Category.

Identifying Supporting Projects

Planning is a process of breaking down an objective from bigger chunks to smaller chunks so that you can see everything that needs to be done to implement the objective successfully. Planning gives you a clear idea of the scope of an objective, how many resources are needed, and whether it can be done within the time frame and budget allocated. It's a lot easier to manage an objective when you can break it down from big to small pieces. You'll notice that the larger the objective, the more parts you need to break it down into, and conversely, the smaller the objectives, the fewer parts you need break it down into.

The first level of chunking we're going to work with is Supporting Projects. These are large chunks that combine to make up your objective. In Figure 9-3, you can see that Carol has broken her Meaningful Objective into four Supporting Projects. Each of these Supporting Projects is necessary for the objective to happen. These Supporting Projects are written in terms of end result statements, as detailed in Chapter 8.

Work joyfully and peacefully knowing the right thoughts and right efforts inevitably bring the right results.
—James Allen

It does not take much strength to do things, but it requires great strength to decide on what to do.
—Elbert Hubbard

Part Three:
Creating an
Integrated
Management
System—The
Processing and
Organizing
Phase

Take Back Your Life!

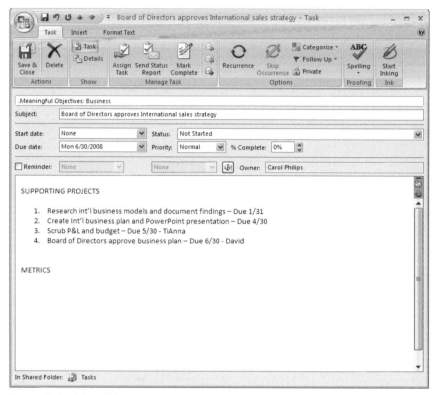

Figure 9-3 Identifying Supporting Projects.

Notice that Carol's Supporting Projects are arranged in sequence so that she can prioritize what has to be done first. She assigned due dates to ensure the objective is completed on time. She also identified to whom she would delegate specific Supporting Projects and entered that person's name next to the project. Later, you will take the Supporting Projects that you want to delegate and add them to your 1:1 categories so that you can track and monitor them. We discuss this later in this chapter in the section titled "Organizing Delegated Actions."

Creating Supporting Projects is the first level of planning you'll do. It helps you identify how big or complex your objectives are, gives you an idea of how much time it will take to complete them, and gets you thinking about what resources you might need to accomplish them. Later in this chapter, you will break these Supporting Projects into Tasks and Subtasks, and finally into Strategic Next Actions. This provides a much more detailed level of planning and prioritizing.

Part Three:
Creating an
Integrated
Management
System—The
Processing and
Organizing
Phase

Exercise 9-5 Expand your Meaningful Objective task, and under the *"SUP-PORTING PROJECTS"* heading, type in the Supporting Projects that will enable you to complete your Meaningful Objective successfully.

- Ensure each Supporting Project is written from the perspective of being outcome related.

- Arrange the Supporting Projects in priority order.

- If appropriate, assign due dates to each Supporting Project.

- Delegate any Supporting Projects that you can by writing the name of the person next to the project.

Example Carol took her new Meaningful Objective "Board of Directors approves international sales strategy" and created four Supporting Projects. Carol then added due dates to each project and decided which ones she was going to delegate. She added the name of the person responsible to clearly identify who she was going to pass it over to.

If for some reason you are having challenges identifying your Supporting Projects, here are several potential solutions:

- There are exceptions, and occasionally you may come across a Meaningful Objective that does not have any Supporting Projects, just Tasks and Subtasks.

- You might need to do a mini "clearing the mind" exercise with regard to your Meaningful Objective. This often helps unblock your thinking and when the list is in front of you, you can easily identify what the Supporting Projects are.

- You might find it hard to identify Supporting Projects because the Meaningful Objective you chose may in fact be a Supporting Project rather than a Meaningful Objective. In can be easy to get these two types of actions muddled up. In the MPS Action Hierarchy Model, (see Figure 8-2 in the previous chapter) the largest, most complex activities start at the top and then chunk down to Strategic Next Actions. You need to identify the correct level on the chart that you're working with. Are you working with the Meaningful Objective level or the Supporting Project level? This makes a big difference, and therefore it is important to ensure your Meaningful Objectives truly are objectives and not Supporting Projects.

Part Three:
Creating an
Integrated
Management
System—The
Processing and
Organizing
Phase

Take Back Your Life!

Identifying Metrics

If your objective is truly meaningful, you'll want to know, on a routine basis, if you're making progress toward it. *Metrics are ways of measuring progress that are accurate and simple.* Sales goals are measured by volume either in dollars or units. Profit goals are measured in percentages or dollars. Metrics keep you honest and allow you and your team to view progress updates without going into all kinds of project plan details. Clients often think they can't measure certain objectives and therefore avoid doing it altogether. We have found that if you approach an objective with the attitude "This can be measured," you'll be creative and find a way that works for you and your team.

Carol stores her business Metrics on a company Microsoft Windows Share-Point site. She copies the links to her Metrics and pastes them into her objective task under the heading "METRICS" so that she can quickly access them when she reviews her objectives each week. See Figure 9-4.

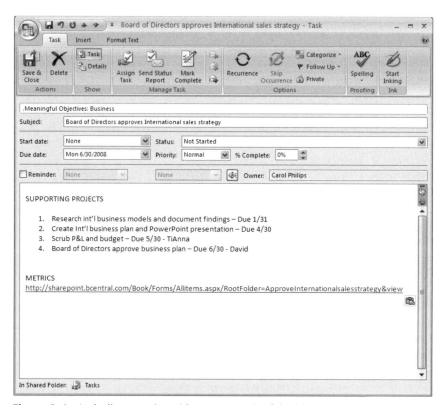

Figure 9-4   Including metrics with your Meaningful Objectives.

Part Three:
Creating an
Integrated
Management
System—The
Processing and
Organizing
Phase

Also, it's a good idea to create your Metrics as you're creating your Meaningful Objectives or certainly before you publish your objectives. Sometimes in the process of developing Metrics you'll discover that your objectives aren't specific or clear enough, and you may need to tweak them a wee bit to create a metric and an objective that work together. Metrics can help ensure your objectives are specific and measurable and progress can be reliably monitored. Metrics can take time to do; however, they support you in creating a high degree of accountability, and so they're well worth the focus.

Some of our clients balk at the idea of using Metrics in their personal life. Even though defining Metrics may not be necessary for all your personal Meaningful Objectives, you'd be surprised at how useful the process can be for many of them. You can track your financial goals, weight-loss goals, and athletic goals (for example, completing a marathon in under 3 hours and 50 minutes could be a specific Metric). You can even track renovating your house using budgets and timelines. We have found that once clients get over the initial discomfort they begin to see the value and use Metrics appropriately.

At this point, we would like to mention that if all you did was track your objectives in your system with Supporting Projects and you did not get round to creating Metrics, you'd still be 100 percent ahead of most of the world. We're setting a very high standard here, and you may not get it all done the first time round; however, it's something to work toward! Be patient with yourself and make sure you acknowledge each step as you move along the journey.

Exercise 9-6   If you have a Metric document on a SharePoint or intranet site, under the *METRICS* heading, go ahead and copy and paste the link into your objective task.

Productivity is a process, not an event. —**Annie McGhee Stinson**

If you have a Metrics document on your hard drive that links to your Meaningful Objective, under the METRICS heading, you can insert the path to the file as a hyperlink.

To insert a hyperlink into a Task, follow these steps:

1.   Open the Task.

2.   Click the Insert tab at the top of the task window.

3.   Click Attach File.

4.   In the Insert File dialog box, browse through your folders to locate the file.

Part Three:
Creating an
Integrated
Management
System—The
Processing and
Organizing
Phase

Take Back Your Life!

5. Select the file you want, and click the drop-down arrow on the Insert button.

6. Select Insert As Hyperlink, as shown in Figure 9-5.

Figure 9-5 Inserting a hyperlink into your objective task.

If you do not have a metric completed for this objective, take a moment to consider what a useful metric would be and if appropriate record a Strategic Next Action (SNA) to start the process of moving the metric forward to completion.

Example   Carol took her new Meaningful Objective "Board of Directors approves international sales strategy" and aligned with her boss on a metric. Her metric was an Excel spreadsheet detailing the milestones to complete the sales strategy ready to present to the board. Carol posted this on Share-Point and inserted a link in her Meaningful Objective to access it easily.

Identifying a Due Date

Review your Meaningful Objective to identify if it has a specific due date other than the end of your fiscal or calendar year. Because you've clarified your Supporting Projects you'll have a better idea of the size and scope of the objective, which will help you assess an appropriate due date. Be realistic when assigning due dates. Check your schedule to ensure that the time-

Part Three:
Creating an
Integrated
Management
System—The
Processing and
Organizing
Phase

line will work given travel schedules, staff meetings, holidays, and other related appointments.

Exercise 9-7 In the Due Date field of your objective task, click on the drop-down arrow and select the appropriate due date, as shown in Figure 9-6.

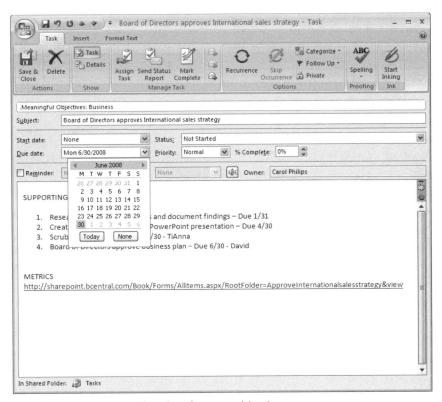

Figure 9-6 Selecting a due date for your objective.

Minimize this objective task for now because you are not yet finished with it.

Example Carol took her new Meaningful Objective "Board of Directors approves international sales strategy" and added a due date of October 21, which was the day the board meeting took place.

Organizing and Planning Your Supporting Projects

In the Workflow Model shown in Figure 9-1, the "Organizing and Planning Meaningful Objectives" section leads to the "Organizing and Planning Supporting Projects" section.

Part Three:
Creating an
Integrated
Management
System—The
Processing and
Organizing
Phase

Take Back Your Life!

Our definition for a *Supporting Project is a complex series of Tasks and Subtasks driven by a Meaningful Objective.*

The five characteristics of a Supporting Project are as follows:

1. Rolls up to an individual Meaningful Objective
2. Is written from an outcome perspective
3. Involves multiple Tasks and Subtasks and requires multiple resources
4. Takes place over time and has specific due dates
5. Includes Metrics

In this section, you organize and plan your Supporting Projects by clarifying the appropriate Tasks and Subtasks, due dates, and Metrics. Carol's Meaningful Objective "Board of Directors approves International sales strategy" has four Supporting Projects, two of which she is personally responsible for completing, one that she delegated to a direct report, and the other that she delegated to her boss. The two projects Carol is responsible for require further planning and need to be broken down into Tasks and Subtasks. To make it easier for Carol to view and manage her project plans, she took the two Supporting Projects she was responsible for and created two separate Supporting Project tasks, which she then categorized under the .Supporting Projects: Business category, as shown in Figure 9-7.

Chapter Nine: Processing and Organizing Categories: (none)

Part Three:
Creating an
Integrated
Management
System—The
Processing and
Organizing
Phase

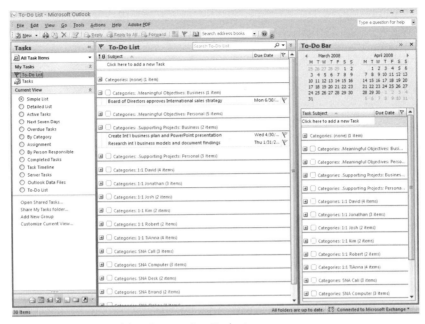

Figure 9-7   Categorizing Supporting Projects.

In Figure 9-7, you can see that Carol's objective "Board of Directors approves International sales strategy" is categorized under .Meaningful Objectives: Business and the two Supporting Projects that she is directly responsible for are separately categorized under .Supporting Projects: Business. (We discuss how to track the two Supporting Projects that Carol delegated in the section titled "Organizing Delegated Actions" later in this chapter.)

Identifying Tasks and Subtasks

The reason Carol separated these two Supporting Projects into their own .Supporting Project category is because each one of these projects requires further planning for her to manage them successfully. Separating them into their own tasks and category provides more room for planning details and calls them out as projects that need to be managed carefully. In Figure 9-8, you can see one of Carol's Supporting Projects, "Create Int'l business plan and PowerPoint presentation," and in the notes section you can see she has two headings: *Tasks and Subtasks* and *Metrics*. Under the Tasks and Subtasks heading, Carol listed all of her Tasks, and then indented the corresponding Subtasks. She put them in priority order and added due dates where appropriate.

Part Three:
Creating an
Integrated
Management
System—The
Processing and
Organizing
Phase

Take Back Your Life!

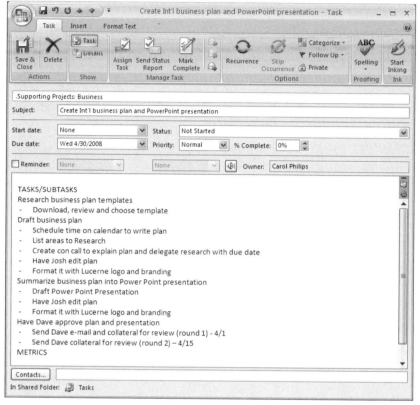

Figure 9-8   Identifying Tasks and Subtasks.

Having the Supporting Projects as their own Task gives Carol plenty of room to plan and review her Tasks and Subtasks and to insert project plan documents and data to support the project if appropriate. It also enables her to see how many projects she is working on at any given time, which in turn supports her in being more discerning about taking on new projects.

Having her Supporting Projects tracked separately makes it easier for Carol to track and manage all of her plans. She could not have done this inside the Meaningful Objectives task as easily as she did inside a separate Supporting Project task, which is why we recommend separating them.

Exercise 9-8   Now, it's time for you to set up your *.Supporting Projects* category and organize and plan the Supporting Projects that you're accountable for. Here are the specific steps to start this process.

1.   Expand the Meaningful Objectives Task that you were just working in.

Chapter Nine: **Processing and Organizing Categories: (none)**

Part Three:
Creating an
Integrated
Management
System—The
Processing and
Organizing
Phase

2. Choose one of the Supporting Projects that you're accountable for, highlight it, and then right-click it.

3. Select Copy from the shortcut menu.

4. Open a new Task by clicking the words Click Here To Add A New Task.

5. Right-click in the Task Subject text box, and select Paste to paste the name of the Supporting Project you've chosen.

6. In the Notes section of this Task, type in two headings, in all capital letters, **TASKS and SUBTASKS** and **METRICS**, as shown in Figure 9-9.

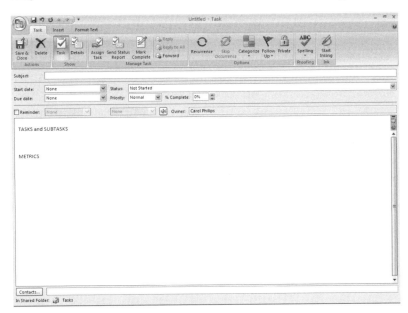

Figure 9-9   Planning Tasks and Sub Tasks.

7. Click Categorize and select either the .Supporting Projects: Business or .Supporting Projects: Personal category.

8. Minimize this Supporting Project task because you are not complete with it yet.

Go back to the Meaningful Objectives task and repeat steps 1 through 8 for the remaining Supporting Projects that you're accountable for. (As a reminder, we cover how to track Supporting Projects you delegated in the section titled "Organizing Delegated Actions" later.)

Exercise 9-9   You're now going to organize and plan the specific TASKS and SUBTASKS and due dates related to your Supporting Project.

Part Three:
Creating an
Integrated
Management
System—The
Processing and
Organizing
Phase

Take Back Your Life!

1. Expand or open one of the Supporting Project tasks that you just created.

2. Under the "TASKS and SUBTASKS" heading, type in a list of tasks that need to be completed for the Supporting Project to be accomplished, and add due dates where appropriate.

3. Under each task, enter relevant Subtasks with due dates.

4. In the Due Date drop-down menu for the Supporting Project, select an appropriate due date.

Complete steps 1 through 4 for each of the Supporting Projects that you are directly responsible for as opposed to Supporting Projects you will be delegating. We will cover how to deal with these in the section titled: "Organizing Delegated Actions."

We would like to point out that Outlook is not designed for comprehensive project planning. If you end up with more than 30 Tasks and Subtasks, we recommend you use Microsoft Project or Office Excel. You can insert these documents into your Supporting Project task as hyperlinks, as shown earlier in Figure 9-5. This is extremely useful because then all of your Supporting Projects are centralized in one place with all the associated action plans attached. This keeps the integrity of your system, ensuring all your actions are centralized in your To-Do List.

Identify Your Metrics

The last step is defining the Metrics you want to use to measure this Supporting Project. Often the metrics you use for the Meaningful Objective can also be used for the Supporting Project.

Carol's Supporting Project "Create Int'l business plan and PowerPoint presentation" has a Metric file in Excel. It lists all the various areas of research that need to be completed and the dates these sections have to be finished. Carol stored this document on the SharePoint site so that each team member involved could update the document. She then copied a link to the SharePoint site into the Supporting Project task, as shown in Figure 9-10. This enables her to quickly link to this document and view what was completed and what's left to be done.

Chapter Nine: Processing and Organizing Categories: (none)

Part Three:
Creating an
Integrated
Management
System—The
Processing and
Organizing
Phase

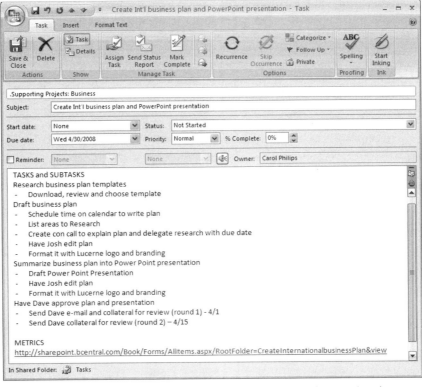

Figure 9-10   Supporting Project, showing Tasks and Subtasks, Metrics, due dates, and category.

Exercise 9-10   If you have an existing Metric document, insert it as a hyperlink into the Supporting Project task under the METRICS heading. To insert a hyperlink into a Task, follow these steps:

1.   Open the Task.

2.   Click the Insert tab at the top of the task window.

3.   Click Attach File.

4.   In the Insert File dialog box, browse through your folders to locate the file.

5.   Select the file you want, and click the drop-down arrow on the Insert button.

6.   Select Insert As Hyperlink.

If you don't have a Metric document for this project, take a moment to consider how you would measure the project and create a document to do that.

Part Three:
Creating an
Integrated
Management
System—The
Processing and
Organizing
Phase

Save the document on your computer or on a SharePoint site and insert the link into your Supporting Project task under the METRICS heading.

> **Example**   Carol created two Supporting Projects that linked to her Meaningful Objective: "Board of Directors approves International sales strategy". She categorized them in her .Supporting Project Business Category. In the notes section of these Tasks you can see she has two headings: "Tasks and Subtasks" and "Metrics." Under the "Tasks and Subtasks" heading, Carol listed all of her Tasks, and then indented the corresponding Subtasks. She put them in priority order and added due dates where appropriate and metrics.

Remember, planning your Supporting Projects is an investment; however, once you've typed in your Tasks and Subtasks and established metrics the majority of the work is done and from here on in you will be reviewing and reprioritizing the list as opposed to doing the initial planning.

What's the Strategic Next Action Without a Dependency?

The secret of getting ahead is getting started. The secret of getting started is breaking your complex, overwhelming tasks into small manageable tasks, and then starting with the first one.
—**Mark Twain**

In the MPS Workflow Model, the Supporting Project category (shown in Figure 9-1) leads to the fourth processing question, "What's the Strategic Next Action without a dependency?" In this section, you identify Strategic Next Actions that move your Meaningful Objectives and Supporting Projects forward. This is the last level of "chunking" you'll do. Without Strategic Next Actions, your Supporting Projects and Meaningful Objectives do not move forward, and so identifying these is critical.

Before you create Strategic Next Actions, we want you to really understand what they are. Our clients often confuse Strategic Next Actions with Tasks and Subtasks, and our experience has taught us to clarify the difference between the three. Defining Strategic Next Actions has the potential to save you an hour a day, reduce fires and crises, and assist you in making your life simpler and more graceful, and so this concept is worth understanding in more depth.

Chapter Nine: Processing and Organizing Categories: (none)

Part Three:
Creating an
Integrated
Management
System—The
Processing and
Organizing
Phase

.

The Strategic Next Action Story

Many years ago, when I used paper to track my life, I lived in Malibu. A friend of mine, Kelly, used to stay in my guest room once a month to go to school. One weekend, she told me that one of the light bulbs in the guest bathroom had burned out. Because I was a good hostess, I wrote down in my paper system, "Change the light bulb."

Kelly came back a month later, and the light bulb was still burned out. Oops—I wasn't such a great hostess after all! I checked my paper organizer, and sure enough, there it was: "Change the light bulb." Hmmm... Why hadn't I done anything? I thought, "What do I need to change a light bulb?" Oh, that's right! I needed a light bulb! Silly me. I crossed off "Change the light bulb," and wrote down "Buy light bulb for guest bathroom."

A month later, Kelly was back, and another bulb had burned out. So now she was in the dark! Oh no! I had an emergency situation on my hands. I looked at my list and "Buy light bulb for guest bathroom" was right there. I'd been to Home Depot two or three times since Kelly last visited. So why hadn't I picked up a bulb? Hmm... Clearly, I could not rely on my memory. I needed a "Things to buy at Home Depot" list!

I quickly drove through the canyon to the hardware store. When I got there, guess what I saw. That's right; long light bulbs, short light bulbs, round light bulbs, push-in light bulbs, and screw-in light bulbs. What kind of light bulb did I require? I had no idea what kind of light bulb I was after. I really needed to write down the specific type of light bulb on my Home Depot list ahead of time to ensure I picked up the right one. Changing this light bulb was turning out to be a bit of a project!

I drove home as fast as I could, marched into the guest bathroom, and looked up. I had cathedral ceilings, so now I needed a ladder! This was getting frustrating because I had lent my ladder to my neighbor Wayne. I picked up the phone and asked Wayne to drop it off for me. Later that day, he brought over the ladder and I was able to retrieve the light bulb and take it to the store. I bought five of the same light bulbs because this was definitely not going to happen again!

To review:

- Situation shows up—light bulb burns out in guest bathroom
- Action: change light bulb
- One month later...
- Action: buy light bulb
- One month later...
- Situation blows up—no lights in the guest bathroom at all
- Action: write a Home Depot list
- Action: write down specifications on Home Depot list

Part Three:
Creating an
Integrated
Management
System—The
Processing and
Organizing
Phase

Take Back Your Life!

- Action: get a ladder
- Action: call Wayne to get the ladder

What did you learn from reading this story?

That's right: you need to stop and pause to think things through when they "show up;" otherwise, they'll "blow up" and take months to complete instead of days! I didn't really take the time to think this one through. I **reacted** and wrote down "Change light bulb." The consequence of not pausing to think was that it took months to handle instead of days. This type of situation happens to us all the time—at work and at home—and it's a huge time-waster!

Defining Strategic Next Actions

How many Strategic Next Actions are there on the list in this story? Take a look and give it your best guess.

Most of our clients say six. However, there's actually only one Strategic Next Action.

To make answering this question a bit easier, here's the definition of a *Strategic Next Action: The next physically doable action with no dependencies.*

The best way to understand this is to appreciate what a dependency is. To change a light bulb, you need to buy a light bulb first, and so changing the light bulb is *dependent* on buying one. A Strategic Next Action doesn't have any dependencies. Take another look at the preceding list and, with this definition in mind, identify the one Strategic Next Action on the list.

The answer is, "Call Wayne to get the ladder." I knew Wayne's number and I knew he worked at home so there weren't any dependencies. All the other steps had dependencies. Changing the light bulb was dependent on buying one, buying one was dependent on having the specific type of light bulb tracked on the Home Depot list, and so forth.

If I'd paused to really think this through, I'd have figured out that "Call Wayne to get the ladder" was my Strategic Next Action. I could've saved myself a whole bunch of time, and the situation would never have blown up!

All day, we write down actions that can't be done because they're loaded with dependencies. *You can't complete an action that has a dependency.* You can only complete an action without a dependency! This is an extremely significant concept to understand, and it's an important practice to help you move forward on your objectives. The time savings are extraordinary, and it makes life simpler and easier.

We can't stress the benefit of this concept enough. You wouldn't believe the number of to-do lists we review in which only 5 percent of the items are actually Strategic Next Actions. Most of them are Tasks and Subtasks with multiple dependencies. These tasks become frustrating and hard to plan, and they end up taking much longer than you think because of their unexpected dependencies.

Having Strategic Next Actions takes away the unexpected and forces you to break down your tasks to the very next physically doable step without a dependency. Your actions will be easier to schedule because you know how long they'll take, they have no unexpected steps, and you can complete them immediately.

Reducing Fires and Crises

In the Sally's story above, the light bulb problem became an issue because she didn't handle it when it showed up. If she'd paused to think and created a Strategic Next Action in the beginning, it would never have blown up, and she wouldn't have wasted her time going to the store without the specification she needed, not to mention taking three months to fix the situation!

We all procrastinate on tasks, opening an e-mail message and thinking, "It doesn't need to be done now. I'll do it next week. It's not important," and closing it back in the Inbox. However, three weeks later, the same e-mail message becomes your next fire and crisis.

When you break down tasks into Strategic Next Actions, you end up reducing the number of emergencies that you have because you handle actions when they show up, not when they blow up. You'll save yourself a whole bunch of time, which helps you take back your life. Imagine an extra hour a day of puttering in your garden, riding your horse, playing golf, eating ice cream, or whatever else puts a smile on your face—that sure sounds good to me!

What we'd like is for you to shift your focus and do your thinking up front instead of after the fact. Changing the timing of your thinking gives you extraordinary rewards. Remember the quote in Chapter 1: "Small things done consistently in strategic places create major impact." Pausing to think and make a decision when an action shows up is a small shift in focus, but it's a profound shift. This concept in and of itself can change your life and the results you accomplish.

Part Three:
Creating an
Integrated
Management
System—The
Processing and
Organizing
Phase

Identifying Your Strategic Next Actions

Our definition for a Strategic Next Action is *the next physically doable action with no dependencies.*

Handle it when it
shows up, not
when it blows up!
—Sally McGhee

The four characteristics of a Strategic Next Action are as follows:

- Rolls up to one of your Supporting Projects or Meaningful Objectives
- Has no dependencies
- Starts with a verb
- Is specific and measurable

For example, "Go to Home Depot and buy a 25-watt, three-way, round, push-in bulb" links to an objective called "Maintain Offenhimer Street home." Or "Send a message to Joe and ask him to review the South Beach Development proposal by January 17" links to "Sign contract with South Beach Development."

When you create your Strategic Next Actions, pause briefly to think them through. It's not always as easy to construct SNAs as you might suppose. For example, "Buy a birthday present for my mom" seems like a clear Strategic Next Action. However, what are you going to buy your mom, and where will you buy it? If you don't know *what* to buy her, you won't know *where* to buy it, and so this task will end up sitting on your list until you make this decision. You could create an alternative Strategic Next Action that helps clarify what to buy her, "Call my dad to get recommendations on presents for Mom." Another alternative is "Go to the Cherry Creek Mall to find a birthday present for Mom." In this scenario, you've decided to wing it and find something at the mall. You don't know what, but you trust that you'll find something! These scenarios are more specific than "Buy a birthday present for my mom," and they'll assist you in completing a task successfully rather than having it sit on a to-do list for months. Remember—you want to create tasks without dependencies because it makes them much easier to schedule and complete.

Here are a few questions to help you test if your next action really is a Strategic Next Action without a dependency:

- What do you need to *do* to complete it?
- What information do you need to *have* with you to complete it?
- Where do you need to *be* to complete it?
- How much *time* will it take to complete it?

Chapter Nine: Processing and Organizing Categories: (none)

Part Three:
Creating an
Integrated
Management
System—The
Processing and
Organizing
Phase

■ Does it *link* to an objective or Supporting Project?

Carol's objective had four Supporting Projects, two of them she was accountable for and two she delegated. To move the projects she was accountable for forward she created Strategic Next Actions for each of these Supporting Projects and categorized them in their own Strategic Next Action categories.

Figure 9-11 shows one of Carol's Supporting Projects: "Create Int'l business plan and PowerPoint Presentation." And then, you can see her corresponding SNA in the SNA Call Category: "Call Christina to see if she has a Business Plan template I can use" (Christina is Carol's neighbor who just wrote a business plan).

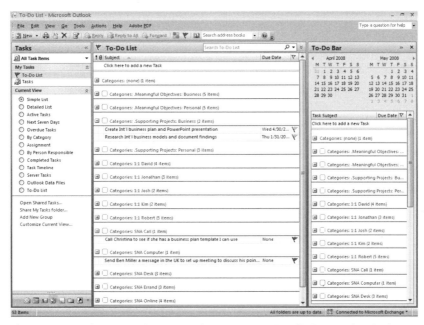

Figure 9-11   The Strategic Next Actions to move Carol's Supporting Projects forward.

You can also see her second Supporting Project: "Research Int'l business model and document findings." And then, you can see her corresponding SNA in the SNA Computer category: "Send Ben Miller a message in the UK to set up meeting to discuss his points of view on Int'l business models."

Strategic Next Actions don't have dependencies, and therefore if you want to move a Supporting Project forward, routinely you have to identify the Strategic Next Actions, track them, and complete them, as demonstrated in

Part Three:
Creating an
Integrated
Management
System—The
Processing and
Organizing
Phase

Take Back Your Life!

the Cycle of Productivity. Remember, Tasks and Subtasks both have dependencies, which means you cannot move them forward immediately, only by creating a Strategic Next Action can you move a project or objective forward. We often say to our clients, *"You don't DO projects and objectives; you can only DO Strategic Next Actions."* If you think about it, you can only plan and manage your Meaningful Objectives and Supporting Projects. You review them, reorganize them, course correct, and meet about them; however, you cannot do any actions related to them because they all have dependencies. You can only do Strategic Next Actions..

The reason we suggest you keep your Tasks and Subtasks in the Notes section of your Supporting Project is because they have dependencies and cannot be completed right away.

As you complete Strategic Next Actions, you unlock the dependencies holding your Tasks and Sub Task static and they can then become Strategic Next Actions without dependencies. At this point, you can move them into an SNA category. We talk more specifically about why we separate SNAs into their own categories in the section titled "Frequently Asked Questions" later in this chapter.

Exercise 9-11   Open each of the Supporting Projects you just created and review the Tasks and Subtasks. Identify the Strategic Next Actions for each one of your Supporting Projects and complete the following steps to turn them into Outlook Tasks in your SNA Categories. (You may find one of your Tasks or Subtasks is an SNA by mistake. This is quite normal, and if that is the case, go ahead and use that as your SNA for this exercise.)

1.   Open a new Task.

2.   In the Subject text box, type the first Strategic Next Action for your first Supporting Project. Make sure it starts with a verb, has no dependencies, and is specific and measurable. Include due dates if appropriate and insert any relevant supporting data that may be required to take the action. Do not categorize this Task yet; you do that in the next section.

3.   For now, minimize the Task.

Repeat steps 1 and 2 until you have SNAs for each of the Supporting Projects you created and they are all minimized.

Go back to the original item you highlighted in Categories: (none). You may find that it is no longer needed because you already created the Meaningful Objective, the Supporting Projects, and Strategic Next Actions. If it is not

Part Three:
Creating an
Integrated
Management
System—The
Processing and
Organizing
Phase

required, delete it. If it is still necessary, turn it into an appropriate Strategic Next Action and categorize it.

Example   Carol's objective had four Supporting Projects, two of them she was accountable for and two she delegated. To move the projects she was accountable for forward she created one Strategic Next Actions for each of these Supporting Projects.

Do It?

In the Workflow Model in Figure 9-1, answering the question "What is the Strategic Next Action without a dependency?" leads to the fifth question "Do it?–If less than two minutes."

If you can complete your Strategic Next Action in two minutes or less, there's no point in recording it in your IMS; it'll take you as long to complete it as it will to track it! The most effective thing to do here is *just do it*. After you've finished it, you can delete it from your list or mark it complete and celebrate a finished cycle of action.

You'd be amazed at how many actions on your To-Do List can be finished in less than two minutes. Our statistics prove that, on average, 30 percent of the items on your To-Do List can be done in less than two minutes. For example, "Order *My Father Is My Teacher* from Amazon.com for my dad's birthday," or "Send a message to Jennifer regarding next week's staff meeting agenda." Completing activities in less than two minutes is a great way to build energy and move forward on your objectives.

Exercise 9-12   In answer to the questions *"Do it–if less than two minutes?"* if you can complete any of the Strategic Next Actions that you minimized, *just do it*! (Nike has the right approach!) And then, delete the SNA Task. If not, move to the sixth question in the workflow model: *"Delegate it?"*

Delegate It?

If you can't do a Strategic Next Action in less than two minutes, the sixth question in the Workflow Model is "Delegate it?" This is another potent filter question that everyone who has the opportunity to delegate can ask more consciously throughout the day.

Our clients move so fast that they literally forget to use the delegate option. Just asking this question is enough for them to stop and consider if they can delegate the Strategic Next Action, and oftentimes they can. Some clients

Part Three:
Creating an
Integrated
Management
System—The
Processing and
Organizing
Phase

Take Back Your Life!

say, "I don't have the time to train other people; I can do it faster myself!" We caution those clients: "If you maintain that focus, you may never be able to delegate effectively and you'll likely get stuck doing what you have always done and so will the people around you!" If you're fortunate enough to have staff to delegate to, take the time to train them so that they can improve what they're doing because, ultimately, this will support you in improving what you're doing. The only person in the way of you delegating effectively might be you!

Exercise 9-13   Ask the question "Can I delegate it?" and if you can delegate any of the Strategic Next Actions that you minimized, go ahead. You can delegate them by sending an e-mail message or making a phone call, and once completed, delete the minimized task. We talk about how to track delegated tasks in the section titled "Organizing Delegated Actions," which follows.

Organizing Delegated Actions

In the Workflow Model, the question "Delegate it?" leads to two different organizing categories, 1:1's and SNA Waiting For. We describe how to use each of these categories in the subsections below.

Using 1:1 Categories   1:1's are recurring face-to-face meetings that take place with key business or personal contacts. If you work in a virtual environment, these may need to take place on the phone. The 1:1 category supports you in preparing for these 1:1 meetings, as well as tracking and following up on Meaningful Objectives, Supporting Projects, and delegated items. Using the 1:1 category is another way to transfer what's on your mind and put it in your system so it's no longer in your head!

Ideally, managers set up regular one-on-one meetings weekly, biweekly, or monthly with their direct reports and their boss so that they can discuss progress related to their objectives. If you're not meeting regularly with your key staff members and boss, we highly recommend scheduling these appointments on your calendar. A face-to-face meeting is a good time to connect in person, and it gives you an excellent idea of how things are going at all levels—objectives, projects, challenges, and work/life balance.

Before a 1:1 meeting, you simply review the 1:1 category for the person for an instant reminder of the items you want to discuss. It's an effortless way to manage these appointments, and it enables you to take your attention off remembering tasks and allows you to put it on the important aspects of running a team, being a leader, and developing your staff's skills and strategies.

Chapter Nine: Processing and Organizing Categories: (none)

Part Three:
Creating an
Integrated
Management
System—The
Processing and
Organizing
Phase

In Chapter 7 you set up your specific 1:1 categories in your Color Categories list. (These categories won't show up on your To-Do Bar until you attach a category to the Task.) Another way to use your 1:1 category is to track Meaningful Objectives and Supporting Projects that you have delegated to your direct reports. Carol delegated two of her Supporting Projects: one to David and one to TiAnna. By tracking these under David and TiAnna's 1:1 categories, Carol indicates that these are projects David and TiAnna are now accountable for and therefore she would not being tracking them in her own Supporting Project category.

For Carol to ensure these projects happen, she holds bimonthly 1:1's with David and TiAnna. By having these items tracked in her 1:1 categories, she can instantly see them whenever she meets with her direct report or boss and discusses progress and improvements and gives support. This is a great way to help keep her staff focused on the important activities and keep her boss updated.

In Figure 9-12, you can see 1:1 categories for David and TiAnna. Under the 1:1 TiAnna category, Carol listed the one Supporting Project that she delegated to TiAnna and two items that she wants to discuss with her. Under the 1:1 David category, you can see the one Supporting Project Carol delegated to him plus three items she wants to discuss with David.

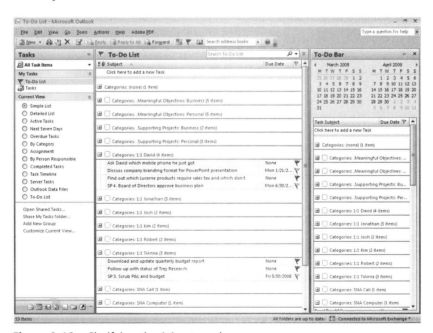

Figure 9-12 Clarifying the 1:1 categories.

Part Three:
Creating an
Integrated
Management
System—The
Processing and
Organizing
Phase

Take Back Your Life!

When adding items to your 1:1 categories, you must be cognizant of timing. Anything you track using this category will not be discussed until your next meeting. If the discussion must happen prior to your scheduled 1:1, you need to use alternative methods of tracking it, such as SNA Computer, SNA Call, or telepathy. Ha! Just checking to see if you're still with us!

You can also use the 1:1 category for personal use: for your spouse, partner, children, and/or community service contacts. Carol has a 1:1 category for her husband! This might sound a little clinical at first; however, it's actually helped their relationship. In the old days, Carol remembered everything she wanted to talk to him about in her head, which often created random, inappropriate discussions about to-do's. For example, when they were skiing—riding on a chair lift and enjoying a wonderful moment—she'd remember that she needed to talk about the flights to London to meet the parents. This was not the right time for the discussion because neither she nor her husband could do much about it on the chair lift without calendars, and it was interrupting a unique moment together.

The alternative was that Carol would forget to talk about topics altogether, and then it would backfire on both of them. Now, she simply sets up a breakfast with him and handles everything at once so that it gets done, and then they go have fun and don't worry about discussing to-do's.

Exercise 9-14   Open the original Meaningful Objectives task that you were working with and look the Notes section. There, you can see your Supporting Projects. If any of these have been delegated to your staff, complete the following steps to track them in their respective 1:1 categories.

1.   Choose one of the Supporting Projects that you want to delegate, highlight it, and then right-click it.

2.   Click Copy on the shortcut menu.

3.   Open a new Task by double-clicking the words Click Here To Add A New Task.

4.   Right-click in the Task Subject text box, and select Paste to paste the name of the Supporting Project you've chosen.

5.   Click Categorize and select the appropriate 1:1 category, as shown in Figure 9-13.

Part Three:
Creating an
Integrated
Management
System—The
Processing and
Organizing
Phase

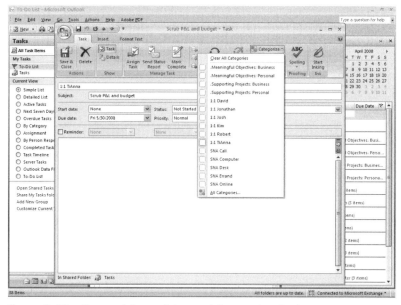

Figure 9-13   Categorizing a delegated Supporting Project.

If any of the minimized Strategic Next Actions Tasks relate to discussions you need to have with any of your 1:1 category people, go ahead and categorize them into the appropriate 1:1 categories.

Example   Carol delegated two of her Supporting Projects: one she delegated to David and the other to TiAnna. Under the 1:1 David category, she categorized one Supporting Project and three SNAs she wanted to discuss with David. Under the 1:1 TiAnna category, Carol listed the one Supporting Project that she delegated to TiAnna and the two SNAs that she wanted to discuss with her.

Using the SNA Waiting For Category   The purpose of the SNA Waiting For category is to track items you're waiting on from people for whom you don't have 1:1 categories. Usually, we're waiting for many miscellaneous actions that don't justify having their own 1:1 category. These types of actions go into the Waiting For category. Here's an example: you recently ordered a book from Amazon and you're waiting for it to arrive. Under the SNA Waiting For category, you could include a Task such as "Waiting for Amazon.com to send leadership book." In the Notes section of the Task, you could insert the confirmation e-mail from Amazon saying the order was received and book is being shipped. And if you wanted to be really organized, you could put a due date on the Task identifying when the book is

Part Three:
Creating an
Integrated
Management
System—The
Processing and
Organizing
Phase

Take Back Your Life!

meant to arrive. If it does not arrive, a reminder will appear, and you can open the Task and respond to the Amazon confirmation e-mail message asking where the book is. Now that's pretty organized!

If you're waiting for someone at work or home to complete an action to assist you to move one of your Meaningful Objectives or Supporting Projects forward and you do not have a 1:1 category set up for that person, the SNA Waiting For category is the place to track that action. Most of our clients did not track Waiting For items until they learned of this category, and then they quickly become Waiting For addicts. It is so wonderful to have a category to track this type of information and get it out of your head and into your system.

Exercise 9-15   If any of your minimized Strategic Next Actions Tasks go into the Waiting For action category, go ahead and categorize them now.

Defer It?

If you can't do a Strategic Next Action in less than two minutes, and you can't delegate it, the seventh question in the Workflow Model shown in Figure 9-1 is "Defer it?" **Defer** means that you are the only person who can complete the Strategic Next Action, and it will take you longer than two minutes to complete. You categorize your deferred next actions into one of the six SNA categories or directly onto the Calendar.

The Strategic Next Action categories are designed around locations where you physically need to be to complete actions. This is different from the categories that most people use to organize their action lists, but we've discovered that clients must be in the right location to complete an action, and so it's simpler to organize the categories in this way. We discuss the Strategic Next Action categories in the following subsections, with an example of how to use each category.

SNA Computer Category

Example: "Review next year's budget to evaluate how to cut out $100,000." You need your computer to complete this Strategic Next Action, but you don't need to be online. Next year's budget is in your My Documents folder, and so, as long as you can turn on your computer, you can complete this action anywhere: on the ferry, on the train, on an airplane, in a hotel room, or at home.

Chapter Nine: **Processing and Organizing Categories: (none)**

Part Three:
Creating an
Integrated
Management
System—The
Processing and
Organizing
Phase

SNA Online Category

Example: "Order leadership book from Amazon.com to send to Jane." Your client contact information is in your Contacts folder, and so all you need is to be online to complete this next action.

SNA Call Category

Example: "Call Brian Johnson to book a client dinner with him and his wife–September 9, 7 PM." Brian's phone number is programmed into your phone, and so all you need is the phone to make the call.

SNA Desk Category

Example: "Complete credit card application." This form is filed at your desk, and so you can't complete this task unless you're at your desk.

SNA Errand Category

Example: "Go to Cherry Creek Mall to buy my mom a present." This requires that you get into your car to drive to the mall to complete the action.

This category is very useful in your personal life. For example, if you shop at Costco for your once-a-month supplies, you can create a Task under SNA Errand that is titled "Costco." In the Task, you can list all the household items you want to purchase. After you synchronize with your personal digital assistant (PDA) and laptop, the next time you're at Costco you can view your SNA Errand list on your PDA to direct your shopping. You can use this method for any errands that are important to you, such as setting up a task for "Videos to watch" with your favorite DVDs listed or "Books to read" with a list of the books you want to purchase.

SNA Home Category

Example: "Paint the garage door." You have the paint, drop cloth, and brush, and so all you need is to be at home to complete this Strategic Next Action.

Exercise 9-16   All of the remaining minimized Strategic Next Actions you created can now be categorized into the appropriate SNA categories or directly onto the Calendar.

To move an SNA Task onto the Calendar, follow these steps:

1.   Click the Calendar icon to view your Calendar.

Part Three:
Creating an
Integrated
Management
System—The
Processing and
Organizing
Phase

Take Back Your Life!

2. Right-click and drag the SNA Task from your To-Do Bar onto the date and time you want the action to appear on your Calendar. When you release the mouse button, a shortcut menu opens.

3. Click Move Here As Appointment With Attachment on the shortcut menu to remove the Task from the To-Do Bar and place it on the Calendar.

Example   Carol created two SNAs for the Supporting Projects that she was directly responsible for. She deferred both of these SNAs: one to the SNA Call Category and one to the SNA Computer Category.

Congratulations! You've just completed your first experience of processing and organizing one of your Meaningful Objectives from the Categories: (none) Collecting Point into the Planning and Action Categories using the Workflow Model. As you can tell, the bulk of the work right now is organizing and planning your Meaningful Objectives and Supporting Projects, and once these are set up, using the model becomes considerably easier and quicker. It takes quite a bit of time to get these all entered; however, it is well worth the investment.

Examples of How Clients Use the MPS Workflow Model

We've listed three tasks that came from clients' Categories: (none) Collecting Points. We're going to take you through the MPS Workflow Model using these examples so that you can better understand how the model works and how easy it can be.

Categories: (none):

Buy dog food

Launch new Web site and corporate identity

Write a proposal for Terry Adams at Proseware

Example: Buy Dog Food

■   What is it? I need to buy more dog food for Maya. We're about to run out.

Chapter Nine: **Processing and Organizing Categories: (none)**

Part Three:
Creating an
Integrated
Management
System—The
Processing and
Organizing
Phase

- Is it actionable? Yes; otherwise, she'll be eating scrambled eggs and toast for breakfast with me and Chris!

- Does it relate to a Meaningful Objective? Yes, I have an objective related to family and friends, and she is part of that objective, which is already listed in my .Meaningful Objectives: Personal category.

- Does it have any Supporting Projects? No, it doesn't.

- What is the Strategic Next Action? Go to Wild Oats food store and buy Maya two bags of Pinnacle dog food.

- Can I do it in less than two minutes? No.

- Can I delegate it? No.

- Can I defer it? Yes, I put it under SNA Errands with a due date of next Wednesday.

Example: Launch New Web site and Corporate Identity

- What is it? Our company recently launched a new version of our Web site. We want to let all our customers know so that they can see it. This involves creating a letter and sending it out to our customers.

- Is it actionable? Yes, the Web site has been completed for a month, and so the letter needs to go out soon, and it's a great marketing opportunity.

- Does it relate to a Meaningful Objective? Yes, it relates to an objective that is recorded in .Meaningful Objectives: Business, "Create and implement upgraded Web site."

- Does it have any Supporting Projects? Yes, and I don't have this tracked.

   I created a new Supporting Project: "Launch upgraded Web site." I defined the Tasks and Subtasks, and I selected a due date. No Metrics are necessary, and I categorized it as a .Supporting Projects: Business project.

- What is the Strategic Next Action? Talk to my assistant and ask her to write the copy for the newsletter regarding the Web site launch.

- Can I do it in less than two minutes? No.

- Can I delegate it? Yes, I tracked this under my 1:1 Jennifer category so that it is ready for our next meeting, which is in two days.

- Can I defer it? Not applicable.

Part Three:
Creating an
Integrated
Management
System—The
Processing and
Organizing
Phase

Take Back Your Life!

Example: Write a Proposal for Terry Adams at Proseware

- What is it? I just opened Proseware as a new account, and the President wants me to work with him and his team.

- Is it actionable? Yes, in fact, this is how I spend 25 percent of my time.

- Does it relate to a Meaningful Objective? Yes, it relates to an overall revenue goal and a product goal to work with senior executives. Already listed in .Meaningful Objectives: Business.

- Does it have any Supporting Projects? Yes, this account becomes one of my projects. Therefore I created a .Supporting Projects: Business category for Proseware and completed the Tasks, Sub Tasks and metrics.

- What's the Strategic Next Action? Type a proposal to Terry Adams detailing the work to be delivered.

- Can I do it in less than two minutes? No.

- Can I delegate it? No.

- Can I defer it? Yes, I recorded it under SNA Computer with a due date of Friday.

Before you complete processing your Categories: (none), we are going to review some of our clients' frequently asked questions. We believe these can make it easier for you to understand and use the model. Then, we give you an exercise to do to complete emptying the items in Categories: (none).

Frequently Asked Questions

Before you start to process and organize your Categories: (none) Collecting Point, we want to review some of the most frequently asked questions from clients. We hope the answer s will assist you as well.

Why Separate Strategic Next Actions from Supporting Projects and Meaningful Objectives?

The intuitive way to organize Strategic Next Actions is to link them directly to your Supporting Project or Meaningful Objective. However, the intuitive way to organize is not always the most productive way to organize! At first, you might feel a little awkward separating Strategic Next Actions from Supporting Projects; however, after a while we think you will get comfortable with it.

You don't do projects. You review, prioritize, and plan projects. You do strategic next actions.
—**Sally McGhee**

Part Three:
Creating an
Integrated
Management
System—The
Processing and
Organizing
Phase

Your objective and project categories, by design, consist of Supporting Projects and Tasks and Subtasks, all of which have dependencies. This means you can't complete anything in these categories. You can review, prioritize, and plan in them, but you can't *do* them! You can only *do* Strategic Next Actions, which is why we separate next actions into their very own categories. This enables you to focus on them and ensure progress toward your goals. If actions are hidden in a project or objectives category, you can't view them easily, and you can't drag them onto the Outlook Calendar to schedule them.

If you use a PDA or Smartphone that synchronizes with Outlook, you have immediate access to your To-Do List and can view your Strategic Next Actions categories. This means that when you're in the airport with an hour to spare, you can pull up your SNA Calls category and get to work on the phone. However, if the phone calls you have to make are hidden in 19 different project tasks, it's unlikely you'll make the effort to find them.

You may have inadvertently created Strategic Next Actions in your Supporting Projects when you broke projects down into Tasks and Subtasks. If you did, you can cut and paste these items into new Tasks and save them in the appropriate Strategic Next Actions categories. In this way, you can make certain that all your Strategic Next Actions without dependencies are in your Strategic Next Actions categories and your Tasks with dependencies are in your Planning Categories.

Planning Categories consist of Meaningful Objectives, Supporting Projects, and 1:1 Meetings; and the Action categories consist of Strategic Next Actions. You'll be using your Planning Categories to plan and prioritize, and you'll be using your Action Categories to take action and get things done. It's actually very simple when you recognize this distinction.

Splitting up Strategic Next Actions into their own SNA categories might feel strange at first, but it's ultimately a very effective process. The answer is to train yourself to *trust in your system*, which might take two or three months to do. So, just be patient, it'll all fit into place, and we're certain you'll be smiling!

Can I Still Associate My SNAs with My Supporting Projects?

If you feel uncomfortable that your Strategic Next Actions are separated from your Supporting Projects, you may want to connect them by including the project name or acronym at the beginning of the Subject line of the SNA

Part Three:
Creating an
Integrated
Management
System—The
Processing and
Organizing
Phase

Take Back Your Life!

Task. For example, "*Publish book*—Create an Excel worksheet to track dead-line dates" creates a link between the objective and the Strategic Next Action. In this way, you can search your To-Do List for Publish book Strategic Next Actions, which is nifty. To perform a project related search in your To-Do List, follow these steps:

1. Go to your To-Do List by clicking the Tasks icon.

2. Under My Tasks, click To-Do List.

3. In the Search To-Do List text box, type the name of the project you want to search for. Outlook automatically displays any Task that has that search word in the Subject line or the Notes section.

Some of our clients are so comfortable with their systems that they don't need this additional step. When they read a Strategic Next Action, it's obvious to them what project it links to. It's up to you what level of detail to include to make your Integrated Management System work for you.

Can I Customize My SNA Categories?

Another awareness clients have when they get more comfortable with processing information in their IMS is how to customize their categories to their specific role and functions. When we work with clients individually, we have the opportunity to do a lot more customization, which offers further value. The Planning and Action Categories that you've created are cross-functional categories; most people work with objectives, projects, e-mail, and errands. However, you might have a specific role—HR, Financial, Sales, Customer Service, or Legal. Roles like these can generate a need for greater customization of categories. You can customize your work around these roles to provide greater application and value. For example, you may want to consider tailoring some of your Strategic Next Action categories around the repetitive functions that your role requires. For example:

- Executive Administrator SNA Calendaring

- HR SNA Resume Reviews

- Accounting SNA Invoice Requests

Rather than figuring out what customized categories you think you may need, you can allow your Tasks to drive these decisions, which makes the process much easier. For example: Imagine you work as a bookkeeper in the financial department of an organization. A request comes in for you to create a customer invoice. Take a moment and ask yourself, "How many of

Chapter Nine: Processing and Organizing Categories: (none)

Part Three:
Creating an
Integrated
Management
System—The
Processing and
Organizing
Phase

these customer invoice requests do I get a day? Am I repeating the same sequence of actions to complete them?"

If you're receiving two or three a day and you follow the same steps to complete them, this would justify creating an "SNA Invoices to be processed" category. You would then be able to schedule one hour on your Calendar and work on all of them at the same time. It's much easier and more effective to work on similar tasks at one time rather than spreading them out throughout the day. Studies have proven switching between unrelated tasks is in effective and time consuming. Working with similar tasks enables you to have all of the tools, information and resources at hand which enables you to work much more efficiently.

This level of customization is very specific to the role and functions you perform, and so we won't be able to go into much detail in this book because there are too may different ways to customize, and our choice might not apply to you. However, McGhee Productivity Solutions specializes in role-related training, and so if you're interested, give us a call. Our contact data is in the back of the book.

Can I Have More Than One Strategic Next Action per Project?

Yes, you can have more than one Strategic Next Action per project, as long as the SNAs have no dependencies. In fact, you can have as many actions as you like. However, we don't normally encounter more than two or three Strategic Next Actions per project at one time. You will find that 95 percent of your project plans consist of Tasks and Subtasks with dependencies. These dependencies are only unlocked when you complete the appropriate Strategic Next Action. In other words, "change the light bulb" was dependent on buying the light bulb. Therefore "change the light bulb" was a Task, and "buy the light bulb" was a Strategic Next Action. When Sally bought the light bulb, that unlocked the Task "change the light bulb" and turned it into a Strategic Next Action. That's why 95 percent of your project plans have dependencies and there are only a few Strategic Next Actions. We're having you pay special attention to identifying and completing Strategic Next Actions because they're the key that unlocks your Tasks and Subtasks, which unlock your Supporting Projects, which finally unlock your Meaningful Objectives.

Part Three:
Creating an
Integrated
Management
System—The
Processing and
Organizing
Phase

Take Back Your Life!

When Do I Transfer a Strategic Next Action into the Calendar?

When you get to the Prioritizing and Planning Phase, you review all of your Strategic Next Actions, prioritizing them and deciding which ones to schedule on your Calendar. If you were to transfer them onto your Calendar now, you'd be prioritizing in a vacuum because you don't yet have a completed To-Do List. After your To-Do List is complete, you can make effective decisions about prioritizing the items to schedule on your Calendar.

After your Integrated Management System is set up, it is easier to identify what actions you want to schedule on the Calendar rather than tracking them on the To-Do List. You'll learn about this process in detail when you learn about the Prioritizing and Planning Phase.

How Do I Insert E-Mail Messages and Documents into Tasks?

Sometimes it's necessary to include supporting documentation to complete a task. Therefore, it's important to be able to insert e-mail messages and files into your Tasks.

Example: "Call Litware regarding licensing contract."

The contract is attached to an e-mail message in your Inbox. By inserting the e-mail message into the Task in your SNA Call category, you'll have the contract handy when you're ready to make the call to Litware. You can just as easily insert files or e-mail messages into Tasks, Calendar appointments, and Contacts. It's a clever little trick that Outlook provides us!

To insert an e-mail message into a Task, follow these steps:

1. Open the Task that you want to insert the e-mail message into.
2. Click the Insert tab.
3. In the Include group, click Attach Item.
4. Browse through the folders and select the e-mail message that you want to insert.
5. Decide whether you want to insert its contents (choose Text Only) or add it as an attachment (choose Attachment), and then click OK.

To insert a document into a Task, follow these steps:

1. Open the Task that you want to insert the document into.

Part Three:
Creating an
Integrated
Management
System—The
Processing and
Organizing
Phase

2. Click the Insert tab.

3. In the Include section, click Attach File.

4. Browse the folders, select the document that you want to insert, and then click Insert.

Does Every Task Require a Due Date?

Not every Task needs a due date. It's easy to assign dates, and it's just as easy to ignore them! Sometimes our clients insist on deadlines, saying, "If I don't give it a due date, it won't get done." However, when we ask, "Do you keep all the due dates you set?" the answer is always, "No!" Therefore, giving Tasks due dates doesn't necessarily ensure that they'll get done!

After all your Collecting Points are empty and your Planning and Action Categories are complete, you'll have a much better idea of what you've agreed to do. At that point, you can prioritize your list and establish realistic due dates; otherwise, you're prioritizing in a vacuum. When you create a due date, you're making an agreement with yourself, and so be discerning when you choose one, and be sure you can keep it. Check your calendar to make certain you have the time, given meetings, vacations, travel, and personal events. Check completion dates on your projects and objectives to make sure your due dates are supporting those deadlines. And finally, check that you can maintain a work/life balance as well as keep your due dates.
As you can see, selecting a due date takes some homework, but once again, taking the time on the front end saves time and disappointment on the back end.

When you're more discriminating about specifying due dates, you'll find it easier to keep them, and you'll begin to recognize how to manage your life so that you can live in balance as well as honor your agreements. Productivity is an art and requires a change in lifestyle.

Can I Choose Multiple Categories?

After three to six months of using your IMS, you'll have more Tasks in your To-Do List, and duplicating them in multiple categories will create confusion and triple or quadruple the size of your lists.

Clients sometimes want to put Strategic Next Actions into multiple categories because they have choices about what actions to take. They could either make a call or send an e-mail message. Our suggestion is to make a decision about which one category to put the Task in, and stick with it. This creates

Part Three:
Creating an
Integrated
Management
System—The
Processing and
Organizing
Phase

Take Back Your Life!

less confusion and reduces the size of your list. Once again, place your decision making on the front end and don't postpone the decision for a future time.

There are exceptions. For example, if you ask all your directs to complete a performance review, you can create one Task to track this and categorize it in all your 1:1 direct categories. Just remember if you delete it in one category, it deletes it in all categories.

How Do I Track Both Personal and Work Items?

There are several solutions to tracking both personal and business Tasks in one system.

Because some personal items you need to do at work, such as "Schedule doctor's appointment" and "Schedule car maintenance," to help you feel more comfortable about using Tasks to track your personal actions, you can mark a Task as private. That way, nobody can view the Task, even if that person has access to your To-Do Bar. When you open a Task, you can see a Private button in the Options category of the Task tab. Click the Private button the mark a Task as private.

You can continue the concept of using individual categories for personal and business objectives to your SNA categories; for example, SNA Call: Personal, SNA Call: Business. The downside to this approach is that you end up with a lot more categories to manage and they become more awkward to review on a PDA. The upside, of course, is that your personal and business items are clearly separated.

You can also create an SNA Personal category and track all personal Strategic Next Actions there, such as phone calls, errands, and computer items. Compared to the previous option, this reduces the number of categories you have and makes them more manageable. If you decide to run some errands, you'll need to view both the SNA Errands and SNA Personal categories to decide which tasks you can do in the time you have and the location you're in.

You can keep your categories as they are and include personal items in your existing categories. When you're at the airport and decide to make some phone calls, you can view the SNA Calls category and choose whether you want to do personal or business calls.

As always, these are personal preferences, and you need to decide what you think will work best for you.

Part Three:
Creating an
Integrated
Management
System—The
Processing and
Organizing
Phase

Each week, you'll be doing a Weekly Review—prioritizing your Strategic Next Actions and transferring the week's actions from the Strategic Next Action categories onto your Calendar. The ultimate destination for a Strategic Next Action is the Calendar, and so it's not so critical what categories you choose for your personal items. It's all about what works best for you.

Emptying Your Categories: (none) Collecting Point

Just for a moment imagine you've now processed all of your actions in the To-Do List using the Workflow Model. Everything you can delete is deleted. Everything you can do in less than two minutes has been done, and everything you can delegate has been delegated. At this point, all that is left are your Strategic Next Actions that take more than two minutes that only you can complete. All of these SNAs directly relate to your Meaningful Objectives or Supporting Projects and are the most strategic actions for you to focus on to move toward your goals. This is a powerful list to have at your fingertips.

You are now ready to complete processing and organizing your Categories: (none) Collecting Point. This takes about an hour. We suggest that you find a time and location where you can have uninterrupted time and be quiet. Do not answer the phone, read e-mail, or take interruptions. Seriously, you need uninterrupted time. Give yourself that gift!

Start with the first item on the top of your Categories: (none) list and work your way down. No need to jump around. You'll complete the entire list anyway, and so everything will get processed. It's an extremely good discipline to go from top down. See if you can do this!

After you start to process an item, don't close it back into Categories: (none). Make sure that you go completely through the Workflow Model. No procrastinating!

We highly recommend that you don't read on in this book until you've emptied your Categories: (none) Collecting Point. This will give you the experience of how to process and organize information effectively. You'll empty a Collecting Point, which is a real motivator, and you'll have set up your IMS so that you can use it moving forward. This is the most exciting part. It feels good when all of your Tasks are categorized in the Planning and Action Categories. Remember, Categories: (none) is only one of your Collecting Points. You still have e-mail, voice mail, notepads, and paper inboxes to empty! So, take the opportunity to completely empty this Collecting Point first!

Part Three:
Creating an
Integrated
Management
System—The
Processing and
Organizing
Phase

Take Back Your Life!

Awarenesses

Here are some of the statements our clients have made after they run through the Workflow Model.

- "Having all my objectives in one category so that I can access them easily was very useful!"

- "Driving all my decisions from objectives will help me stay on track."

- "Once I started breaking down my tasks, I realized I had a lot more projects than I thought."

- "Keeping all of my Tasks and Subtasks in a Project category reduced my original To-Do List. Now, I just need to focus on my Strategic Next Actions to move them forward, which is less overwhelming."

- "Chunking down to Strategic Next Actions is extremely useful, and it creates a more powerful To-Do List."

- "I never knew how to use categories in the To-Do List before...Categories rock!"

- "I like having my personal and business items all in one place."

- "Synchronizing this list with my Blackberry will help me when I am traveling."

- "I feel more relaxed and in control of my life, knowing my commitments are organized in one place."

What Changes Will You Make?

Take a moment to think about the changes you want to make as a result of reading this chapter, such as setting up Planning and Action Categories in the To-Do Bar, creating Strategic Next Actions without dependencies, using 1:1 categories, and following the Workflow Model to process and organize information.

In the To-Do List in Outlook, open the IMPROVING PRODUCTIVITY task that you created in Chapter 4, and under the heading "Processing and Organizing," enter the specific actions that you want to do to support the this piece of the Processing and Organizing Phase. After you've entered the changes you want to make, please close the Task and keep it in Categories: (none). You'll be referring to it again at the end of Chapter 12 and incorporate it into your list of personal objectives. Carol's processing and organizing actions are shown in Figure 9-14, for example.

Chapter Nine: Processing and Organizing Categories: (none)

Part Three:
Creating an
Integrated
Management
System—The
Processing and
Organizing
Phase

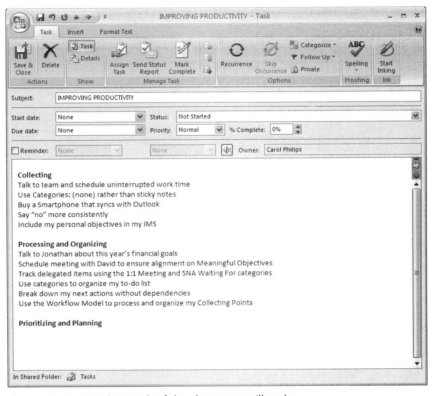

Figure 9-14 Keeping track of the changes you'll make.

Here's what some of our clients have to say:

- "Use the categories to help me organize my To-Do List."

- "Use the 1:1 categories to track my direct report's objective and delegated items."

- "Have my objectives tracked right in front of me so that I can see them daily."

- "Create Strategic Next Actions without dependencies so that I know I can take action immediately."

- "Link Metrics into objective and project Tasks so that they are immediately available."

- "Track Tasks and Subtasks inside of the project Task so that everything is in one place."

- "Organize Strategic Next Actions categories by location."

Part Three:
Creating an
Integrated
Management
System—The
Processing and
Organizing
Phase

Take Back Your Life!

Success Factors for Processing and Organizing Categories: (none)

Before you move on to setting up your Reference System, here's a summary of the key topics discussed in this chapter.

- Schedule uninterrupted time to process and organize your Collecting Points. Schedule a daily, recurring appointment for one hour to do this.

- Use the Workflow Model to clarify your commitments and communications. This model makes it a lot easier to get through the Processing and Organizing Phase simply.

- Process Tasks one item at a time, starting at the top of the list. This ensures you empty the Collecting Point and get into good habits.

- Use the Planning and Action Categories to organize your actions in the To-Do List.

- Remember, Meaningful Objectives and Supporting Projects are Planning Categories. They're loaded with dependencies, and they're not Strategic Next Actions.

- Strategic Next Actions are Action Categories and do not have dependencies.

- Organize all of your Tasks in the To-Do List so that your list is centrally located, accessible, and flexible.

- Identify personal behavior changes so that you can successfully maintain your system going forward.

Congratulations! You've set up 50 percent of your Integrated Management System, and you're probably much clearer about what you're doing and how it's going to help you take back your life and create more productive time.

Part Three:
Creating an
Integrated
Management
System—The
Processing and
Organizing
Phase

Take Back Your Life!

Chapter Ten

Improving Your Reference System

Chapter Ten: Improving Your Reference System

Part Three:
Creating an
Integrated
Management
System—The
Processing and
Organizing
Phase

How would you like to have an additional five weeks each year? According to our company's statistics, clients spend 60 minutes a day, on average, finding and filing information. After our clients improve their Reference System and learn how to use the Search Desktop function, that number can be reduced to 10 minutes a day. That's a 50-minute savings every day of the week. Almost five weeks a year! Now *that's* something worth working toward!

In this chapter, you learn how to create an effective Reference System and how to use Windows Desktop Search. Some of you may find that you can use a very simple system for filing and primarily use the desktop search feature for finding all your information. Others will find that they need a more robust system for finding and filing and want to take the time to fine-tune their digital Reference System.

Now for some of you, your Reference System is working and you're able to find most everything you need when you need it; however, we think you'll still find some really effective pointers in this chapter to take our system to the next level. And if your system is not working, this chapter will be incredibly useful and will result in big-time savings and a huge reduction in frustration.

The Difference Between Action and Reference Information

Before we start to talk about improving your Reference System, let's be clear what a Reference System is and how it differs from an Action System. The key distinction between a Reference System and an Action System is that the Reference System stores **reference information** and the Action System

Part Three:
Creating an
Integrated
Management
System—The
Processing and
Organizing
Phase

Take Back Your Life!

stores **action information**. We know this sounds simple, but you wouldn't believe the number of clients who get this confused.

Action Information is data you must have to complete an action, such as, "Call Jeremy to go over the sales proposal." It's essential that you have the sales proposal with you when you make the call; therefore, this is classified as action information. "Call the landscaper to review the quote for the dog run." You must have the dog run quote to make the call, and therefore the quote is also action information. In both these examples, the proposal and the quote would be stored and tracked in your Action System. Your Action System includes the Outlook To-Do Bar, Daily Task View, and Calendar.

Reference information is not required to complete an immediate action. Its material you may want to access later, and so it's stored in your Reference System.

David Hamilton is a financial director, and one of his deliverables is creating annual budgets for six of his company's departments. After these budgets are distributed his job is complete and so he stores them in his My Documents folder, in a top-level folder named Finances, and within a subfolder named Departmental Budgets. Inevitably, he is asked questions that require him to refer to these documents, and he also uses them at the end of the year to create the following year's budgets. However, no immediate action items are required related to these budgets; therefore, he stores them in his Reference System.

Karen Berg, a mother at home, loves to cook. She collects recipes that arrive by e-mail from friends. She stores them in her Personal Folders list, in a top-level folder named Personal, and in a subfolder named Cooking. Karen doesn't use these recipes daily; she only goes to this folder when she needs a particular recipe, and so keeping the recipes in her Reference System works well for her.

When you can start to discern the difference between action information and reference information, you'll be able to set up your Reference System with a greater level of confidence.

Using Search Functions to Find Information

Setting up an effective Reference System can take two to four hours on average to do, and so before we get into how to do that, we are going to discuss using the Microsoft Windows Desktop Search function so that you can

Part Three:
Creating an
Integrated
Management
System—The
Processing and
Organizing
Phase

determine if this will enable you to find and file information without having to adjust or set up a new Reference System.

If you are using Windows XP you will need to download Windows Desktop Search to access the Search Box. And if you are using Vista, there is no need to download anything because Desktop Search is a core feature of that operating system.

Once you have Windows Desktop Search on your system, you can access the search function by using the Instant Search box as shown in Figure 10-1 below. This search box is always accessible from the Inbox, Calendar, Contacts, Tasks, Notes, Folder List, and Journal, which makes life simpler. From the Search box, you can access the Windows Desktop Search, which enables you to customize your search, allowing you to look through e-mail messages, appointments, files, and even attachments. You can search just e-mail or all of Outlook, or your entire desktop.

To access the search functions, follow these steps:

(These instructions are from the Calendar view in Outlook, but you can get to the search pane from the Inbox, Calendar, Contacts, Tasks, Notes, Folder List, and Journal.)

1. Click the Calendar icon.

2. Click the drop-down arrow to the right of Search Calendar, and select Search Desktop.

3. Windows Desktop Search opens (Figure 10-1). You can choose your selection criteria by typing the search word, and then choosing the location (Desktop, Outlook, e-mail) and the type of item (document, e-mail, or picture) you're looking for.

Part Three:
Creating an
Integrated
Management
System—The
Processing and
Organizing
Phase

Take Back Your Life!

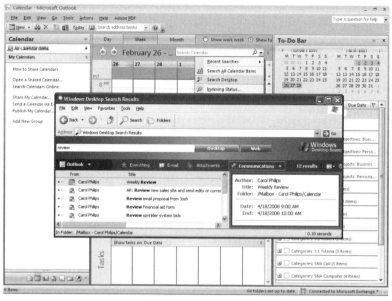

Figure 10-1 In the Windows Desktop Search, you can choose what to look for and where to look for it.

This new search capability is fast and easy to use, and some of our clients find that it works so well that they do not need to update or create a new Reference System. However, some of our clients still have trouble finding and filing and want to fine-tune their Reference Systems, or they're committed to emptying their Collection Points and want a better system to make that process easier. Although a search function is great at finding data, it does not help you file information, and some of our clients want to create a better way to do this so they can save time and energy.

How to Improve Your Reference System

Improving your Reference System takes five simple steps:

1. Identifying existing reference locations

2. Reviewing the six reference locations we recommend

3. Consolidating your system

4. Creating a folder hierarchy

5. Setting up your Reference System

1. Identifying Existing Reference Locations

Before you start to create your Reference System, identify where you are currently storing your data so that you can identify if these locations are working for you, and, if not, you can fine-tune them. When we ask clients how many reference locations they have, they reply, "Two or three: e-mail, My Documents, and paper notepads." On closer scrutiny, it can be as many as 16 to 20! This is a huge discrepancy!

We'd like you to take a moment and scan through your life—from home to work—and identify as many places you can think of where you're storing reference information. Use the following list to write them down. If you have a file cabinet at home and one at work, that counts as two separate locations on your list, so be aware of having duplicate systems for personal and for business. If you run out of steam, Table 10-1 shows a list of potential reference points to help jog your memory.

In your thirst for knowledge, be sure not to drown in all the information.
—**Anthony J. D'Angelo**

1.	11.
2.	12.
3.	13.
4.	14.
5.	15.
6.	16.
7.	17.
8.	18.
9.	19
10.	20.

Part Three:
Creating an
Integrated
Management
System—The
Processing and
Organizing
Phase

Take Back Your Life!

Table 10-1   Potential Reference Locations

Sticky notes on your monitor	Papers on desks at home and/or work
Business cards in your wallet	File folders on your Windows desktop
Inbox	My Documents
Microsoft Windows SharePoint	Personal digital assistant (PDA)
Personal Folders	Multiple notepads
Microsoft Office Word documents	Paper filing system at home and work
Paper address book at home	Briefcase
Kitchen drawer	Refrigerator magnet
Archive boxes in the garage	Kitchen counter
Microsoft Office OneNote	PDA Notes application
PC Notes application	Paper pictures
Digital pictures	Digital music
CDs and tapes	Stacks of magazines

Seeing how many places you're storing information and how spread out your system is can be very revealing! When our clients realize how extensive their systems are, they immediately want to consolidate and simplify.

2. Reviewing the Six Reference Locations We Recommend

In this section, we review six of the most commonly used reference locations. This will assist you to decide how best to consolidate your existing locations to a minimum number.

The six locations are the following:

1. Folder List—tracking e-mail messages

2. Contacts—tracking contacts

3. My Documents—tracking documents

4. SharePoint/Groove—tracking shared documents and folders

5. OneNote—tracking meeting/call notes/ideas

6. Filing cabinet—tracking paper

1. Folder List

The Folder List is the ideal location to store e-mail. It's easy to drag messages from your Inbox directly into this folder. You need to decide which folder in the Folder List you want to use to set up your e-mail Reference Sys-

Chapter Ten: **Improving Your Reference System**

Part Three:
Creating an
Integrated
Management
System—The
Processing and
Organizing
Phase

tem: the Mailbox, the Archive Folders, or the Personal Folders. This is one of the easiest Reference Systems to work with, and you can get tremendous value from it when it's set up and running smoothly.

The Folder List contains three possible locations in which to set up the e-mail Reference System: your personal Mailbox, Personal Folders in your computer, and Archive Folders. Which folder you use depends on how much time you want to spend synchronizing your local folders with the server, how accessible you want your data to be, and the policies in your company about where to store personal and business e-mail.

Unless you have a valid rationale for using your Mailbox or Archive Folder, such as if you're using two different computers and need to access these folders from both, and if you are using a laptop, we strongly recommend using the Personal Folders list to set up your e-mail Reference System, for these reasons:

- You have access to the information 24/7, which is extremely useful when traveling.

- You're not using valuable e-mail storage space, which can be an issue for some people.

- Most companies allow personal e-mail to be stored as long as it's on your hard disk and not the company server.

Our computers are automatically backed up once a week, and so we're extremely confident about using our hard disk to store our e-mail Reference System. However, if your company doesn't back up your hard disk, and doesn't allow you to use a third-party vendor to back up your hard disk (for IT reasons), you should reconsider where to store both business and personal e-mail.

If you have no issues with synchronization, e-mail storage space, and 24/7 access, using your Mailbox or Archive Folder works just fine. Some of my clients like to use the Archive Folder instead of the Mailbox folder because it's stored as a .pst file, which gives them unlimited storage. In an Exchange Server environment, this file is connected to the server, so you won't have 24/7 access when you travel. After you have decided where to locate your e-mail Reference System, you can then begin to create the folders you want to use to store your data. We talk about creating an effective folder hierarchy in the next section.

Part Three:
Creating an
Integrated
Management
System—The
Processing and
Organizing
Phase

Take Back Your Life!

2. Contacts Folder

The Contacts folder is the ideal location for personal and frequently used business contacts. We've found that most companies allow you to keep track of personal contacts in your Contacts list on your hard disk. We recommend that you check to ensure that you're complying with corporate policies. Also, most personal digital assistants (PDAs) and smartphones will synchronize with your Contacts, enabling you to have access to them 24/7 if needed. Being able to synchronize your PDA or smartphone with Outlook makes this reference location a very useful one both personally and professionally.

You can also give other people access to your Contacts list so that they can share it with you. For example, you could give your administrator access to your contacts so that she can add new contact data for you or use your contact information when setting up meetings. When you're sharing a Contacts list, we suggest you set up guidelines about how to sort the contacts so that all users do it consistently, making it easier to find data. Do you file them by last name, first name, or company name? Will you use categories, and, if so, which ones? After you decide how to use contacts, sharing the information becomes very easy and saves considerable time. For example, rather than your administrator asking you for contact data, she can look in your Contacts instead. Very simple, very effective.

There are lots of ways to benefit from having reference information in your Contacts list. Here are a few examples from clients:

- Keeping directions in Contacts. When you're driving to a business or friend's house you can use your PDA to view directions. Microsoft MapPoint and Windows Live Local are great sources for directions and maps which then can be linked to or copied and pasted into your Contact record.

- Posting birthdays in Contacts so that they appear on the Calendar. By opening a contact, clicking the Details tab, and entering a date in the Birthday field, you can have a reminder appear on the Calendar for that day.

- Including clothes sizes for family and friends. When you're shopping and see a potential wardrobe gift, you'll have the data handy.

- Tracking client/vendor conversations if you don't use a customer relationship database. We have clients type their notes directly into their contact when they're on a call with a client. When they call the client again, their comments from the previous call are handy in the contact.

Part Three:
Creating an
Integrated
Management
System—The
Processing and
Organizing
Phase

- Remembering vaccinations for children and pets.

- Recording equipment warranty expiration dates, and contact information, such as a Help Line number.

If you're connected to a server on a corporate network, you'll see two Contacts folders in the Folder List; one is for global Contacts, which is shared by all employees in your company; the other folder is only on your computer, and so you alone can see it. If you're not connected to a server, you'll have only one Contacts folder, which is located on your computer.

Carol has two Contacts folders in her Folder List: Contacts under the Mailbox heading, which is located on her hard disk, and Contacts under the Public Folders heading, which is located on the server. She uses the Contacts list on her hard disk to store her personal information and her frequently used business contacts. She uses the Contacts list in the Public Folders to share business contacts. Carol can access this list only when she's connected to the server, and so she keeps her frequently used business contacts in the Contacts folder on her hard disk. That way she can access this information when she's no longer connected to the server.

Carol uses her contact list religiously. When she and her husband got their first dog, she immediately created a new contact to track the dog's birth date, vaccinations, and other relevant data. This proved to be incredibly useful when she found herself at the vet's office. The doctor asked questions about vaccines and Carol was dumbfounded until she remembered her Contacts in her Pocket PC! Organization strikes! It took her 15 seconds to locate the data in her Contacts, saving her from making phones calls that could have been unsuccessful causing another trip to the vet!

Carol never worries about birthday reminders because once she enters them into her Contacts list, they automatically show up on her Calendar. And having directions in her Contacts helps her get to her appointments on time. Carol synchronizes her laptop with her PDA so that when she's in the car, her PDA helps her get where she's going. Carol is directionally challenged, and so having directions handy is beneficial to her.

You can also use categories in your contacts to make it easier to find contacts or to create mailing lists. In Figure 10-2, you can see contacts grouped by categories.

Part Three:
Creating an
Integrated
Management
System—The
Processing and
Organizing
Phase

Take Back Your Life!

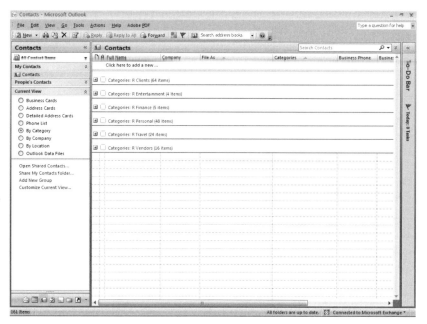

Figure 10-2   Viewing contacts by categories.

As an example of how useful grouping contacts can be, imagine you need to call a contractor for some home maintenance and you can't remember his name. Rather than scan your entire Contacts list, you can look in the "Home" category.

We have a client who has an "Entertainment" category in which he tracks favorite restaurants and theaters in the cities he travels to. This makes booking reservations much easier. Another client uses a "Friends & Family" category to help her create her Christmas card and gift list each year. The category reminds her to whom she wants to send cards and gifts. She also uses this list to print out Christmas card envelopes.

There are lots of good reasons to view contacts by categories. However, for this view to work effectively, you must categorize each contact you create. If you don't do this consistently, your system will break down. Be careful. Only use categories if they add value; otherwise, they'll become one more thing for you to do.

To view your contacts by categories, click By Category in the Navigation Pane to the left of the Contacts list.

Chapter Ten: Improving Your Reference System

Part Three:
Creating an
Integrated
Management
System—The
Processing and
Organizing
Phase

3. My Documents

Your My Documents folder is the ideal location for storing documents: Microsoft Office Excel worksheets, Microsoft Office PowerPoint presentations, Word documents, Portable Document Format (PDF) files, and pictures and music files.

Many of our clients store e-mail messages that have large documents attached in their e-mail Reference System. We suggest you save these documents *separately* in your My Documents Reference System, and delete them from the e-mail message. This can reduce the size of your Inbox and any other locations where you are storing attachments that could be stored in your Documents Reference System. There are a few exceptions to this rule, however. Sometimes you will want to keep a document with the e-mail message because it is relevant to the message and therefore important to keep together. In this case, you can save the document both in My Documents and also in your E-mail Reference System with the message. That way, it's in two places. You can be confident that you'll find it either way.

The key to an effective My Documents Reference System is how you set up the folder hierarchy so that you can easily file and find information. Simplicity is the key here, and of course less is more. We discuss folder hierarchy in the next section.

4. SharePoint and Groove

Many companies now use Microsoft Windows SharePoint sites to help their intact workteams share, view, and edit documents, calendars, and tasks. These sites dramatically reduce e-mail and attachments, and they support team collaboration. For example, team members can easily access SharePoint sites and view or download documents from document libraries rather than sending information back and forth by e-mail. Team members can easily post documents to be viewed on the SharePoint site and send links to the documents, which reduces the size of e-mail messages. And, when teams are collaborating on documents, they can easily edit documents on the site, either directly or by checking out the document. This supports version control, ensures team members are always seeing the latest document, and reduces e-mail traffic because editing is done directly on the site and not via e-mail. Team members can save multiple documents from SharePoint to Outlook and have SharePoint alert them when these documents have been updated.

Part Three:
Creating an
Integrated
Management
System—The
Processing and
Organizing
Phase

Take Back Your Life!

SharePoint is a fantastic product for information sharing and team collabo-ration. If you work on a team, SharePoint is an essential tool for increasing team productivity. It works and there is no way around it except for Groove.

Microsoft Office Groove is another tool that makes shared reference infor-mation and team collaboration easy. Even if team members work for differ-ent organizations, work remotely, or work offline, they can access Groove sites, which is extremely useful. Groove is a more dynamic product than SharePoint is because it provides more extensive features related to collabo-rating, editing, and updating documents. Pretty much everything that SharePoint can do, Groove can do better, particularly when it comes to team collaboration on documents, actions, and calendars.

These two products work really well, and we highly recommend you inves-tigate using one or the other for managing your shared reference informa-tion and for team collaboration. And if you're a smaller business, hosted SharePoint providers enable you to use this service.

5. OneNote

Microsoft Office OneNote is designed to capture, share, and organize refer-ence information. It also communicates with multiple Microsoft Office applications. For example, OneNote integrates with Contacts and your Cal-endar allowing you to create synchronized notes page in your OneNote notebook that are also linked to a specific contact record or a specific appointment. This enables you to have notes particular to an appointment in the appointment as well as in OneNote and notes particular to a contact in the contact as well as OneNote. The benefit of this is that when you're in a meeting, you and other attendees can easily access these notes in the appointment. Because they are also connected to OneNote, if you forget which appointment the notes are in, you can easily find them in OneNote via search functions.

With OneNote, you can synchronize tasks you capture in notes with the To-Do Bar. This enables you to keep all of your actions in your Action System and references in your Reference System.

If you have a Tablet PC, OneNote allows you to store both typed and hand-written notes, enabling you to eliminate paper notepads completely.

Because OneNote synchronizes with Outlook, it is a seamless note-taking device. When you're in meetings, rather than using your notepad, you can use OneNote to take typed or handwritten notes (see Figure 10-3).

Part Three:
Creating an
Integrated
Management
System—The
Processing and
Organizing
Phase

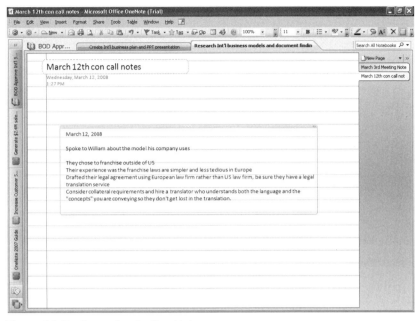

Figure 10-3   Example of a OneNote page.

You can file by the date or name of the meeting, whatever naming convention works for you. During your meetings when you come across actions that need to be recorded, you can track these in OneNote, and because of the synchronization capabilities, you can easily copy these to the To-Do Bar so that all your actions are centralized in one place, and you still have a record of this in your meeting notes. (See Chapter 12 for more information about how to capture actions from OneNote).

When the meeting is completed, if you want to share your meeting notes with the team, you can send any note page as an e-mail message directly from OneNote, and recipients do not have to have OneNote to receive and open the notes.

OneNote also has a powerful search function, and so it is easy to find your notes, unlike finding notes in a paper notepad. And when you are in OneNote and want help on how to use it effectively, you can easily access the OneNote 2007 Guide. In Figure 10-3 in the bottom left corner, you can see a vertical tab labeled OneNote 2007 Guide.

Between the search function, note-taking capabilities, synchronization with Outlook, and the ability to move actions to the To-Do List, OneNote is a very productive tool to use for storing reference information.

Part Three:
Creating an
Integrated
Management
System—The
Processing and
Organizing
Phase

Take Back Your Life!

6. File Cabinet

A file cabinet is the best location to file papers, though you wouldn't know it from the stacks of papers in some of our clients' offices! Although most of us are working toward eliminating paper, some of our clients still live in a paper world and need to have good paper Reference Systems. In the section titled "4. Creating a Folder Hierarchy that Works" later in this chapter, we review how to create a Folder Hierarchy that makes it easier to file and find papers.

These are the six locations our clients use most commonly. You may have other locations you want or need to use to support your professional or personal life, and that is fine. Hopefully, these six will give you some ideas of how you can consolidate and minimize your existing locations.

3. Consolidation

Most of our clients are storing reference information in a lot more than six places—sometimes as many as 25. Now that you have some idea of the most commonly used reference locations you can start to identify how to consolidate yours to a smaller number of locations. For example, you can move documents from your desktop to My Documents. You can transfer phone numbers written on sticky notes into your Contacts list, you can replace paper notes with OneNote, and you can use SharePoint or Groove to keep shared information. There are many options to help you consolidate; simply use your IMPROVE PRODUCTIVITY task to make a note of these actions to remind you what you want to do.

4. Creating a Folder Hierarchy That Works

After you have decided which locations you're going to use for your reference information, the next step is creating the right kind of Folder Hierarchy so that you can file and find the data easily and effortlessly. There are millions of ways to store reference data. For example, you can file by a person's name, alphabetically, by project, chronologically, or using a combination of all of these. There are many ways to do it. You need to find a Folder Hierarchy that fits your needs and reflects your work style and circumstances.

Whatever you do, we recommend creating your Folder Hierarchy first, before you file data. Most of our clients create their Folder Hierarchy as they go along, and when data shows up that does not fit into their current system, they simply create a new folder to file it in. This is reactive, creates mul-

Part Three:
Creating an
Integrated
Management
System—The
Processing and
Organizing
Phase

tiple folders, and does not guarantee you can find the data in the future given how spontaneous the hierarchy is.

By creating a Folder Hierarchy first, you're creating a natural filtering system for your information. If you then replicate this hierarchy across all of your reference locations, you do not have to rethink where you file a document or note because your hierarchy is always the same.

Organizing Your Folders by Meaningful Objectives

There are many ways to create a Folder Hierarchy, and we've seen and used many of them over the years. We're going to recommend a somewhat radical approach: create your hierarchy around your Meaningful Objectives. This creates a strong filtering system causing you to think twice before filing data that does not relate to your objectives. Now, of course, you can create additional folders to track management data that is outside of your objectives; however, the bulk of your folders would be objective related. This causes you to maintain a focus on your Meaningful Objectives whether you are dealing with reference information or action information. It is consistent with the Cycle of Productivity and Action Hierarchy Model, which are the cornerstones of your Integrated Management System (IMS).

The way to do this is to set it up so that your top-level folders match your Meaningful Objectives and your subfolders match your Supporting Projects. Remember, your objectives are your North Star and guiding light.

A Folder Hierarchy based on your objectives supports a very clear focus and causes you to be more discerning about the information you keep and the information you delete. When you try to file an e-mail message that doesn't relate to one of your objectives, you need to ask the question, "Why am I filing something that doesn't relate to one of my objectives?" By focusing primarily on your goals, you can dramatically reduce the amount of information you're filing, and by duplicating this taxonomy across all your reference locations, you'll discover that finding and filing become second nature. It also reinforces your focus on your Supporting Projects.

In Figure 10-4, you can see Carol's e-mail Reference System in the Folder List under Personal Folders. Carol has five top-level folders, and under each of these folders are a number of subfolders. Notice that the names of the top-level folders mirror Carol's business Meaningful Objectives on her To-Do List, and her subfolders mirror her Supporting Projects. One of Carol's top-level folders is titled "Personal," and the subfolders under this folder mimic her personal objectives.

Goals provide the energy source that powers our lives. One of the best ways we can get the most from the energy we have is to focus it. That is what goals can do for us; concentrate our energy.
—**Denis Waitley**

Part Three:
Creating an
Integrated
Management
System—The
Processing and
Organizing
Phase

Take Back Your Life!

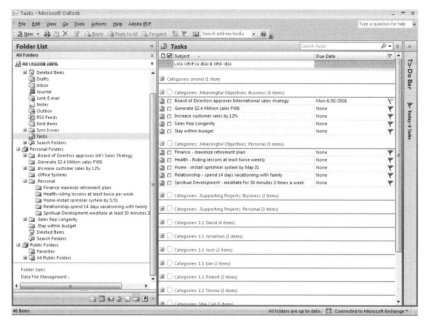

Figure 10-4   Carol's Reference Folder Hierarchy maps to her personal and business objectives.

We think you'll be surprised by the benefits of setting up your Folder Hierarchy by Meaningful Objectives and Supporting Projects. In a world full of distractions, it's essential to keep redirecting your thinking to what's important. After all of your Reference Systems are set up with this Folder Hierarchy, you'll be reminded of your objectives and projects every time you go to find or file something. This is very powerful and helps you consistently redirect your attention. This kind of Folder Hierarchy has integrity and truly helps you focus on your most important activities.

Adding Some Function and Role Folders If Appropriate

If your Meaningful Objectives and Supporting Projects folders really represent what you're doing, you won't need additional folders for functions or roles. Sometimes, the fact that you need these additional folders is an indication that your objectives are not clear and could use a little adjustment.

However, we've come across situations in which a few additional function and role folders came in handy. For example, you might need to store information related to company policies, such as parking regulations, retirement plans, cafeteria coupons, and company gym use. These can be filed in a "Company Policies" folder, or in a folder that indicates to you that it stores general information about corporate guidelines.

Part Three:
Creating an
Integrated
Management
System—The
Processing and
Organizing
Phase

Using Your File Hierarchy Consistently Across Systems

You have several locations you can choose to store information: Personal Folders, Contacts, My Documents, SharePoint, OneNote, and paper files. After you have a Folder Hierarchy set up, we suggest you take this very same folder structure and use it across all of your systems. You can literally take the same taxonomy you used for your Folder List and set up the exact same top-level and sublevel folders in My Documents, OneNote, and SharePoint. You won't believe how simple that makes filing and finding! You're creating a path that will become automatic so that using it becomes habit and you won't have to think twice.

5. Setting Up Your Reference System

The most time-consuming element of setting up your IMS is creating your Collecting System, Action System, and Reference System. When you have these set up, you're golden!

Setting up your Reference System is much like setting up your Collection System. You need to analyze where you're capturing data and decide which of those buckets you want to eliminate, which you'll keep and combine, and what new systems you want to create.

Of course, all of us have time, but the truth is we just don't want to spend our time improving our Reference System—it appears so insignificant compared to other tasks. For most of us, this is really low on the priority list, not to mention dull, boring, monotonous, and for some people, just plain confusing. However, when you can save 50 minutes a day by having a system that works, there's really no excuse!

Where do you start? We suggest you pick a reference location, such as My Documents, and then by using capital letters to distinguish from your existing folders, type in your objectives, one per folder. Create your Supporting Projects as subfolders. Then, you can drag your old files into the new Folder Hierarchy. At the same time, you can do a little house cleaning, deleting the items that don't fit in with your objectives or Supporting Projects. In Figure 10-5, you can see Carol's My Documents folder that uses the same Folder Hierarchy she used in her Personal Folders. Both sets of folders map to the objectives in her To-Do List. This is extremely simple and extremely powerful.

Part Three:
Creating an
Integrated
Management
System—The
Processing and
Organizing
Phase

Take Back Your Life!

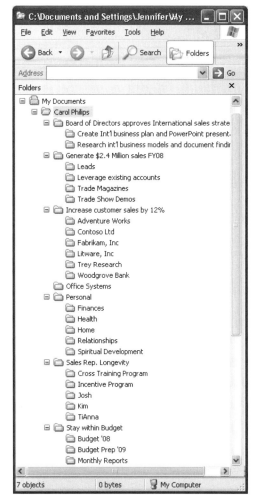

Figure 10-5 Carol's My Documents Folder Hierarchy maps to her personal and business objectives.

Tips for Using Your Reference System

Stop Using Your Inbox as a Reference System!

Some of our clients use their Inbox as their e-mail Reference System because using Personal Folders wasn't effective. And truth be known, for some of you, using e-mail as a Reference System is not effective either! We of course always recommend moving your reference e-mail out of the Inbox so that you can have the pleasure of an empty Inbox and truly use it as a Collection Point, not a Reference System.

With Windows Desktop Search, finding information is becoming a lot easier. Therefore, storing reference information in one folder works really well, especially if you do not want to use a more comprehensive reference structure.

Here is a somewhat radical approach: create a folder named "E-Mail Reference" and move all of your e-mail messages into it that are past three months old. When we mention this, some of our clients have a hernia. "You've got to be kidding!" We show them their e-mail and their Folder List and politely say, "There is a vertical line in the middle that separates your e-mail and your folders, and we're asking you to move your e-mail from the right side of the line to the left side of the line." From the looks on their faces, you'd think we'd asked them to delete all their e-mail! Obviously, that line is a powerful boundary! This points to the fact that some of our clients are really attached to the way they are doing things; nothing wrong with this. However, if what you are doing is not producing the results you want you may want to consider changing what you're doing. Just a thought!

Remember, your Inbox is part of your Collecting System. It's not part of your Reference System. To keep the integrity of your IMS, we urge you to use your Personal Folders as part of your Reference System and leave the Inbox as part of your Collecting System. You can sort just as easily in the Personal Folders list as you can in the Inbox, and if you store your e-mail in an Archive .pst folder, you can dramatically reduce storage issues in your main e-mail file.

We have clients who resist moving e-mail out of the Inbox because leaving messages in the Inbox has become a habit. These clients say that an empty Inbox wouldn't motivate them. But you can't pull the wool over our eyes! We've never worked with a client, ever, who on emptying the Inbox, didn't have a humongous smile on his or her face and an expression that said, "I didn't realize how good I'd feel. I haven't had an empty Inbox since the day I started, 10 years a go!" The problem is that we forget how good it feels to have an empty Inbox. Use your e-mail as a Collecting Point and store reference information in the Reference System. You'll feel better!

Determine What to Keep and What to Delete

This topic is really for the "keepers" who are reading this chapter. Our company's statistics show that, on average, people working in companies save 20 to 30 percent of their e-mail per day. That's a lot of e-mail, and for those of you who are "keepers," this percentage is much higher.

Part Three:
Creating an
Integrated
Management
System—The
Processing and
Organizing
Phase

Take Back Your Life!

Here are some questions to ask to help you discern what to keep and what to delete:

- Does this e-mail information relate to an objective I'm currently working on?

- Can I find this information somewhere else, such as on a Web site, on an intranet, or from a colleague?

- Will I refer back to this information in the next three months?

- Am I required to keep it? Is it legal, HR, or financial?

The cry of a keeper is, "But you never know when I might need it!" We ask that when you answer the preceding questions, you remove this sentence from your mind. Answer the questions logically rather than from your emotions or your fear! We know this is hard to do when your habits are so strong, but if you always do what you've always done . . . you know the rest by now!

It's so easy to store data today, dragging it into your folders in nanoseconds! However, it's not so easy to go through your folders and clean them out. That takes hours! If you take the time to pause and ask the four previous questions, you make decisions on the front end so that you won't have to make them on the back end, when it'll take a lot more time! Don't be afraid to make best friends with your Delete key, and it is OK that you're no longer the person to whom everyone comes to find the e-mail they deleted! You weren't hired as a librarian.

Keep Your Folder List Current

Changes will happen in your world. You'll complete objectives, you'll take on new ones, your direct reports will change, reorganizations will happen, you might move, or you'll have a new baby. As these events happen, you'll need to adjust your Meaningful Objectives, which then must be reflected in your Reference System. At the same time, you'll want to delete or archive completed objectives and Supporting Projects so that they're not clogging up your system. It's important to keep this connection between your current reality and your folder structure; otherwise, you'll end up carrying around unrelated files for years, which will distract you from your focus on objectives.

When you get used to having a Reference System, you'll find it pretty easy to maintain. Once a year you clean it out and put in your new Meaningful Objectives and Supporting Projects.

Part Three:
Creating an
Integrated
Management
System—The
Processing and
Organizing
Phase

Keep Your System Simple

You want your Folder Hierarchy to be really simple so that you can file in your sleep. Hundreds of file folders means hundreds of decisions about filing and finding, and lots of time dragging files between long lists of folders. It's so much simpler to minimize the number of top-level folders and, if necessary, increase the number of second-level folders. We've consistently found that less is more when it comes to filing.

Some of our clients have an extremely simple Folder Hierarchy. They have four folders—Q1-07, Q2-07, Q3-07, Q4-07—to represent the four quarters of the year. E-mail search functions are so good that they don't need anything more complex. There's nothing wrong with easy!

The most uncomplicated system we've seen consisted of a single folder titled "Reference." This client stored e-mail in it and used the Search function to find specific e-mail messages. This is extremely simple, and if it works for you, keep doing it. There is beauty in simplicity.

Ensuring your E-Mail Reference System is Set Up

Before you move onto the next chapter, we want to make sure you set up or improve your e-mail Reference System in the Folder List. This is extremely important to do because in the next chapter you'll be organizing your Inbox and filing all your reference e-mail messages. To be able to file them easily you'll want your e-mail Reference System set up and working.

Plan on reserving one or two hours to complete setting up your new e-mail Reference System. How long it takes depends on the size and quantity of your existing e-mail Reference System. We recommend that you set up your top-level folders first. Each top-level folder represents one of your Meaningful Objectives. If you have eight objectives, you'll have eight top-level folders. We suggest you use the same nomenclature that you used in the Meaningful Objectives category on your To-Do List. Then, set up subfolders under each objective folder to represent your Supporting Projects, using the same nomenclature used in your Supporting Projects category. For example, if your first objective has four Supporting Projects, you'll have one top-level objective folder with four subfolders representing the Supporting Projects.

If you have a large number of e-mail reference files, we suggest creating your new objective folders using a period (.) at the beginning of the file name so that they are alphabetized at the top of the folder tree. Typing folder names

Part Three:
Creating an
Integrated
Management
System—The
Processing and
Organizing
Phase

Take Back Your Life!

in all capital letters can help you distinguish your new folders from the old ones. After you've created your Folder Hierarchy by objectives and Supporting Projects, you can then drag your old files into the new folders.

To create a new folder, follow these steps:

1. Select the folder that will contain the new folder.

2. On File menu, select New, and then click Folder. Or you can right-click and select New Folder.

3. In the Create New Folder dialog box, enter the name of the new folder, and then click OK.

Eventually, you'll want to go into each of your personal folders and give them a good pruning. This is always an extraordinary eye-opener! Our clients typically find that they're not using 50 percent of what they're filing.

To summarize, there are many ways reduce the time you spend filing and finding information: you can use the new Windows Desktop Search feature in Outlook, you can reduce the number of locations you store in, you can create a Folder Hierarchy that filters your filing and simplifies it. Make sure whatever you do, you customize it to your work style and situation.

What Changes Will You Make?

Once you make a
decision, the uni-
verse conspires to
make it happen.
--**Ralph Waldo
Emerson**

In your Outlook To-Do List, open the task named IMPROVING PRODUC-TIVITY. This is the location you created to capture all the behaviors you'll do differently as a result of learning the Three Phases for Creating an Integrated Management System. Under the heading "Processing and Organizing," list the changes that you want to make to set up your Reference System effectively. For example, Carol's processing and organizing actions are shown in Figure 10-6.

Chapter Ten: Improving Your Reference System

Part Three:
Creating an
Integrated
Management
System—The
Processing and
Organizing
Phase

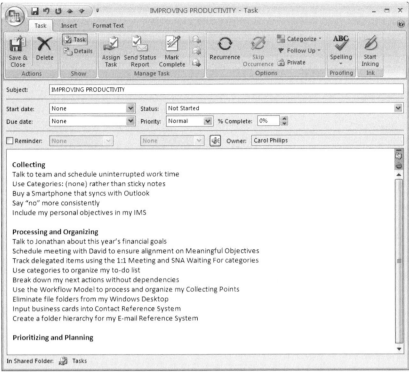

Figure 10-6   Keeping track of the changes you'll make.

Here are a few examples from our clients:

- "Set up Personal Folders so that I can stop using my Inbox as a Reference System, and start using my Personal Folders instead."

- "Reduce my 45 top-level folders to 17 so that it's easier to file and find!"

- "Synchronize my Folder Hierarchy between my Personal Folders and My Documents."

- "Set up SharePoint for my team so that we can share documents using the same Folder Hierarchy."

- "Enter my names and addresses into Contacts so that I have one central place for them instead of multiple buckets."

- "Find out if I can integrate my personal contacts into my Contacts file on my hard disk."

- "Keep action information with actions in the Action System and reference information in the Reference System."

Part Three:
Creating an
Integrated
Management
System—The
Processing and
Organizing
Phase

Take Back Your Life!

■ "Categorize my contacts to make it easier for me to find them."

■ "Load OneNote and review tutorial."

Success Factors for Improving Your Reference System

With an effective Reference System, you can find and file critical data easily and dramatically reduce the amount of time you spend doing so. It's well worth putting the time and effort in on the front end because you'll have extraordinary time savings on the back end.

As you set up your Reference System, remember these key items:

■ Understand the difference between action and reference information so that you know what data to store in which system.

■ Decide what locations you're going to use to store information and minimize the list to six systems, if you can.

■ Create a clear Folder Hierarchy based on objectives, functions, and roles so that you're driving your IMS from this focus whatever hierarchy works best for you.

■ Use 15 or fewer top-level folders so that you can simplify your system.

■ Mirror your Folder Hierarchy across systems to create a consistent taxonomy that makes it easily to find and file data.

Now, the moment you've all been waiting for: processing and organizing e-mail. Hold onto your hats, and prepare to get friendly with the Delete key!

Part Three:
Creating an
Integrated
Management
System—The
Processing and
Organizing
Phase

Take Back Your Life!

Chapter Eleven

Processing and Organizing Your E-Mail

Part Three:
Creating an
Integrated
Management
System—The
Processing and
Organizing
Phase

E-mail is one of the biggest challenges facing our organizations today. Our clients often comment, "We get too much of it, we can't keep up with it, but we can't stop doing it. We're addicted!" Many companies are now questioning the value of e-mail and how to bring it back into balance. An information technology (IT) director recently commented to us: "E-mail has become unproductive. We're overusing the Cc line, sending messages that aren't valuable, and spending too much time with our heads stuck in the Inbox." It would appear on the surface that e-mail is a big problem. However, is e-mail really the problem, or is it our approach to e-mail?

In the 21st century, technology has eliminated many personal boundaries, and a lot of our clients have allowed e-mail to drive their behavior instead of the other way around. As in dealing with interruptions, if you don't consciously set boundaries for yourself, the world will set them for you. You have probably experienced working on e-mail at home, late at night, early in the mornings, during meetings, and while on telephone conference calls. Some of our clients have smartphones or personal digital assistants (PDAs) and process their e-mail while driving the car or standing in line at the grocery store!

We've discovered that e-mail is not the problem companies are facing today. The issue is the behaviors employees have adopted and developed around responding and approaching their inboxes. Companies readily adopted and deployed communication software company-wide; however, this was done with little or no education. In the absence of education, it is not surprising that e-mail communication has become a problem. The first step to controlling e-mail is re-examining your approaches, recognizing that they may not be working, and replacing them with behaviors that you can use to manage

Part Three:
Creating an
Integrated
Management
System—The
Processing and
Organizing
Phase

Take Back Your Life!

your e-mail more effectively, not just as individuals but as teams and organizations. E-mail is a powerful tool that has the ability to increase productivity; a little education goes a long way and that's what this chapter is all about.

We review how to use the E-Mail PASS Model, which includes learning to create meaningful e-mail messages; the most appropriate use of the To, Cc, and Subject lines; and what questions to ask before clicking Send. We also review the McGhee Productivity Solutions (MPS) Workflow Model and the Four Ds for Decision Making, which you can use to process and organize your Inbox effectively so that you can empty it successfully into your Integrated Management System (IMS). (Yup, we did use the word *empty*!) When you've learned how to do this, you'll find that it can relieve a tremendous amount of stress and help you make better choices about what your priorities are and how to get them done.

If you have hundreds of e-mail messages in your Inbox, there's hope in sight. The search for the empty Inbox is close at hand, and there's gold at the end of the rainbow! Many of our clients go to bed at night with an empty Inbox! Even if your Inbox is already clear, read on, because we'll be introducing some very nifty MPS tips and tricks that we think you'll definitely find valuable.

E-Mail Is a Communication Tool

Perhaps we have all forgotten that e-mail is primarily a communication tool. The purpose of communication is to exchange information so that it's clearly understood. Therefore, one of the main functions involved in processing and organizing your e-mail is communicating effectively. Communication is an art we can practice and improve. If your messages are not clear, your recipients will not be clear, and effective action will not take place.

We're certain you've gotten e-mail messages and said to yourself, "What is this, what does it mean, and why did I get it?" Having spent too much time trying to figure out what the message is about, you likely close it back into your Inbox, merrily on your way to hundreds, if not thousands, of other e-mail messages. On the flip side, think about the number of times you've sent an e-mail message that came back with questions because you didn't write the message clearly enough to begin with.

Part Three:
Creating an
Integrated
Management
System—The
Processing and
Organizing
Phase

Introducing the MPS E-Mail PASS Model

The MPS E-Mail PASS Model is designed to help you think about your e-mail communications before you send them. The result is clearly defined messages that produce effective action with the minimal number of communication cycles. By writing effective messages, you can actually reduce the number of e-mail messages you receive in a day.

Creating Meaningful E-Mail Using the MPS PASS Model

The E-Mail PASS Model consists of four questions. We'll review them one at a time, and if you want to pick out an e-mail message to practice on, choose one that is complex and that would take more than two minutes to write. In other words, choose a really meaty, chewy example so that you can experience the value of this model. Obviously, using this model for an e-mail message that requires a one-sentence reply would be overkill; however, we all have messages that require some thought, and this model is designed to support that thinking process.

The E-Mail PASS Model questions are as follows:

P   What's the **Purpose** of your communication and does it relate to a Meaningful Objective?

A   What **Action** is involved and does it have a due date?

S   What **Supporting** documentation do you need to include?

S   Have you effectively summarized your communication in the **Subject** line?

    Did you use the *To*, *Cc* and *Bcc* lines effectively?

What Is the Purpose of Your Communication?

To help you clarify the purpose of your communications, first identify the Meaningful Objective the e-mail message relates to. If it doesn't relate to one of your objectives, you'll want to look at renegotiating or disengaging from it. If it does relate to one of your objectives, ask the question, "What's the outcome you want to produce as a result of this message?" Once you're clear on the outcome and have thought it through, you can write your e-mail communication.

Notice that we haven't asked you to complete the To line, the Cc line, or the Subject line at this point. We suggest you write your e-mail communication

If any man wishes to write a clear style let him first be clear in his thoughts.
—Johann Wolfgang Von Goethe

Part Three:
Creating an
Integrated
Management
System—The
Processing and
Organizing
Phase

Take Back Your Life!

first. Once you've clarified the outcomes of the message, you complete your Subject line, To line, and Cc line.

Susan Burk, an IT program manager, received an e-mail message from her boss asking her to update him on the Microsoft Outlook Migration project. She realized she didn't know the status of the project and needed to get accurate data. She started to type a quick message to Jennifer, her assistant, to find out what was going on. John interrupted her and said, "Let's just pause and think about this for a moment." Susan looked at him a bit surprised. In her mind, she was mumbling, "Hey, this is a simple enough e-mail. I can do this on my own, thank you very much!"

John asked her two questions, "What objective does this relate to?" and "What is the outcome you really want?" As Susan stopped to think about the communication and these questions, she realized that what she really needed was to receive a reoccurring, monthly project status report. This would enable her to monitor what was going on, and if the report was posted on SharePoint, she and her boss could access it whenever they needed it. Her eyes lit up! This was a much better solution. She grinned and said, "OK, perhaps I need to think through these communications a bit more!"

Exercise 11-1   Pick an e-mail message that requires a comprehensive communication, take a moment to establish the outcome for your message, and then write the reply in the body of your e-mail.

What Action Is Involved and Does It Have a Due Date?

What type of action do you want the recipient or recipients to take as a result of your communication? By clearly stating the action, you have a better chance of it getting done.

Following are the four most common e-mail actions that we recommend.

1. **Action**   The recipient has to take a physical action step: order an extension cable. Write a review. Read proposal. Book a meeting for Management Team.

2. **Respond**   The recipient needs only to respond to your communication. There's no action to complete: "Let me know if you can attend the staff meeting at 9 A.M. on Friday."

Part Three:
Creating an
Integrated
Management
System—The
Processing and
Organizing
Phase

3. **Read**   The recipient needs only to read the information. There is no need to take action or respond: "Read sales plan before our next STP meeting on April 20."

4. **FYI only**   The recipient needs to file the information for future reference. There is no need to take action, to read, or to respond: "Enclosed is your approved expense report for your records."

The reason to identify the type of action you're asking the recipient to perform is to eliminate any confusion or guessing about your expectations. In many cases, the benefit is as much for you as it is for the recipient! In Susan's example, she realized, with a little thought, that asking one of her direct reports to post a regular status report on the SharePoint site was a much more effective action than was asking her assistant to find out what was going on with the project. If Susan hadn't thought this through, she wouldn't have reached that conclusion. Think about your communication and clearly identify the action you want the recipient to complete.

Susan decided that her action was to delegate her task to Joe Healy one of her direct reports. She asked him to create the report for the Microsoft Outlook Migration project and post it each month to SharePoint, enabling her and her boss to access it easily.

Clarifying dates can help recipients prioritize their tasks more effectively. If everything you delegate is absent of a timeline, you're relying on the recipient's best judgment to know what your priorities are. That's not a fair request to make of everyone. Most people need clear direction. Also, we do not assume that all tasks require due dates because not all of your actions need them.

When using timelines be discerning and make sure they mean something. It's easy to use due dates, and it's just as easy to overuse them. If you don't hold people accountable to your timelines, they'll eventually come to the conclusion that your timelines don't mean anything. One day, when you give a date that really matters and your team don't respond, you'll wonder why. Don't give out timelines unless you're willing and able to follow up on them.

You can't expect others to keep their due dates if you don't keep yours. Remember, "What's good for the goose is good for the gander." When you demonstrate being accountable to timelines, other people around you will aspire to do the same.

Part Three:
Creating an
Integrated
Management
System—The
Processing and
Organizing
Phase

Take Back Your Life!

Finally, be sensitive when giving out timelines to recipients who don't work for you. It's important to mention a timeline so that everyone is aware of the impact if a task misses a deadline. However, you can't reinforce a due date outside of your own team unless you're working on a project with mutual benefit to both parties.

Exercise 11-2   Take a moment now to review your e-mail message and clarify the action. Then, revisit the deadline of the related Meaningful Objective and evaluate if the action needs to happen by a specific date to ensure that the objective stays on track. Check the Calendar to ensure that the timeline will work, given staff meetings, vacations, and other appointments. When you're clear that your due date is realistic, go ahead and add it to your message.

Example   Susan wanted Joe to create a Microsoft Outlook Migration project monthly status report. She wanted it posted to the SharePoint site by the fifth of each month and to have the first report completed in April. With this done, Susan could get back to her boss on time and it would give her regular data so that she could ensure the project stays on track.

What Supporting Documentation Do You Need to Include?

Identifying the supporting information that the recipient requires to complete the requested action successfully reduces the likelihood of your message coming back to you with questions, creating additional e-mail.

Recently, we asked our operations manager at our company to create a cash flow analysis report. We attached an example of the report we wanted her to complete. This enabled her to accomplish the request without sending further e-mail messages inquiring about layout, data to include, comparisons, and time frames. Once again, moving your thinking to the front end saves you time and effort on the back end.

Exercise 11-3   If you need to include supporting documentation in your e-mail message, you can either type it in the body of the communication, attach a file (a Microsoft Office Excel worksheet, a PDF file, a Microsoft Office Word document, a Microsoft Office PowerPoint presentation, and so on), or insert an item (Inbox, Contacts, reference, or e-mail files). To attach a file or an item, open a new e-mail message, and on the Message tab in the Include group, select one of the following choices on the Ribbon:

- Attach File to insert a file from your computer

Chapter Eleven: Processing and Organizing Your E-Mail

Part Three:
Creating an
Integrated
Management
System—The
Processing and
Organizing
Phase

■ Attach Item to insert an item from your Folders List in Outlook

Example   Susan inserted a monthly status report template into her message so that Joe could view a sample of what she was looking for, and she told him which SharePoint site to post the finished report on. Figure 11-1 shows Susan's e-mail message. This type of information reduced all kinds of guessing on Joe's part, making it easier for him to duplicate the report and post it where Susan could find it.

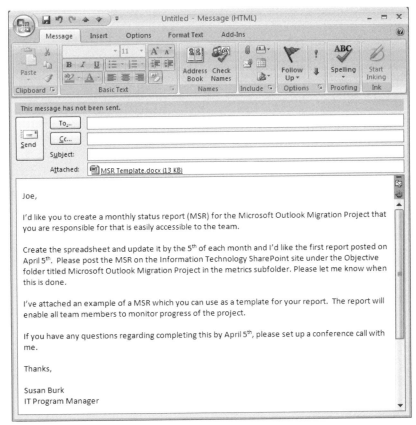

Figure 11-1   Susan's e-mail message clarifies purpose, action, and supporting documentation.

Have You Effectively Summarized Your Message in the Subject Line?

After you've completed writing your e-mail communication, you can then summarize your message using the Subject line. Our clients often fall into

Part Three:
Creating an
Integrated
Management
System—The
Processing and
Organizing
Phase

Take Back Your Life!

the trap of trying to construct Subject lines first because it seems the intuitive thing to do. However, we've observed them consistently changing their subject lines after they've completed writing their communications. We suggest you construct your communications first, and then do your summary in the Subject line afterward. You will find that after you've clarified your outcomes and action and due dates it is a lot easier to create meaningful subject lines.

Three elements make a good Subject line:

1. Clarify the Meaningful Objective or Supporting Project that the e-mail message relates to.

2. Clearly indicate the action requested.

3. Identify a due date, if there is one.

An example Subject line might be "Microsoft Outlook Migration. Create monthly status report on SharePoint, by April 5."

There are four different types of action that you can use in your Subject lines.

1. **Action Requested**   The recipient has to complete an action before he or she can respond. Example: AR: Outlook Migration: post monthly report to SharePoint starting April 5.

2. **Response Requested**   The recipient needs only to respond. No action is required. Example: RR: When do you need the PP slides for your Oct. vendor meeting?

3. **Read Only**   The recipient is required to read the document. Example: RO: Performance Review encl. for Holly Henson August 10 mtg.

4. **FYI only**   The recipient doesn't need to read the document, but can file or delete it. Example: FYI: Updated P&L report for your Q1 records.

Imagine if you could sort your Subject lines by action—'Action Requested', 'Response Requested', 'Read Only' and 'FYI Only' or if you could sort them by the objective or due date. Clearly written subject lines speed up your ability to process and organize your e-mail effectively. The objective lets you know immediately what it relates to. The action lets you know what your responsibility is. The due date enables you to look at your Calendar and Task list to see if it is possible to complete on time. Taking the time to create clear subject lines makes e-mail communication more effective and increases the chance that your e-mail will be responded to.

Chapter Eleven: Processing and Organizing Your E-Mail

Part Three:
Creating an
Integrated
Management
System—The
Processing and
Organizing
Phase

Another helpful tip is to use "EOM" at the end of your Subject line. EOM stands for End Of Message. By using EOM, you're informing the recipient that the message in the Subject line is complete and the recipient doesn't need to open the e-mail. For example: "AR: Fabrikam. Book 1 hour review mtg. with Peter Houston by June 15th. EOM." This is a courtesy and it saves time for the recipients.

You'll want to be sensitive when using Subject-line acronyms: Action Requested (AR), Response Requested (RR), Read Only (RO) or End of Message (EOM). Recipients will not know what you mean unless they've received training. Your best solution, especially with people outside of your team, is to avoid using acronyms altogether and stick with the basic three Subject line elements: objective, action requested, and due date. This type of subject line is clear and universally understood. If in doubt, spell it out!

Just as it's easy to overuse due dates, it's easy to overuse Subject lines so that they become meaningless instead of meaningful. One of our clients so overused the "Action Requested" Subject line that it now holds no value and people disregard it. Be discerning about how you use the Subject line, reinforce its value by reminding people when they are using it appropriately and reminding them when they're using it inappropriately.

Exercise 11-4   Create a subject line for your message. Include the Meaningful Objective or Supporting Project, action, and due date if appropriate.

Did you Use the To, Cc and Bcc lines Effectively?

The Purpose of the To Line

The To line and the Subject line are intrinsically linked. The Subject line clarifies the action that the recipients on the To line have to take. Therefore, be aware of who you're placing on the To line and ensure that they are responsible for the action in the Subject line.

Here are two simple and useful questions to help you filter To line recipients.

- Does this e-mail communication relate to the recipient's objectives?
- Is this recipient responsible for the action in the subject line?

If the Subject line requests an action, each individual on the To line is responsible for taking that action. Some people send e-mail messages with four or five people in the To line in the hopes that one of them will respond. Usually, each person receiving the message assumes that someone else on the To line will reply, and no one ends up responding. Be thoughtful and

Part Three:
Creating an
Integrated
Management
System—The
Processing and
Organizing
Phase

Take Back Your Life!

respectful when you assign recipients to the To line. People will observe your thoughtfulness and the results will be more effective.

If the action in the Subject line relates to multiple recipients who need to take different actions, clarify this in the body of the e-mail message so that everyone is clear exactly what's needed. Figure 11-2 provides an example of a message with multiple recipients who must take different actions.

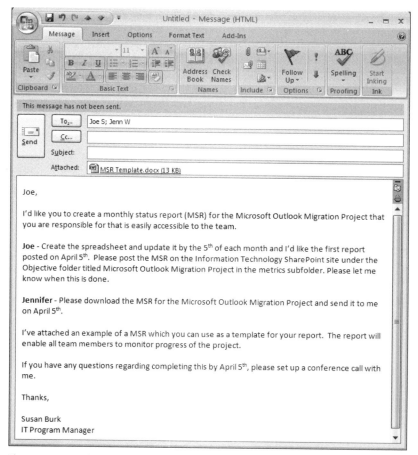

Figure 11-2 This e-mail message demonstrates how to make it clear that multiple recipients are required to take different actions.

Example Susan put Joe on the To line because he was responsible for creating the status report. She also put her assistant, Jennifer, on the To line because she wanted Jennifer to download a document and send it to her. Susan clarified Jennifer's action in the body of the e-mail message, as shown in Figure 11-2.

Part Three:
Creating an
Integrated
Management
System—The
Processing and
Organizing
Phase

The Purpose of the Cc Line

E-mail we've been carbon copied on dominates our e-mail boxes and is an endless source of frustration and unproductive behavior, although it really doesn't have to be. The Cc line is only a courtesy copy, which means it needs to be read or filed, and no action or response is required. The Cc line is linked to the Subject line only by the objective and not by the action. Therefore, a useful question to help you filter your Cc line recipients is, "Will this e-mail impact the recipient's objectives?"

If you ask this question whenever you're about to type a person's name in the Cc line, you'll end up sending considerably less e-mail. We consistently question our clients' use of the Cc line, and 8 times out of 10, they don't need to use it. Take the time to pause and ask the question, "Does this communication impact the recipient's objectives?" If it doesn't, or you don't know what the recipient's objectives are, refrain from including the recipient on the Cc line. Believe me; you're not helping people by sending them information that doesn't impact their objectives. You're just giving them more work to do and more distractions to overcome. Don't be part of the e-mail problem. Be part of the solution by demonstrating effective use of the Cc line.

Exercise 11-5   Assign the appropriate To and Cc contacts to your message. Do not send the message yet because we're not quite finished.

The Purpose of the Bcc Line

If you want to protect a distribution list and keep individuals from receiving a Reply or Reply All, we recommend you use the Bcc line. Individuals on the Bcc line will not get messages if folks on the To or Cc line hit Reply and Reply All. It's important that you are aware that if anyone on the Bcc line hits Reply All, everyone on the To and Cc lines will receive that reply.

Other than that, we do not recommend using the Bcc line. For example, if you have an HR situation and you want to blind copy the HR manager, we recommend that you send your message, and then go to the Sent Items box and forward the e-mail to the HR manager. This way you ensure there are no ramifications or concerns. As we say to our clients, "Be very, very careful when using the Bcc line."

Part Three:
Creating an
Integrated
Management
System—The
Processing and
Organizing
Phase

Take Back Your Life!

Questions To Ask Before Sending E-Mail Messages

The three final questions to ask before sending your e-mail message are these:

■ Does your e-mail message PASS?

■ Have you written the message so that it will not come back to you with questions?

■ Do you need to track this e-mail message in one of your 1:1 or SNA Waiting For categories?

This is your last chance *before* clicking Send to ensure that your message is clear and will produce the results you intend.

1. Does Your E-Mail Message PASS?

The PASS test is your final check to ensure that your e-mail message will be clearly understood.

To take the test, ask these questions:

P   Have you communicated your **purpose** and made sure that it relates to an objective?

A   Have you communicated the **action** requested?

S   Did you include the appropriate **supporting documentation**?

S   Have you summarized the message effectively on your **Subject** line?

Did you use the *To*, *Cc* and *Bcc* lines appropriately?

Figure 11-3 shows Susan's message after she applied the PASS test.

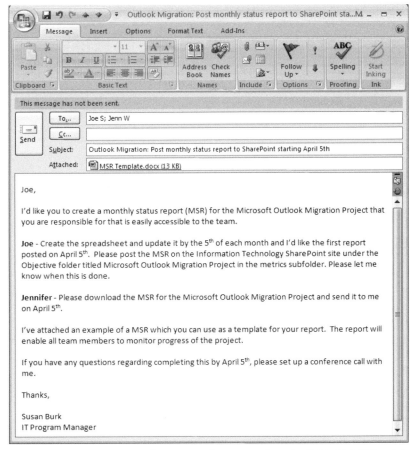

Figure 11-3 Susan's e-mail message demonstrating the E-Mail PASS Model questions.

2. Have You Written the Message so That It Won't Come Back to You with Questions?

When we ask clients this question, they inevitably go back and edit their message to make it clearer. This is not only polite and respectful, but it also reduces the volume of e-mail exchanged. When your communications are clear, people can move forward with requests instead of e-mailing you back and forth to gain clarity.

Don't underestimate this question. Just recently, we worked with a CIO and asked him this question repeatedly. He was a fast-thinking person who was having trouble understanding why we wanted him to slow down and put so much thought into his messages. At the end of the day, he received several

Part Three:
Creating an
Integrated
Management
System—The
Processing and
Organizing
Phase

Take Back Your Life!

responses to his e-mail messages with questions asking for more information and clarity. He raised one eyebrow and said, "Wow! You weren't kidding. I really do need to be clear to ensure I don't get e-mail responses asking questions! I suppose I better change my standard for what clear means."

Writing e-mail messages so that recipients understand what you mean and don't need to ask questions is not as easy as people think. It takes pausing and collecting your thoughts. To do this you need a quiet, uninterrupted environment because processing e-mail during meetings, when you're talking on the phone, driving in the car, or late at night doesn't support this process. Writing clearly is a skill and it takes practice and concentration.

3. Do You Need to Track This Message in One of Your 1:1 or SNA Waiting For Categories?

This question reminds you to consider if you want to track a delegated item. If you trust your team members to do what they say they will do, there is no need to follow up with them. We recommend tracking delegated items if you need to follow up because the action affects the completion of your objective. Or track the item if you question a team member's ability to complete the item on time and you want to make certain the person does, or if you're training a new team member to be accountable. However, you don't want to police people by tracking everything you delegate just because you can! It's important to trust the people you're working with, and only track a delegated task if you have a specific reason to do so.

If you want to track the e-mail message you just wrote, we suggest that you Cc yourself so that the e-mail goes back to your Inbox, and from there you can either transfer it into one of your 1:1 categories or to your Waiting For category.

Exercise 11-6   Make any adjustments to your e-mail communication so that it does PASS and will not come back with questions. If it is a delegated item that you want to track, copy yourself in the Cc line so that it returns to your Inbox, and then you can move it into a 1:1 or Waiting For category. We will show you how to move messages into your 1:1 or Waiting for Category in the section titled "Dragging E-Mail to the To-Do Bar or Calendar."

Now that you have completed creating an e-mail message using the PASS Model you may notice that it took you a wee bit longer to do than usual. However, after you get the hang of it, it'll move faster. And when you write clear, purposeful e-mail, you'll end up reducing the amount of mail you

Chapter Eleven: Processing and Organizing Your E-Mail

Part Three:
Creating an
Integrated
Management
System—The
Processing and
Organizing
Phase

receive and the amount of mail you send. You'll reduce cycles of action and make progress toward your Meaningful Objectives. When it comes to processing e-mail, slowing down does, in fact, help you speed up!

Unfortunately, some people have allowed the speed of technology to dictate the pace at which they work. But just because technology moves fast doesn't mean that you have to. Your best results will come from pausing and giving yourself time to think.

The more you practice and demonstrate writing clear, meaningful e-mail messages, the more those around you will take note. Demonstration is one of the most powerful instigators of change. When you're consistent in your behaviors, others will start to do the same. It's inspiring to work with people who go the extra mile and demonstrate excellence. This is another example of how "small things done consistently in strategic places create major impact"!

Many of our clients have shared with us that they want support with changing e-mail habits and have requested products that would help them reinforce new behaviors. In response to this request, we created our Take Back Your Life! 101 E-Mail Webinar Series. There are three 1 hour webinars in the series: Storing E-mail So You Can Find It Fast, 'Writing E-mail that Gets Results, and Getting to Zero in Your Inbox. You can purchase and download each webinar individually or as a series from the Products page on our Web site at *www.mcgheeproductivity.com*, or go to the MPS Products page in the back of this book. The feedback we're getting is that they are assisting new and current customers to create and maintain new e-mail habits that increase productivity, save time, and support work-life balance. Check them out!

Preparing to Process and Organize Your Inbox

Before you start to process and organize your Inbox, we are going to review some of the technical instructions that will be essential to implementing the MPS Workflow Model. In the following subsections, we run through how to set up your To-Do Bar so that you can use it effectively as part of your Action System. We show you how to drag and drop e-mail messages onto your To-Do Bar and Calendar and how to insert e-mail messages into existing Tasks and Calendar appointments.Finally, we discuss the difference between organizing your To-Do Bar by dragging and flagging. All these sections support using your IMS and getting your Inbox to zero.

Part Three:
Creating an
Integrated
Management
System—The
Processing and
Organizing
Phase

Take Back Your Life!

Setting Up the To-Do Bar

If you look at the control panel shown in Figure 11-4, you can see the To-Do Bar on the right-hand side of the Calendar. With this bar, you can easily view your "Total Life To-Do List" with all of the relevant Planning and Action Categories. The beauty of the To-Do Bar is that it's accessible not only from the Inbox, but also from the Calendar, Tasks, and Contacts. This means that whichever part of Outlook you're working in you can easily add Strategic Next Actions (SNAs), delete SNAs, or plan and prioritize them onto your Calendar. The To-Do List, which you've used up until now, is basically the same list with the following exceptions: the To-Do List can be accessed only from Tasks and it shows both completed and active Tasks and has more real estate to work with. The To-Do Bar does not show completed Tasks and is accessible from all parts of Outlook and has less real estate. Our clients use both of these lists depending on what type of work they're doing; it's a matter of preference and work style as to which list you use and when you use it.

Following are the technical instructions to set up your To-Do Bar. For reference, see Figure 11-4.

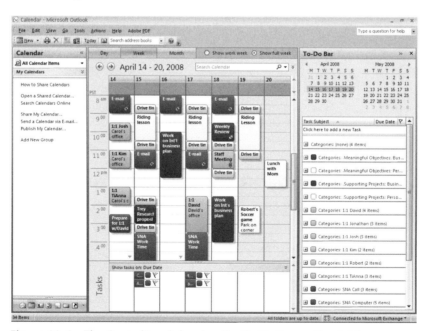

Figure 11-4   The ControlPanel showing the To-Do Bar on the right.

Chapter Eleven: Processing and Organizing Your E-Mail

Part Three:
Creating an
Integrated
Management
System—The
Processing and
Organizing
Phase

Adding Click Here To Add A New Task and Changing Custom to Customize Current View

If you don't see the words Click Here To Add A New Task at the top of the To-Do Bar, follow these steps:

1. Right-click the Subject heading above Categories: (none), and select Custom or Customize Current View. If you see Custom instead of Customize Current View, be sure to follow step 4 below.

2. In the Customize View: To-Do List dialog box, click the Other Settings button.

3. In the Other Settings dialog box, in the Column Headings And Rows section, be sure both Allow In-Cell Editing and Show "New Item" Row are selected, as shown in Figure 11-5.

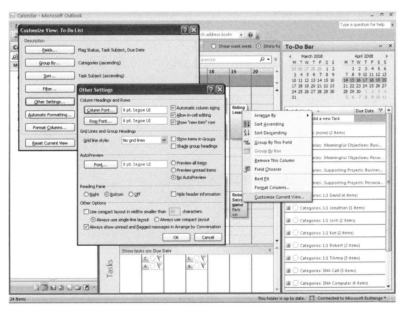

Figure 11-5   Adding Click Here To Add A New Task to the To-Do Bar.

4. In the Other Options section, be sure the Always Use Single-Line Layout is selected.

5. Click OK.

6. Click OK again.

7. The words Click Here To Add A New Task will appear below your field headings and above Categories: (none).

Part Three:
Creating an
Integrated
Management
System—The
Processing and
Organizing
Phase

Take Back Your Life!

To-Do Bar Fields and Grouping by Categories

The next two settings are necessary to choose the To-Do Bar fields and to group your Tasks by categories. Follow these steps:

1. Go to the To-Do Bar, right-click the words Click Here To Add A New Task, and then click Customize Current View on the shortcut menu. Here you will choose the fields to view in the To-Do Bar and group your actions by category.

2. In the Customize View: To-Do List dialog box, click Fields.

3. Under the heading Select Available Fields From,choose All Task Fields from the drop-down menu.

4. In the Show These Fields In This Order section, select Icon and Due Date.

5. Under the heading Select Available Fields From, choose All Mail Fields from the drop-down menu.

6. Select Task Subject and add to the Show These Fields In This Order area. Rearrange your fields so they're listed in the order shown in Figure 11-6 and then click OK.

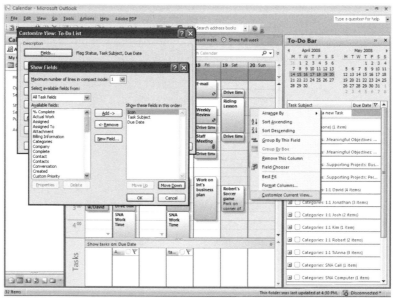

Figure 11-6   Selecting the To-Do List fields

7. In the Customize View: To-Do List dialog box, click Group By.

Chapter Eleven: **Processing and Organizing Your E-Mail**

Part Three:
Creating an
Integrated
Management
System—The
Processing and
Organizing
Phase

8. In the Group By dialog box, in the Group Items By drop-down menu, select Categories, and in the Expand/Collapse Defaults drop-down menu, select All Collapsed, as shown in Figure 11-7. Then, click OK.

Figure 11-7   Grouping tasks by categories.

9. Click OK again.

Attaching Contacts to Your Tasks

To complete the final setting that allows you to attach contacts to your Tasks, follow these steps:

1. On the Tools menu, click Options.

2. In the Options dialog box, on the Preferences tab, in the Contacts And Notes section, click the Contact Options button.

3. In the Contact Options dialog box, in the Contact Linking section, select Show Contact Linking On All Forms, as shown in Figure 11-8, and then click OK.

4. Click OK again.

Part Three:
Creating an
Integrated
Management
System—The
Processing and
Organizing
Phase

Take Back Your Life!

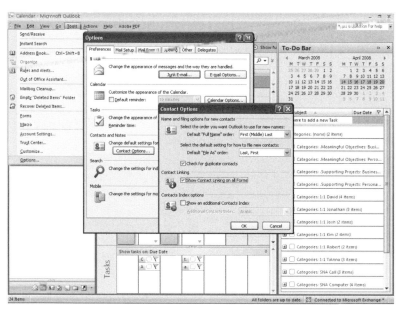

Figure 11-8   Linking contacts to your Tasks in the To-Do List.

Dragging E-Mail to the To-Do Bar or Calendar

To set up an effective Integrated Management System, we recommend you predominantly use dragging as a method for organizing e-mail. Our productivity philosophy is based on you emptying Collection Points, centralizing your action list, and having all the data you need to complete an SNA attached to the SNA, and dragging facilitates this. You can drag an e-mail message from the Inbox directly onto your To-Do Bar and into your Planning and Action Categories or onto your calendar as an appointment. This is a pretty cool feature.

In Figure 11-9 Carol received an e-mail reminding her to edit the Adventure Works proposal, which was posted on a SharePoint site. Carol could not do this SNA in less than two minutes or delegate it, so she had to defer it to do herself. She dragged the e-mail into her SNA computer category, added a due date and inserted the proposal from SharePoint; she now had everything she needed to complete the action in one place. Dragging e-mails enables you to remove them from your inbox and puts them in your To-Do Bar as a task; from here you can respond to them as you would an e-mail which is really useful.

Part Three:
Creating an
Integrated
Management
System—The
Processing and
Organizing
Phase

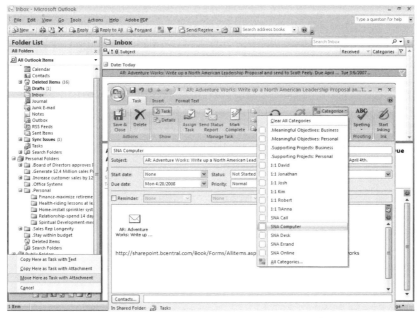

Figure 11-9   Dragging an e-mail on the To-Do Bar into a Planning or Action Category.

To drag an e-mail into your one of your Planning and Action Categories on your To-Do Bar follow these steps:

1. Right-click and drag the e-mail to the Task icon in the Folder List.

2. From the shortcut menu, choose Move Here As Task With Attachment.

3. In the Task window, the e-mail Subject line appears in the Task Subject line, and the e-mail is inserted into the task as an envelope icon.

4. Review your subject line to ensure it says want you want and if not you can change it.

5. Click Categorize on the ribbon and select the appropriate Planning and Action Category.

6. Click Save and Close.

You can just as easily drag and drop e-mails onto your calendar as you can the To-Do Bar. Carol received an e-mail related to completing her performance review and submitting it online by Friday at 3 p.m. This was a SNA she could not do in less than two minutes or delegate so she had to defer it to herself. She wanted to make sure she got it done on Friday so she dragged

Part Three:
Creating an
Integrated
Management
System—The
Processing and
Organizing
Phase

Take Back Your Life!

and dropped the e-mail onto her calendar on Friday at 1 p.m. and created an appointment for 1 hour to make sure she completed it. The e-mail attached itself to the appointment so that when she got to the appointment, she could open the e-mail, find the link to the intranet site, and complete the review online. By using this method, you can move action-related e-mail out of your Inbox and place it where you can do something with it to complete it.

To drag an e-mail onto your Calendar, follow these steps:

1. Right-click and drag the e-mail message to the Calendar icon.

2. On the shortcut menu, click Move Here As Appointment With Attachment.

3. In the appointment window, the e-mail Subject line appears as the appointment Subject line, and the e-mail is inserted into the appointment as an envelope icon, as shown in Figure 11-10.

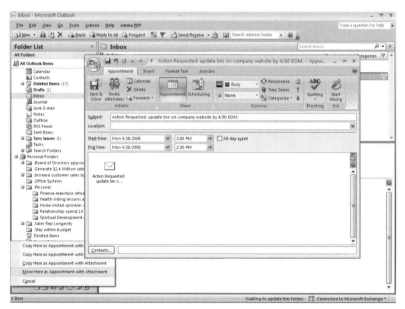

Figure 11-10 Dragging an e-mail message to the Calendar.

4. Review your Subject line to ensure it says want you want, and if not, you can change it.

5. Click Save and Close.

Part Three:
Creating an
Integrated
Management
System—The
Processing and
Organizing
Phase

Inserting an E-Mail Message or Document into an Existing Task

One of the cool things about Tasks is that you can insert files and contacts and e-mail messages into them, making it easy to have the supporting information you need to complete your Strategic Next Actions. Carol received an e-mail message related to her 401(k) plan detailing her different investment options. Carol has an existing Task in her 1:1 Jonathan category to talk to him about an investment strategy. Carol thought it would be a good idea to include this message in her conversation with Jonathan, and so she decided to insert it into that Task so that she can refer to it when she is in her 1:1 meeting with him.

You have a choice when inserting e-mail messages into Tasks. If the information you need is in an attached document in the e-mail message, you can either insert the entire e-mail message, which includes the attachment, or you can insert the attached document only. If you don't need the body of the e-mail message and only need the attached document, you can first save the document in your My Documents Reference System, and then link the document to the Task. This way, the document is in two places. When you delete the Task, you'll still have access to the document in your My Documents Reference System. Or if you want the e-mail message and the document, you can insert the message into the Task and the document will go with it.

To insert an e-mail message or its attachment into an existing Task, follow these steps:

1. Double-click an existing Task.

2. In the Task, click the Insert tab, and choose Attach Item from the ribbon.

3. In the Insert Item dialog box, select Inbox.

4. Locate the e-mail message that you want to insert, and click it once to select it.

5. In the Insert Item dialog box, in the Insert As section, select either Text Only or Attachment, as shown in Figure 11-11.

6. Click OK.

Part Three:
Creating an
Integrated
Management
System—The
Processing and
Organizing
Phase

Take Back Your Life!

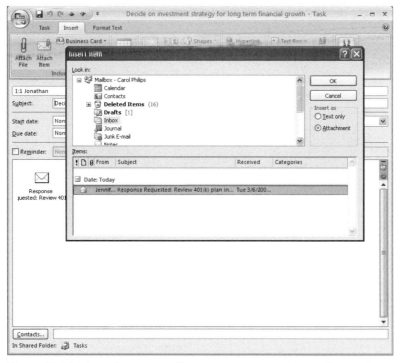

Figure 11-11 Inserting an e-mail message or an e-mail attachment into an existing Task.

Inserting an E-Mail Message or Document into an Existing Calendar Appointment

Some of the e-mail you receive will be information that you'll want to have handy during meetings or phone calls. For example, Carol Philips received an e-mail message outlining the agenda for a Friday staff meeting. Carol wanted to make sure she had the agenda available on Friday, and so she inserted the message into the staff meeting appointment on her Calendar, as shown in Figure 11-12. With this setup, she can open the appointment on Friday and double-click the e-mail icon, and the agenda immediately shows up on her screen. It takes less than two minutes to complete, and places the data where it is most useful, and minimizes what Carol has to do to find it on Friday at the start of the staff meeting.

When you insert an e-mail message into an existing appointment, you have two options: you can insert the text, or you can insert the entire e-mail message. When you include the whole e-mail message in an appointment, you can open the message and respond to it or just view the information in it.

Part Three:
Creating an
Integrated
Management
System—The
Processing and
Organizing
Phase

When you insert the text of a message only, you can't respond to the message, but you can see the text. This is useful in relation to using a PDA or smartphone. When you synchronize with a PDA, the text of the message shows up in the appointment so that you have it available. If you insert an e-mail message, you cannot open the message from a PDA. Based on how you are going to view this information you need to discern whether you insert text or the e-mail message itself.

In the example, if Carol inserts the Friday staff meeting agenda as text into the appointment, she can view the agenda on her PDA, which is pretty cool. Another example of using text on a PDA is when you go on trips, you can insert the travel data as text into your travel appointments, such as air, hotel, and car rental confirmations. It's much easier to view your PDA when you're on the road than it is to use your laptop. This information is extremely helpful, and having it readily available saves time and makes you look good! It's very important to look good and have the latest equipment, you know!

To insert an e-mail message or its text into an existing Calendar appointment, follow these steps:

1. Double-click an existing Calendar appointment.
2. In the appointment, click the Insert tab, and select Attach Item from the ribbon.
3. In the Insert Item dialog box, select Inbox.
4. Locate the e-mail message that you want to insert, and click it once to select it.
5. In the Insert Item dialog box, in the Insert As section, select either Text Only or Attachment, as shown in Figure 11-12.
6. Click OK.

Part Three:
Creating an
Integrated
Management
System—The
Processing and
Organizing
Phase

Take Back Your Life!

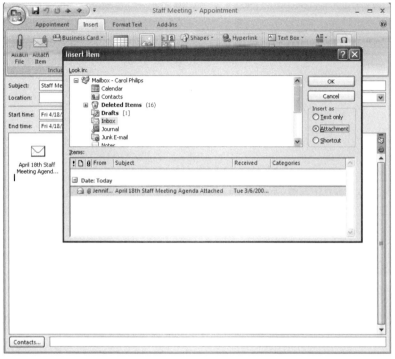

Figure 11-12   Inserting an e-mail message or the text of a message into an existing Calendar appointment.

Flagging

Flagging an e-mail message creates a synchronized link between the item in the Inbox and the To-Do Bar; it does not create a Task or an appointment, and the e-mail message stays in the Inbox. In Figure 11-13, you can see that Carol flagged an item in her Inbox; you can see the flag on the far right-hand side of the message "Create Sales Proposal Templates for new products." Carol wants to discuss this item with Kim in their next 1:1 meeting, and so she categorized it under her 1:1 Kim category. You can see the item appears under this category in the To-Do Bar and stays in her Inbox. If Carol were to click the item in the To-Do Bar, it opens as an e-mail message not as a Task, and this enables Carol to respond to the e-mail immediately. However, she cannot insert or add any supporting information.

Chapter Eleven: Processing and Organizing Your E-Mail

Part Three:
Creating an
Integrated
Management
System—The
Processing and
Organizing
Phase

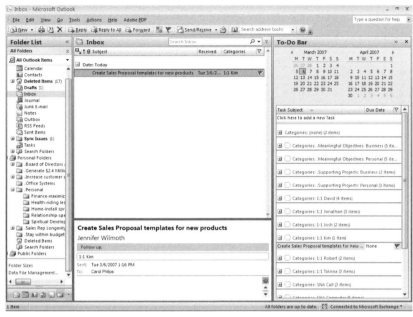

Figure 11-13   A flagged e-mail message in Carol's Inbox.

If you are going to be flagging e-mail, we suggest you have the Flag Status Field and the Category field showing in your Inbox. To add these fields, follow these steps:

1. In the Inbox, right-click the Subject heading, and then click Customize Current View.

2. In the Customize View: Messages dialog box, click Fields.

3. In the Select Available Fields From section, choose All Mail Fields To Add Flag Status. Choose Frequently-Used Fields from the Select Available Fields From section to add Categories.

Part Three:
Creating an
Integrated
Management
System—The
Processing and
Organizing
Phase

Take Back Your Life!

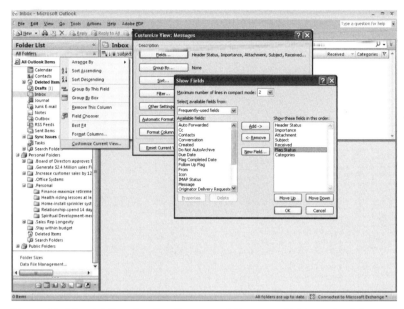

Figure 11-14 Adding the Flag Status and Category fields to the Inbox.

To flag and categorize an e-mail message onto the To-Do Bar, follow these steps:

1. In the Inbox, click the Flag Status field of the message, and the flag will turn red.

2. In the Inbox, right-click the Categories field of the message, and then select a category. This e-mail message will show up on your To-Do Bar under the category you selected with no due date. See Figure 11-15.

Part Three:
Creating an
Integrated
Management
System—The
Processing and
Organizing
Phase

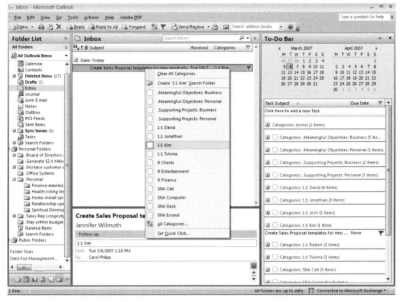

Figure 11-15 Flagging and categorizing an e-mail message onto the To-Do Bar.

Why We Recommend Dragging Instead of Flagging

Dragging is not as intuitive as flagging, but dragging provides you with some very strong advantages.

■ You can drag e-mail to the To-Do Bar as well as to the Calendar.

■ You can create Tasks that capture relevant Supporting Information needed to complete SNAs.

■ You can empty the Inbox by moving action material to your Action System and reference material to your Reference System.

■ You have only one location for storing your Planning and Action Categories, not two, and so all of your action items are in one central location.

■ If you delete a flagged e-mail message by accident, you remove it from the To-Do Bar without notification or warning.

■ With flagging, you end up with two Planning and Action Categories to review, one in the Inbox and one in the To-Do Bar, and they are *not* identical. When you add Tasks to your To-Do Bar, they do not show up in your Inbox categories; they show up only on the To-Do Bar.

Part Three:
Creating an
Integrated
Management
System—The
Processing and
Organizing
Phase

Take Back Your Life!

We believe these advantages make dragging the primary method to use. Flagging does have value, and we write about this in the section titled "When Can I Use Flagging Effectively?" later in this chapter. Of course, you can use a hybrid approach, mixing both dragging and flagging.For now it is simpler to choose one method and stick with that until you become an Outlook Power User and can use both effectively.

Using the MPS Workflow Model to Process and Organize E-Mail

You've now learned how to create meaningful e-mail messages using the E-Mail PASS Model, how to set up your To-Do Bar, and the few essential technical features for moving e-mails onto the To-Do Bar and Calendar. Now you're ready to go to work on processing and organizing your e-mail using the MPS Workflow Model.

Quick question: Does your e-mail come to you in the order in which it needs to be done? Now that would be a great software product! Until such a time, you have to process and organize your e-mail so that you can prioritize when to take the necessary actions.

Most of you probably scan your e-mail throughout the day, jumping around your Inbox and opening and closing messages without taking any action. We call you people "jumpers," and you know who you are! The more you do this, the quicker it is for your Inbox to grow in size and the more time you are spending on nonproductive actions. For some people, the Inbox grows to as many as 7,000 e-mail messages. To get through large volumes of e-mail, you need a system for managing messages. The Workflow Model can help you process and organize your mail using a systematic approach so that you can empty the Inbox regularly.

Reviewing e-mail during meetings, in between meetings, and while you're on the phone is not a productive way to process mail. We recommend quiet time during which you can concentrate, pause, and think clearly. Therefore, the first step in processing and organizing e-mail effectively is to schedule at least one hour of uninterrupted time each day to get through your e-mail. You will discover over time how much time you need to book and when the best time to book it is. Some clients like to process e-mail first thing in the morning, whereas others prefer the end of the day; you'll discover what works best for you. This doesn't mean you cannot monitor your e-mail during the day; however, processing e-mail is a completely different skill from monitoring and it requires your full attention.

Part Three:
Creating an
Integrated
Management
System—The
Processing and
Organizing
Phase

The second step is to sort your e-mail into the order in which you want to process it, organizing it by date, subject, or person. You'll be processing your e-mail messages one at a time, starting at the top of the list. This means that after you open an e-mail message, you will not close it until you have decided what the action is and transferred it into the appropriate bucket, be it your delete bucket or an SNA bucket. Basically, you're not allowed to close it back into the Inbox! Now for you "jumpers," during this exercise, we want you to refrain from jumping; work *one e-mail at a time in sequence.* Don't move to the second e-mail message until the first is processed. We know this will be challenging; however, it is well worth the discipline.

The shortest way to do many things is to do only one thing at a time.
—Sydney Smiles

Now you're ready to start working through the MPS Workflow Model. Double-click your first e-mail message and let's get cracking.

What Is It?

Is the e-mail message you've selected reference or action, big or small, a Meaningful Objective or Supporting Project, personal or business? When you're clear what the message is, move onto the next question in the Workflow Model.

Is It Actionable?

Given everything else on your plate right now, is it appropriate for you to take on this action? If not, you have three options:

- File it in your new, improved E-Mail Reference System.
- File it in your SNA Someday Maybe category (we discuss how to do this in the following sections).
- Swiftly delete it, never to be seen again! (We'd like you all to become much more familiar with your Delete key!)

All of these options remove the e-mail message from your Inbox. If you want to take action on this e-mail, move on to the next question.

Does It Relate to a Meaningful Objective?

Ensure that the action this e-mail message requires maps to one of your personal or business Meaningful Objectives. If it doesn't map to one of your Meaningful Objectives, question why you want to take action on it. Just because a message shows up in your Inbox doesn't mean you need to act on it. Be discerning about what you put your energy into. At the end of the day,

Part Three:
Creating an
Integrated
Management
System—The
Processing and
Organizing
Phase

Take Back Your Life!

you're measured on your objectives (at work), and so it's important to stay focused on them and not get distracted into other areas.

This is also true of your personal life. Because you're not measured on your objectives, it's easy to abandon the goals you've created and get lost in distractions. Asking whether the message relates to a Meaningful Objective helps you pause and question how you're using your time and energy.

The question "Does it relate to a Meaningful Objective?" leads to both a "yes" and "no" option. If the answer is "no," we suggest you first look to *disengage* from the commitment altogether. This involves contacting the respective stakeholder to let the person know and creating ways of doing this that have integrity. In some cases, you may not be able to disengage from the action because it is too far along the process and you have to complete it. At this point, you can consider *renegotiation*, finding out if the action can be completed later or changing the scope to make it easier to complete along with your other objectives. It can be uncomfortable to back out of an agreement you've already made. However, if you ask this question *before* you make agreements, you can ensure that you only involve yourself in commitments that link to one of your Meaningful Objectives. The key here is asking this question upfront so that you can let people know right away if you can assist them or not.

By disengaging from commitments that don't focus on your objectives, you free up your time and energy, making it easier to stay focused on the objectives you have already agreed to accomplish.

If your e-mail communication does map to one of your Meaningful Objectives, move on to the next question.

What Is the Strategic Next Action Without a Dependency?

Take a few moments to clarify what your Strategic Next Action is. Make sure it is a one-step item with no dependencies so that you can complete the action immediately. We don't want you to put off this decision and close the e-mail message back into the Inbox.. After you've created your SNA, you're ready to move onto the next section of the Workflow Model, which we call the Four Ds for Decision Making. This helps you decide whether to complete your SNA right away, delegate it, or defer it. We will pick up this discussion regarding what to do with your SNA in the section titled "Do it...If it Takes Less Than Two Minutes."

Part Three:
Creating an
Integrated
Management
System—The
Processing and
Organizing
Phase

Using The Four Ds for Decision Making

The latter part of the Workflow Model is also called the Four Ds for Decision Making, and you can effectively process and organize your e-mail by simply following these four Ds. This part of the Workflow Model is easy to use and helps with large volumes of e-mail that require rapid decisions.

The four Ds are as follows:

- **Delete** it.
- **Do** it if it takes less than two minutes.
- **Delegate** it and, if appropriate, track it in your 1:1 Meeting or SNA Waiting For category.
- **Defer** it to one of your SNA categories on the To-Do Bar or transfer it to a specific time on your Calendar.

Delete It

Deleting e-mail is not easy for all of us, and it has a lot to do with past experience. Some people are extremely uncomfortable letting go of information, and for good reason. Remember your very first job. Perhaps you were incredibly nervous and wanted to do everything right. It was your fourth day and your boss asked you for a document you didn't have. You'd deleted it two days earlier! He was unhappy you couldn't produce the document and made a big, huge fuss about it. You felt disappointed and beat yourself up for getting rid of it. After this experience, you decided never to delete anything ever again to ensure you didn't have to repeat the experience.

However, not all people are the same. If you delete a document, it doesn't necessarily mean it's going to come back to bite you! What happened 10 years ago may not happen today. So, ask yourself, in all honesty, how many times have you referenced the e-mail messages you've saved? We'd guess maybe 10 percent of the time! The truth is that you really don't get paid to file, you get paid to complete Meaningful Objectives successfully. So, be watchful of how much e-mail you file, how much you use it, and how long it takes you to find it.

Did you know that, on average, clients delete 50 percent of their e-mail? (Deep breaths now, in and out!) For those of you who are uncomfortable deleting e-mail, there are four questions that can help you determine what to keep and what to delete. (Keep breathing!)

Part Three:
Creating an
Integrated
Management
System—The
Processing and
Organizing
Phase

- Does this e-mail information relate to a Meaningful Objective I'm currently working on?

- Can I find this information somewhere else? On a Web site, on an intranet, or from a colleague?

- Will I refer back to this information in the next three months?

- Am I required to keep it? Is it legal, HR, or financial?

There are exceptions to all of these questions and you have to be discerning about what those are. The point is to be conscious about why you are keeping messages that you don't really need. We find these questions assist clients to let go of e-mails that don't support their primary focus.

Have you ever lost your entire Inbox in the past as a result of an application crash or virus? Remember what happened? Most of my clients say, "Nothing! I was so surprised. I just got on with business as usual." So, don't be afraid to step outside of your comfort zone, let go of the "keeper" role, and see what happens. We think you will be pleasantly surprised.

Do It

A "Do It" action is a Strategic Next Action that you can personally complete in less than two minutes. On average, clients complete 30 percent of what's in their Inbox in less than two minutes. It's motivating to complete this many cycles of action, and it proves how much you can get done in less than two-minute cycles.

Here's an example of a "do it in less than two minutes." In an e-mail, my assistant asked me to send her an updated schedule for the book-editing project. I had the updated schedule in my Reference System in My Documents. There was no point in typing this action onto my To-Do Bar; it would have taken longer to do that than it would have taken to send the schedule to her.

If it takes less than two minutes, just get it done and get it out of your Inbox. If it takes three minutes, that's fine, too. You don't have to be too rigid about the time limit. The key is to complete an action if you can complete it faster than you can track it.

We used to work with stopwatches, timing clients while they processed their e-mail. It was inspiring how much they'd get done in two minutes or less. Often, clients would try to convince us that a reply or an action would

Chapter Eleven: Processing and Organizing Your E-Mail

Part Three:
Creating an
Integrated
Management
System—The
Processing and
Organizing
Phase

take longer, and so we'd say, "Let's time it and see." Voila! It was almost always completed in less than two minutes.

You can also scan an e-mail message in less than two minutes to decide if you really need to read it. Clients say to us, "Oh, I need to defer this e-mail. It will take me 15 minutes to read!" We always suggest scanning it in two minutes or less to decide if you need to spend 15 minutes reading it. Often, the scanning is enough to decide that you do not need to read it. We all underestimate what we can do in less than two minutes.

If you can complete your SNA in less than two minutes, do it now. If not, move to the next question in the Four Ds for Decision Making.

Delegate It

A "Delegate It" action is a Strategic Next Action that you can delegate to someone else. Often, we forget to ask ourselves whether we can delegate an action. We're moving so fast that it doesn't occur to us. Just recently, we worked with a client and asked this question four times in 30 minutes. Each time, the client was able to delegate the item and was thrilled to have one less thing to do.

Let's look at how to organize your delegated items in more detail. Carol received an e-mail message from one of her most important clients, Scott Seely, who works for Adventure Works. He requested that she create a sales proposal for a leadership meeting he was having, and he detailed exactly what he wanted in the body of his e-mail communication. Carol recognized that she could delegate this to Josh, her sales director. In less than two minutes, Carol wrote an e-mail message to Josh delegating the task. She decided to track the action to ensure Scott got the proposal, and so she included herself on the Cc line. When the e-mail message arrived in her Inbox, she transferred it into her 1:1 Josh category on the To-Do List and placed a due date on it to ensure Josh completed it on time. This is a very nifty technique that enables you to record items you've delegated so that you can easily follow up with them during your 1:1 meetings.

Now if Carol had moved an e-mail message into one of her 1:1 categories and that task needed to be followed up on before her next 1:1, she could put a due date on the Task with a reminder. The reminder then automatically pops up on the reminder date, and if she clicks the reminder, it takes her to the Task and to the e-mail message she embedded as shown in Figure 11-16. She can then forward this e-mail message asking if the task is going to get done on time.

Part Three:
Creating an
Integrated
Management
System—The
Processing and
Organizing
Phase

Take Back Your Life!

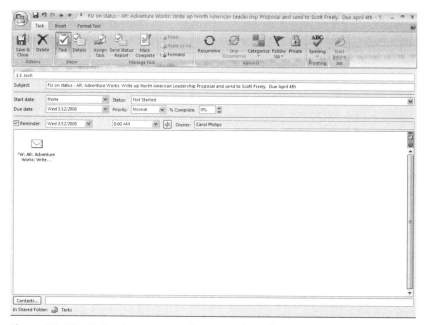

Figure 11-16 Following up on tasks you assigned to your 1:1 category with reminders.

The Subject line Carol created for the e-mail message was "AR: Adventure Works: Write up a North American Leadership Proposal and send to Scott Freely. Due April 4." This heading clearly states what Josh has to do. If your Subject line isn't useful, you'll want to modify it. A comprehensible Subject line is important because in your 1:1 meetings you'll want to avoid having to open and read an e-mail message to clarify its discussion point. You want the Subject line to do that for you. This kind of preparation on the front end saves you time on the back end. Are you tired of hearing that message yet?

If your Strategic Next Action is a delegated item that you want to track in your 1:1 category or Waiting For category, go ahead and Cc yourself and send the e-mail. When the e-mail message arrives back in your Inbox, you can then transfer it into the appropriate 1:1 or Waiting For category using the dragging method. Ensure that your Subject line in the Task reflects the item you want to follow up on, a due date is set if appropriate, and you have all the supporting information you need attached. See Figure 11-11 and the appropriate instructions as a reference for dragging e-mail onto your To-Do Bar.

Clients often ask us, "Why do I need to Cc myself? Why not drag and drop the message from the Sent Items folder?" Imagine that you've sent

Part Three:
Creating an
Integrated
Management
System—The
Processing and
Organizing
Phase

your e-mail, and you're about to go to the Sent Items folder to drag it into your SNA Waiting For category when the phone rings. You answer the call and get involved in a conversation and completely forget to transfer the e-mail from the Sent Items folder to the To-Do Bar. The only way to ensure you don't forget these e-mail messages is to Cc yourself *before* you send e-mail. This way the messages come back into your Inbox to remind you to file them. Once again, a little bit of effort on the front end saves work on the back end.

If you cannot delegate this e-mail, move to the next question.

Defer It

A "Deferred Action" is a Strategic Next Action that you can't complete in less than two minutes and that you can't delegate. Therefore, the only option left is for you to complete it personally. This is where the buck stops and the real work begins, especially if you're an individual contributor who has no staff to delegate to.

The number of deferred Strategic Next Actions you have may depend upon your role in the company. Our executive clients delegate most of their tasks, which means they end up with very few deferred items. However, individual contributors, with no one to delegate to, can end up with a considerable list of deferred Strategic Next Actions. The good news about deferred items, however, is that they've gone through a tough prioritizing process to get on to your list, and so they're important tasks to record and complete. You filtered out all the activities that did not relate to your Meaningful Objectives, items that could be deleted, items that could be completed in less than two minutes, and items that could be delegated. The end result of this process is a list of deferred Strategic Next Actions that only you can complete and that will take more than two minutes.

Our statistics prove that, on average, 50 percent of most people's e-mail can be deleted, 30 percent can be completed in less than two minutes or delegated, and 20 percent can be deferred. That means that out of 100 e-mail messages you receive, only 20 of them end up being deferred items in your SNA categories.

Here's an example of a deferred Strategic Next Action: Carol received an e-mail message from John Emory, a Web site project manager, asking her to spend 20 minutes reviewing the new sales site for her edits and corrections, which were due by April 15th. Carol couldn't delete the task, or do it in less than two minutes, or delegate it. She personally had to do it, and so she

Part Three:
Creating an
Integrated
Management
System—The
Processing and
Organizing
Phase

Take Back Your Life!

transferred the e-mail message into her SNA Online category, with a due date of April 15th. In this case, the e-mail Subject line that John wrote related to the action Carol had to take, and so she didn't have to change the Subject line.

Carol's next e-mail message was from her CFO and asked her to scrub her portion of the sales budget and return it by the end of the month. Carol could not do this in less than 2 minutes or delegate it, and so she was going to have to complete this herself. She needed an hour to do it, and she also needed the budget handy to review it. Carol right-clicked and dragged the message to her To-Do Bar, changed the subject line to "Spend one hour scrubbing sales budget," included a due date of May 1st, and then inserted the Excel worksheet she needed to scrub and an e-mail message from one of her directs listing last year's shortages. In Figure 11-10, you can see how to insert e-mail messages into your Tasks, and in Chapter 9, Figure 9-5 demonstrates how to insert files into your Tasks.

If your e-mail message is a deferred action, transfer it into the appropriate Strategic Next Action category on your To-Do Bar. When it's transferred, check that your Subject line details the Strategic Next Action, starts with a verb, clearly communicates the action, and has no dependencies. Select a due date if appropriate, and insert any supporting information you require to complete the action. (If you need a reminder about inserting, see the section above, "Inserting an E-Mail Message or Document into an Existing Task")

You've now successfully completed processing one of your e-mail messages. I hear you saying, "That took a while!" You're right. However, when you get the hang of this model, you can move through it quickly and process at least 60 e-mail messages an hour. By pausing to use the Four Ds for Decision Making, you're making effective decisions and moving e-mail out of your Inbox.

Processing and Organizing Your E-Mail for 30 Minutes

OK, you're now ready to fly solo and process your e-mail using the Four Ds for Decision Making. You'll do this for 30 minutes because we want you to discover exactly how many messages you can process in that time frame. For example, if you receive 60 e-mail messages a day and can process 30 messages in 30 minutes, you can estimate you'll process your e-mail in one hour a day. That's important information to know!

Chapter Eleven: **Processing and Organizing Your E-Mail**

Part Three:
Creating an
Integrated
Management
System—The
Processing and
Organizing
Phase

You'll also learn that using the Four Ds for Decision Making is invigorating because you make a decision for each message and move it out of your Inbox. If your Inbox is particularly full, don't worry; you'll work on emptying your Inbox later in this chapter, but for now we want you to experience processing e-mail for just 30 minutes.

Get a timer and set it for 30 minutes or use your computer's clock. Sort your e-mail in the view you want to work with: by sender, by date, or by Subject line. Work one e-mail message at a time until the alarm goes off or 30 minutes has elapsed on your computer's clock.

A few guidelines before you start. When you open an e-mail message, do not leave it in the Inbox, make sure you take action and move through the Four Ds for Decision Making. Watch yourself when you want to avoid dealing with a message. Push through your reluctance and keep focused on making decisions and transferring mail out of the Inbox. We've never found an e-mail message that couldn't be deleted, done, delegated, or deferred. Somewhere, there's always an answer for every message, but you might need to dig for it. Don't get caught up in responding to an e-mail message if it takes more than two to three minutes. See if you can delegate it or, if not, defer it to one of your SNA categories. No jumping around now—one e-mail at a time, starting from the top. Away you go!

Awarenesses

After 30 minutes is up, take the total number of e-mail messages you started with, deduct the current number, and subtract the number of new e-mail messages that came in over the last 30 minutes. This will give you the total number of e-mail messages you processed in 30 minutes. It's extremely useful to see how many you can handle in that short a time period, and observe what it's like to make effective decisions on each and every message you touch. Hey, we bet you are surprised by how many you processed and organized in 30 minutes.

So, what were your awareness's while doing this?

Here's what our clients have to say:

- "It's much easier than I thought to complete e-mails in less than two minutes."
- "I deleted at least half of them!"
- "I'm concerned about moving everything onto my To-Do Bar."

Part Three:
Creating an
Integrated
Management
System—The
Processing and
Organizing
Phase

Take Back Your Life!

- "I like being able to track delegated items in my 1:1 categories."

- "I got a lot done in a concentrated period of time!"

- "It worked to force myself to make decisions for each and every e-mail message."

- "It was easy to transfer reference material into my new Reference System."

- "I like writing clearer Subject lines."

- "I used the Cc line a lot less!"

- "Deferring e-mail messages to my To-Do Bar was useful."

- "I still have 2,000 e-mail messages to go, and at 60 an hour, that's 16 hours!"

- "I was surprised how many e-mail messages I receive that don't relate to my objectives!"

- "It takes discipline to make decisions about what to do with each and every e-mail message in my Inbox."

- "Most of what was in my Inbox was reference material that I hadn't filed."

Now that you know how many e-mail messages you can process in 30 minutes, we want you to apply that to the number of e-mail messages you actually receive a day and calculate how much time you'll need per day to process your e-mail. Make sure you answer this question accurately and avoid guessing on the basis of the number of e-mails that are currently in your Inbox. If you have 500 or more messages in your Inbox, it can feel like you're receiving hundreds a day. However, you may actually be receiving only 50 a day, and so don't go by the total volume. Find out how many you actually receive a day.

When you know what your daily volume is, you can calculate how much time you'll need to schedule to process your e-mail each day. You might be pleasantly surprised at this number. If you receive 60 messages a day and you're able to process 60 messages an hour, you'll be able to complete your e-mail in one hour each day. The empty Inbox is in sight! All you need to do is book an hour of uninterrupted time each day and follow the Four Ds discipline. This habit will keep your e-mail under control and your Inbox empty. If you have a higher daily e-mail volume, you'll learn, later in this chapter, how to reduce the number of incoming messages.

Part Three:
Creating an
Integrated
Management
System—The
Processing and
Organizing
Phase

By now, we hope you're realizing that by changing your approach to how you process and organize your e-mail you can change your relationship with it. You can gain control of your e-mail and have it be a productivity tool that serves you. Education is a powerful tool, especially when clients are motivated to change.

Frequently Asked Questions

Before you continue processing and organizing the rest of your Inbox, we'd like to address some of the most frequently asked questions we receive from clients. We believe that these answers can help you approach your e-mail more effectively and make it easier for you to empty your Inbox. We're going for the empty Inbox here. We want you to imagine being at zero e-mail at least once daily. Visualize a completely white screen. Your Inbox is so empty that it echoes!

When's the Best Time to Process E-Mail?

Before we answer this question, we want to clarify the difference between processing your e-mail and monitoring your e-mail. Processing requires uninterrupted time, allowing you to make effective decisions and create meaningful e-mail communications. Monitoring e-mail is reactive, allowing you to scan your mail for emergency situations and communications from senior staff. You might also monitor your e-mail because you need a distraction. There's nothing wrong with that as long as you know what it is you're doing, and don't get addicted to it! When you've set aside time to process and organize your e-mail, you can still monitor it during the day. Just be clear that monitoring and processing are not the same activity.

We recommend that you create recurring appointments in the Calendar to process and organize your mail. Estimate how much time you'll need based on the figures you calculated earlier. We schedule an hour a day for e-mail processing because we receive 50 to 60 messages each day. Then, evaluate the best time of day to schedule uninterrupted e-mail processing time. Consider when your prime meeting times are so that your e-mail appointment won't compete with other activities. This takes some thought if you have a busy schedule.

Sally processes her e-mail from 8 to 9 a.m. because her meetings generally start at 9 or 9:30. "I have the energy at 9 a.m. to make 60 decisions, and I'm relaxed enough to pause and think about what I am doing."

We are what we repeatedly do. Excellence, then, is not an act, but a habit.
—**Aristotle**

Part Three:
Creating an
Integrated
Management
System—The
Processing and
Organizing
Phase

Take Back Your Life!

Look through your Calendar and find a good time to set up a reoccurring appointment for yourself. Make these appointments important so that you don't give them away for other meetings. Be ruthless because that's what you'll need to do to make e-mail work and inspire those around you to do the same.

If you work with a team of people in close physical proximity, ask them to avoid interrupting you during your e-mail processing time. Let them know that if they interrupt you, they'll get a gentle reminder to come back later. You have to be prepared to reinforce your request or people won't take you seriously.

If you're a customer service agent, dealing with electronic customer requests, an hour a day of e-mail time will not work for you. You'll need to be working on your e-mail for most of the day, excluding breaks. Specific roles require more customized e-mail solutions.

What's an Appropriate Amount of E-Mail to Receive?

The volume of e-mail you receive depends on your role and function, but, in general, from 50 to 120 messages a day is a good range. Anything more becomes unmanageable because it takes too long to process each day.

Some of our clients receive up to 300 messages a day, and although they want to receive less, they spend most of their time justifying why they need to get 300 messages. This is understandable, given how much time they've invested in dealing with this kind of volume. We have to gently remind them, "If you always do what you've always done, you'll always get what you've always got." Therefore, you have to do something different for change to take place, and to do something different, you have to let go of something you're currently doing. Deep down, they know they'll need to let go of this to be open to the possibility of receiving less.

As you know, success in a company isn't based on the volume of e-mail you can handle each day. It's based, instead, on your ability to achieve your objectives within budget, timelines, and resources. You have other activities you have to do besides e-mail, and so you need to monitor how much time you spend processing messages. If you receive 40 to 60 e-mail messages a day, it will take you an hour to process your messages, which is very doable. Receiving 60 to 120 messages is still doable, but more time consuming, taking you up to two hours a day to complete. We suggest you err on the side

Part Three:
Creating an
Integrated
Management
System—The
Processing and
Organizing
Phase

of less is more when it comes to e-mail. Anything you can do to reduce volume will be productive.

How Do I Reduce the Volume of E-Mail I Receive?

Daily mail volume is not difficult to reduce when you're willing to make behavioral changes. Here are a few changes you might consider.

- Send less e-mail.
- Write clear e-mail messages so they don't come back with questions.
- Use the Cc line only when it impacts the recipients' objectives.
- Unsubscribe from newsletters and subscriptions.
- Meet with your team to discuss when to Cc.
- Clarify roles so that you're not getting mail that someone else really needs to get.
- Resist getting involved in e-mail threads that don't impact your objectives.
- Post information on an internal Web site so that employees pull the information from a site instead of the company pushing it through mail.
- Establish an e-mail protocol so that team members know when to use e-mail rather than instant messaging, landline phone calls, or cell phone calls.

There are hundreds of ways to reduce mail. You must first have a very clear intention to reduce it, and then you'll start to find solutions that'll help you. Without an openness to change, it won't happen. So, be open to the possibility. Reducing your e-mail volume can only increase your productivity.

Can I Customize My Own Subject Lines?

Of course you can, and you can request others customize their Subject lines, too. Imagine that you're in the Finance Department of a company, for example, and you ordinarily receive three to five invoice requests each day. Because it's easier to process these requests in a single batch rather than one by one, you can ask internal customers to start the Subject line of an invoice request with the words "Invoice Request." With this system, you can quickly transfer these messages into an SNA Invoice Request category to be processed once a week at a specific time. The same applies to any repetitive

Part Three:
Creating an
Integrated
Management
System—The
Processing and
Organizing
Phase

Take Back Your Life!

task, such as "Résumés to be reviewed," "Calendar appointments to be booked," or "Expenses to be approved."

Another form of customization is using different e-mail addresses to capture repetitive tasks. For example, if you spend eight hours every Thursday handling accounting tasks, you cab set up an alternative e-mail address named "accounting@cpandl.com." Your internal clients would send all accounting requests to that address. On Thursday, you'd simply download the *accounting@cpandl.com* e-mail and handle the requests. In emergencies, clients could use your regular address, which you download daily. Any kind of customization that helps you use your time more effectively is useful.

Didn't I Only Move E-Mail from the Inbox to the To-Do Bar?

Yup, it sure seems like you did nothing more than move e-mail messages from one location to another! But be careful not to underestimate the value of what you've done. You didn't just move e-mail; you processed and organized it using the Four Ds for Decision Making. The end result of this process is an extremely well prioritized To-Do List. You determined if the e-mail related to one of your Meaningful Objectives. You created a Strategic Next Action without a dependency. You confirmed that you couldn't do the task in less than two minutes and that you couldn't delegate it, and so you decided you had to defer it. You transferred it into a specific SNA category with a clear Subject line and included a due date and supporting documentation (if it is needed). We wouldn't say you only moved it from the Inbox to the To-Do Bar. Far from it!

Acknowledge what you did. You created a centralized, easily accessible To-Do List that is prioritized and directly maps to your objectives. You still have one step to go, of course, which is to schedule these Tasks onto the Calendar, as you'll see in Chapter 12.

How Will I Remember to View the To-Do List?

Most of our clients have depended on their Inbox and their memories to track their action steps. Therefore, using the To-Do List to centralize their actions feels uncomfortable. Some clients have never used the To-Do List, and so they're especially anxious about remembering to look at it. Their concern is valid, much like when you put your car keys in a new location at home. Will you remember where you put them? If you put your car keys in the same place each time, it won't take long to remember where they are. In fact, in two or three days, you become dependent on the new location, and you'll say, "Don't move my keys!"

In the Prioritizing and Planning Phase, you'll be setting up a recurring Improving Productivity appointment on your Calendar. You'll use this appointment to prioritize and plan your tasks from the To-Do Bar onto your Calendar. You'll have plenty of time each week to work with your To-Do List, and it won't be long before it becomes a habit, and your To-Do list becomes your best friend.

When Do I Put E-Mail Messages onto the Calendar versus onto the To-Do List?

So far, we've asked you to transfer all of your deferred Strategic Next Actions onto the To-Do List because until you've captured all of your agreements from all of your Collection Points, you're prioritizing in a vacuum! After your To-Do List is complete, you can decide whether to transfer a Task onto the Calendar or onto the To-Do List. The Calendar is the last place a Task goes. When it's scheduled on a date in the Calendar, you're making an agreement to do it on that day. Use the Calendar with great respect. It's not a place to put a Task that you think you only might get done. It's a place to schedule a Task because you've promised to do it on a particular day. More on this topic in Chapter 12.

If you receive an e-mail message that turns out to be a Strategic Next Action that can be deferred but that must be completed on a particular day, simply transfer it from the Inbox directly onto your Calendar for that day. To transfer an e-mail message onto the Calendar, follow the steps given in the section titled "Inserting an E-Mail Message into an Existing Calendar Appointment" earlier in this chapter.

The Tasks on your To-Do List do not have to be done immediately. You're waiting to transfer them onto the Calendar as they come due. More on this concept in Chapter 12.

Can I Use the E-Mail Notification Options?

Clients ask us if it's OK to use the Outlook feature that alerts them to the arrival of a new e-mail message. We highly recommend that you don't use these features except in an exceptional circumstance, or if your role requires it. Being notified when an e-mail message comes in is an interruption and a distraction. You need to stop what you're doing, scan the message, and decide if you'll take action on it right away. Taking action distracts you from

Part Three:
Creating an
Integrated
Management
System—The
Processing and
Organizing
Phase

Take Back Your Life!

what you're doing. If you don't take action, you're still reminded that the e-mail needs attention, and you'll track it in your head as well as tracking it in your Inbox. All of our clients want to reduce this level of interruption and distraction, so why create more? We recommend you turn off all e-mail reminders.

If you process and organize your e-mail once a day and successfully reduce your messages to zero, there's no purpose in reviewing each e-mail as it arrives other than to distract you. You've spent a full day in meetings without access to your computer, and so you can certainly go eight hours without looking at mail! If you have no valid reason for the chime, eliminate it and create more uninterrupted time for yourself. You'll scan e-mail anyway, and so you don't need each and every e-mail that arrives to remind you! This is your chance to drive technology instead of having it drive you.

When Can I Use Flagging Effectively?

By using flagging, you can quickly link an e-mail message to the To-Do Bar without creating a Task. If you have a Strategic Next Action where there is no Supporting Information, flagging is an excellent choice. If you have to respond to an e-mail communication that will take more than two minutes, you could defer it by flagging the message, categorizing it into your SNA E-Mail category and changing the subject line to capture the appropriate action. In this way, all of the flagged items become e-mail messages to respond to and won't require supporting information.

If you are in a role where you work primarily from e-mail and do not need to enter any independent Tasks on to the To-Do Bar or do not need Supporting Information to complete your Strategic Next Actions, flagging is excellent. Also, if you do decide to work primarily with flagging, your Inbox can be sorted by Planning and Action Categories. This creates a Categories: (none) section that holds all of your unprocessed e-mail, making this your main e-mail Collection Point. Even though your entire Inbox will not be empty because it will have your Planning and Action Categories in it, your Categories: (none) can then become your Inbox and you can empty this, which means you can still work on the concept of an empty Inbox.

If you're a power user of Outlook, we still suggest dragging as your primary method. However, you can include flagging as a supplemental feature supporting work style preferences and personal customization of your IMS.

Part Three:
Creating an
Integrated
Management
System—The
Processing and
Organizing
Phase

Can I Organize My E-Mail in the Inbox and Not Use the To-Do Bar?

Certain roles and work situations may cause you to use only the Inbox as your "Total Life To-Do List" instead of the To-Do Bar. These roles are usually customer service related and require you to be in your Inbox all day. Your work is answering e-mail, and therefore you have little use for the To-Do List.

Instead of entering Meaningful Objectives and Supporting Projects as Tasks on the To-Do Bar, you would enter them as Subject lines in e-mail messages and categorize them in your Inbox under your Planning and Action Categories as you do in the To-Do Bar. The only difference is that all entries have to come by e-mail and you cannot create Tasks in which you can insert documents and other e-mail messages and write notes. If you do not need to do that, flagging and organizing in the Inbox will work well for you. The theory is exactly the same, it is just a lot more simplified, and in certain roles this can work exceedingly well.

Emptying the Inbox and Getting to Zero

If you still have e-mail in your Inbox, let's see what you can do to get it to zero. (If your Inbox is empty, skip ahead to the section titled "What Changes Will You Make?" later in this chapter.)

We encourage you to take the time right now to get your e-mail message count to zero. You can do it! We've worked with people who have as many as 7,000 messages in their Inbox and they got to zero, and so we know you can.

Here are three steps you can follow to help you eliminate e-mail.

1. Identify the "shelf life" of your e-mail. It can be anywhere from one week to two months or more, depending on your role. (Legal and financial roles have strict rules with regard to how long to keep e-mail.) After a certain point, e-mail is no longer meaningful, and so there's no point in keeping it unless it's helpful to have as reference information. Sort your Inbox by the oldest e-mail first, and then eliminate all of the out-of-date e-mail. This can dramatically reduce your volume.

   Erasing lots of e-mail can be scary, but ask yourself, "What am I willing to let go of to get what I want?" Remember Linda from Chapter 1? She elim-

We're drowning in information and starving for knowledge.
—**Rutherford Rogers**

Part Three:
Creating an
Integrated
Management
System—The
Processing and
Organizing
Phase

Take Back Your Life!

inated 1,991 messages in one press of the Delete key! If this makes you very nervous, create a new Archive Folder. Use the date range of filed e-mail as your folder title. Drag the old e-mail into the folder. You can always go back to it later. Meanwhile, it's not cluttering up your Inbox.

2. When you've eliminated the outdated shelf life e-mail, go through what's left and delete Calendar notices, Inbox full notices, E-mail messages from anyone who's left the company or moved to a different department, and project-related messages for projects that are now complete. Do whatever you can do to eliminate unwanted e-mail quickly.

3. Identify how much e-mail you have left and calculate how long it will take you to empty your Inbox. If you have 400 messages and you can process 60 an hour, it will take you 6.6 hours to get to zero. However, you need to ask yourself whether that time is worth it. What could you do in six hours that would add more value than processing e-mail does? After you've answered these questions, you can choose to work through your messages or delete and archive even more e-mail, leaving only the last week's worth of messages to process.

If you have hundreds or thousands of messages in your Inbox, processing the 60 new messages for the day won't help you get to zero. You need to eliminate the buildup to really get on top of your e-mail. When you get to zero, you'll be motivated to stay there because there's nothing like a blank e-mail screen to ease your mind and put a smile on your face! Go for it!

What Changes Will You Make?

Take a moment to reflect on what changes you'll make as a result of reading the topics in this chapter:

- Using the E-Mail PASS Model to write more meaningful e-mail communications

- Properly using the To, Cc, Bcc, and Subject lines

- Using the Four Ds for Decision Making

- Reducing volume

- Scheduling e-mail processing time

In the To-Do List in Outlook, open the IMPROVING PRODUCTIVITY task that you created in Chapter 4, and under the heading "Processing and Organizing" enter the specific actions that you want to do to support the comple-

Chapter Eleven: Processing and Organizing Your E-Mail

Part Three:
Creating an
Integrated
Management
System—The
Processing and
Organizing
Phase

tion of the Processing and Organizing Phase. For example, Carol's choices are listed in Figure 11-17.

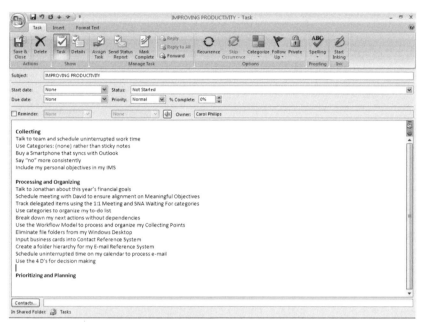

Figure 11-17 Keeping track of the changes you'll make.

After you've recorded these changes, close the Task back into Categories: (none). You'll refer to it again at the end of the Prioritizing and Planning Phase.

For inspiration, here are few examples of what our clients have written:

■ "Use the Delete key!"

■ "Handle e-mail in less than two minutes."

■ "Schedule uninterrupted time to process e-mail."

■ "Be way more careful about how I use the Cc line."

■ "Meet with my team to clarify e-mail standards and reinforce them."

■ "Save attachments into My Documents instead of my Personal Folders E-mail Reference System."

■ "If I can do it in less than two minutes, do it."

■ "Scan long messages in less than two minutes to establish if I really need to read them."

Start with doing what's necessary; then do what's possible, and suddenly, you are doing the impossible.
—**Saint Francis of Assisi**

Part Three:
Creating an
Integrated
Management
System—The
Processing and
Organizing
Phase

Take Back Your Life!

- "Never close an e-mail message back into the Inbox. Make a decision and do something with it."

- "Talk to my team about how we Cc so that I can reduce my e-mail volume."

- "Use dragging to defer tasks into the SNA categories."

- "Don't save e-mail messages that don't relate to my Meaningful Objectives."

Success Factors for Processing and Organizing E-Mail

Here are success factors that you should keep in mind when you process and organize e-mail.

- Use the E-Mail PASS Model to help you create meaningful e-mail messages so that recipients understand your communication and its purpose. By writing clear e-mail messages, you can effectively move toward your objectives and reduce e-mail volume.

- Use the To, Cc, and Bcc lines effectively to reduce e-mail and increase the effectiveness of your communications.

- Use the Subject line to help recipients anticipate the purpose of your e-mail even before they read your message.

- When you open an e-mail, make a decision using the Four Ds for Decision Making: delete it, do it in less than two minutes, delegate it, or defer it to a SNA category. Never close an e-mail message back into the Inbox!

- Schedule uninterrupted time to process and organize your e-mail each day so that you can empty the Inbox. If you can process 60 messages in an hour and you receive 50, it'll take you less than an hour to process your e-mail for the day.

- Ask your direct reports and co-workers to respect your scheduled e-mail processing appointments.

Each person can choose to become part of the e-mail solution. The results are so huge that it's impossible to ignore them and hard not to be motivated by them. Our statistics prove that departments can reduce the total number of e-mail messages in employees' Inboxes by as much as 81 percent, reduce daily e-mail volume by as much as 26 percent, and increase work/life bal-

Part Three:
Creating an
Integrated
Management
System—The
Processing and
Organizing
Phase

ance by as much as 25 percent. Education works, and so take the time to change your approach and work with your team to help them do the same. Everyone will benefit and you'll inspire change throughout your company.

To reinforce the behavioral changes you learned in this chapter, we developed an add-in software product, Take Back Your Life! 4Outlook Plug-In. This product makes it much easier to file and find information, use the PASS model, move e-mails into the Task list, reduce key strokes, and offers coaching support. You can download this from the Products page on our Web site at *www.mcgheeproductivity.com*, or go to the MPS Products page at the back of this book. This product currently runs on Microsoft Office 2000, 2002, and 2003. We're just completing the 2007 Microsoft Office version. Stay tuned.

On to the final chapter, "The Prioritizing and Planning Phase."

Creating an Integrated Management System— The Prioritizing and Planning Phase

Part Four:
Creating an
Integrated
Management
System—The
Prioritizing and
Planning Phase

Chapter Twelve

The Prioritizing and Planning Phase

Chapter Twelve: **The Prioritizing and Planning Phase**

Part Four:
Creating an
Integrated
Management
System—The
Prioritizing and
Planning Phase

The purpose of the Prioritizing and Planning Phase is to assist you in getting the right things done while experiencing freedom and work/life balance. We believe there's a paradigm shift that needs to take place for you to experience this kind of freedom and stability. Most of us are living in an illusion, hoping that one day we'll get it all done. The truth is you'll *never get it all done and you'll always have more to do than ou can ever hope to do*. When you really get this concept, you can finally let go of it and you'll see how funny it is that you tried so hard to achieve something so impossible. Then, you can start to rebuild how you're managing your life so that you can achieve freedom and work/life balance.

This paradigm shift comes only when you truly accept you cannot get it all done. When you get that, you can then choose the most strategic things you want to do and let the rest go. Unfortunately, because our to-do lists are limitless and have no boundaries, many of our clients are still trying very hard to complete them, and they feel guilty when they don't, hoping one day they'll figure out how to do it. There are no silver bullets; the bottom line is you will never get it all done! And therefore the only choice *you have is to be more strategic about what you decide to do*, in other words be discerning and truly prioritize what is most important.

The Calendar unlike the To-Do List, does have boundaries, and these are the kind that cannot be moved. Therefore, we recommend that when you prioritize and plan you use a combination of the Calendar and the To-Do List because one tempers the other and reminds you that you cannot get it all done, therefore supporting you in the behavior of being more strategic about what you choose to do. Ever heard the expression "You can't do everything, but you can do anything you choose to do?"

Part Four:
Creating an
Integrated
Management
System—The
Prioritizing and
Planning Phase

Take Back Your Life!

We also look at how to sustain and maintain your Integrated Management System (IMS) so that you can stay on track with your Meaningful Objectives and maintain the experience of freedom and personal balance. This process is called the Weekly Review and it is the most important habit to maintain after you finish reading this book. To complete a Weekly Review you'll learn how to create a BaselineCalendar, handle meeting requests, proactively plan your Meaningful Objectives (MOs) and Supporting Projects (SPs) so that they stay on track, and prioritize and schedule your Strategic Next Actions (SNAs) onto the Calendar. This is the last of the three phases for creating an Integrated Management System and will help you maintain an experience of control, focus, and balance.

Are You Planning from Your Calendar or Your To-Do List?

One of the most important aspects of the Prioritizing and Planning Phase is coming to grips with the reality of using a calendar to support accomplishing your Meaningful Objectives and maintaining balance. A calendar has clear boundaries: you have only 24 hours in a day. No matter how well you manage them, you can't make them 25. Conversely, they won't become 23 if you mismanage them.

One of the reasons clients aren't getting everything done is because they're not using their calendars to book their daily activities. Consequently, such actions as processing e-mail and completing Strategic Next Actions happen after hours or get squeezed around meetings and sometimes happen during meetings! Clients wonder why this occurs, and it truly is simple: if you don't book time to process e-mail during the day, you'll be doing it in between meetings, late at night, or early in the mornings, none of which supports being present or balanced.

The problem isn't lack of time; the problem is that clients plan their To-Do List in their heads instead of planning their activities in their calendars, and therefore they plan more than they can do. If you schedule what you have to do on your Calendar, you'll know if you can get it done. We often say to clients, *"You can't do everything, but you can do anything, as long as it fits in your Calendar."* In other words you need to decide what the most strategic activities are that you need to complete and continuously plan these activities on your Calendar. If these activities don't fit into your Calendar, you then have to move to a higher level of strategizing and planning. The Calendar forces you to make these tough decisions, and that's what prioritizing is all about. You'll end up having to say no to more things, which means you'll be able to

Chapter Twelve: The Prioritizing and Planning Phase

Part Four:
Creating an
Integrated
Management
System—The
Prioritizing and
Planning Phase

say "yes" to the most important things. The Calendar forces a level of reality that causes you to be more honest and live more in your integrity and ultimately supports you in being accountable and getting what you want.

Sally was working with a group of executives in Chicago last year and one of the participants came in late for the session; she had been up since 4 A.M. doing her e-mail. At one point during the day Sally asked everyone in the room, "How many of you book daily appointments on your Calendar to process e-mail?" No one raised a hand. Then, she asked, "When do you do your e-mail?" Eileen exclaimed, "4 A.M.!" Other replies were, "At home in the evenings or early in the mornings." She then asked the group, "How many of you plan 'Strategic Next Action' work time on your Calendar?" Again, no one raised a hand. Sally asked, "When do you do your Strategic Next Actions?" The responses were, "In-between meetings," "On the fly," "After work," and "Maybe not at all." If you aren't planning your day, you can be sure someone else will plan it for you, and their plans aren't likely to reflect your priorities or objectives.

Sally asked Eileen why she did her e-mail at 4 A.M., and she replied, "I don't have time during the day." Sally said, "I'd like you to consider that you do have time. The problem is that you don't book the time on your Calendar." Eileen looked confused and said. "You mean, if I scheduled time to process e-mail during the day, I'd get it done during the day?" She thought for a moment, contemplating whether to believe in this concept, and then responded, "Then I'd have to book my meetings around my e-mail time. But I have so many meetings!" Sally chuckled, "Keep doing what you're doing and you'll keep getting the same results. You have lots of meetings because you book lots of meetings. If you booked e-mail time during the day, you'd need to be more strategic about which meetings to attend." *If you don't calendar your work during the day, it won't happen during the day.* It's all about managing what you agree to do so that you can get it done in the time you have.

The truth is that you'll always have more meeting requests than you can accommodate, you'll consistently frustrate co-workers because you're not available, and you'll forever have more to do than you can do. Sound familiar? These are realities that we all need to embrace, accept, and come to peace with. Remember, you all have more to do than you can ever hope to do. You can't change these facts, but you can change what you agree to do based on your objectives and the amount of time you have available.

Your head and your To-Do List have no boundaries; they're limitless. Reality lies only in the Calendar because it has time limits. Use it as a prioritization

Part Four:
Creating an
Integrated
Management
System—The
Prioritizing and
Planning Phase

Take Back Your Life!

tool, and it will assist you to be much more strategic about what you can and cannot do. Remember there is a 75 percent greater chance that your tasks will get done if they are planned on your Calendar as opposed to being on your To-Do List. We'd be working with the calendar based on this statistic alone!

Using Your Calendar to Prioritize and Plan

Imagine looking at your time as though it was money. Your Calendar is your bank account, and your appointments and your To-Do List are bills. Each day, 24 dollars are deposited into your bank account. That's your daily allowance, and you'll never be able to increase it! Every time you book an appointment, you're paying a bill and your bank balance decreases. The more bills you pay, the less time you have.

To balance your accounts, you need to reconcile what you've agreed to do on your To-Do List with the time you have available on your Calendar. By balancing these two, you can quickly identify if you've spent more money than you have or if your account is in balance. When you know this, you can course correct and get yourself back on track. The challenge with time is that you can't buy more of it! This means you need to be conscious of the time you have and use it wisely. If you overcommit, there's nothing you can do but renegotiate your commitments or sleep fewer hours!

Now when it comes to the credit card, we're all having a fine old time spending money. "Yes, I'll complete that budget. I'll give you a call back. Let's have dinner soon. I'll get that report done, finish that project, and fix the car." We're unconscious of what we're spending until the statement comes in and we need to pay the bill, and then we get conscious in a hurry!

By planning your activities on the Calendar, you're able to see clearly how much money you've spent and what is left to spend. It's very hard to know what you can and can't do if you don't know how much money you have. Time and money are very similar in that regard. They both have limits, and so they both require conscious prioritization and planning to create balance.

To support you in bringing more awareness to your Calendar, we'd like you to do a simple exercise. For one week, track how you spend your time each day and record it on your Outlook Calendar. Record everything you do, and we mean *everything*. Here's an example.

- Showered and dressed: 40 minutes
- Prepared and ate breakfast: 30 minutes

Chapter Twelve: The Prioritizing and Planning Phase

Part Four:
**Creating an
Integrated
Management
System—The
Prioritizing and
Planning Phase**

- Did e-mail for 30 minutes

- Drove to work: 25 minutes;made calls on cell phone and looked at e-mail on smartphone

- Waited in line to get my morning latte: 15 minutes, and looked at e-mail on smartphone

- Did e-mail: 15 minutes, then got interrupted with a call

- Did a phone call: 10 minutes

- Handled a walk-in interruption: 10 minutes

This is a very simple exercise, but it can be extremely revealing, just like tracking how much money you spend in a week! Before you can really start to plan your Calendar, you have to have a baseline for what you are actually doing, and most of us are not conscious of how we really spend our time.

After you've tracked your activities for a complete week, you'll be able to analyze what you spent your time doing, how long it takes, and whether it truly maps to your personal and professional objectives. This part can be quite revealing. From this experience, you can determine activities you want to stop doing, activities to keep doing, quicker ways to get things done, and better times of the day to complete tasks. This exercise also prepares you for creating a **BaselineCalendar**, which you do next.

Setting Up Your BaselineCalendar

With a BaselineCalendar, you can be more conscious of exactly what you need to do in a day and make sure you block out time on your Calendar to get it done. You identify the essential reoccurring activities that you need to perform weekly, monthly, and yearly, and ensure that you book them onto your Calendar. Essential reoccurring activities could be processing e-mail, downloading and processing voice mail, holding monthly 1:1s with your staff, attending quarterly management team reviews, picking up your kids, or exercising three times a week. After these activities are booked on the Calendar, you can clearly see how much time you have left. From there, you can plan and prioritize your To-Do List, transfer SNAs onto the Calendar, and decide whether to accept additional meeting requests.

To discover what your BaselineCalendar activities are, ask yourself the question "How much reoccurring time do I need, weekly, monthly, and annually, to ensure that my personal and business objectives get completed?" Each person has a different set of circumstances. You may have to drop off or pick

Part Four:
Creating an
Integrated
Management
System—The
Prioritizing and
Planning Phase

up your children, keep exercise appointments, or attend horseback riding lessons. You may receive 120 e-mail messages a day and need two hours of e-mail processing time, and you may have five direct reports and need to meet each of them regularly every month for an hour. You might have annual planning meetings or staff meetings. Your specific objectives affect which activities you need to plan routinely on your Calendar.

BaselineCalendar Activities

Following is a list of potential BaselineCalendar activities to consider.

- Processing e-mail: at least 1 hour a day

- Emptying additional Collecting Points: at least 30 minutes every other day, depending on volume

- Weekly Review time to update your Integrated Management System: 1 hour, once a week

- 1:1 Meetings with your direct reports, boss, and others: decide if you want to split these appointments up or do them all in one day

- Staff meetings: once a month, for a day

- Quarterly strategic team planning meeting: once a quarter for a day

- Annual strategic team planning meeting: once a year for a day

- Reading time: 2 hours, every other week

- Vacations: twice a year

- Exercise time: 1 hour, three times a week

- Riding lesson every Saturday morning

- Pick up kids at 4:30 P.M. on the way home: Monday, Wednesday, and Friday

- Church and community service

- Walk the dogs: three times a week

Take a moment and list in the following chart the recurring activities that you want to include on your Calendar and make sure they really represent your Meaningful Objectives, both personal and business. Realize that after you put them on the Calendar, you're making a commitment to complete them. The Calendar is a prioritization tool. Only place items on the Calen-

Part Four:
Creating an
Integrated
Management
System—The
Prioritizing
and
Planning Phase

dar that are critical to complete and support your Meaningful Objectives. Everything else stays on your To-Do Bar until it becomes a priority to calendar.

	Baseline Calendar Activity	Length of Time	Recurrence
1			
2			
3			
4			
5			
6			
7			
8			
9			
10			

When you start to schedule baseline activities on the Calendar, you'll want to consider the best time to book them by identifying what fits into the rhythm of your business and personal life. This takes a little thinking. For example, with regard to e-mail processing, you'll want to pick a time when you're least likely to get interrupted and won't have consistent scheduling conflicts.

Carol Philips, for example, reserves from 8 to 9 A.M. three days a week to process her e-mail because she starts her meetings at 9 A.M. and on days when she has riding lessons, she does e-mail from 11 A.M. to 12 P.M. Her staff tends to use the 8 to 9 A.M. time slot to get uninterrupted work done, as well. Carol schedules two hours of Strategic Next Action work time every other day. 1:1s with her direct reports happen once a month on a Monday, and her staff meetings occur once a month on a Friday. She has riding lessons twice a week, getting her into the office at 11 A.M. Figure 12-1 shows an example of her work week. Notice that she includes travel time to and from her lessons, client meetings, and her staff meetings. This gives her a realistic view of her plans so that she knows what else she can and cannot do that day.

Part Four:
Creating an
Integrated
Management
System—The
Prioritizing and
Planning Phase

Take Back Your Life!

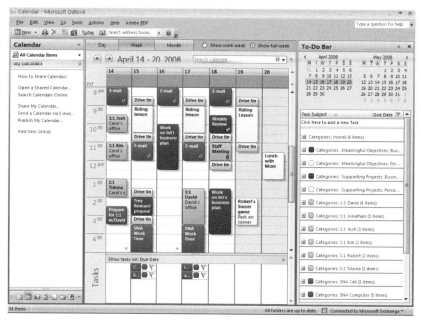

Figure 12-1   Carol's work week.

To book your reoccurring activities, go to the Calendar and select Show Work Week to the right of the Day/Week/Month tabs to see a week at a glance. To view Saturday and Sunday as part of your week, click the Show Full Week option. We encourage you to use the full week view to support your focus on work/life balance.

We'd like you to plan your BaselineCalendar using the list you created earlier. If you have a heavy meeting schedule, you need to book these new appointments weeks out. If that's the case, go ahead and plan them in the future. We know it takes courage to book your Calendar in advance, but to ensure that you complete these actions, it's necessary to schedule them. Calendar away!

Including Travel Time

We often see Calendars in which meetings are booked back to back. There's no way someone can be on time leaving a meeting at 3 P.M. and starting another at 3 P.M. In Figure 12-1, you can see that Carol marks in the travel time to get to and from her meetings. This ensures that she's on time and doesn't have to rush or make excuses for being late.

You can also schedule domestic travel by scheduling drive time to and from the airport, time spent checking in, and time going through security. This

Chapter Twelve: The Prioritizing and Planning Phase

Part Four:
Creating an
Integrated
Management
System—The
Prioritizing and
Planning Phase

ensures you know when to leave and shows how much time you have in the car and standing in security lines. This seems so obvious, but you'd be surprised how many Calendars we see in which travel time isn't scheduled. Clients figure out in their heads when to leave (often at the last minute), or they accidentally book meetings they cannot attend because they didn't mark on their Calendar the time they needed to leave for the airport. It's a simple discipline, but it helps keep your Calendar realistic. Once again, more thinking on the front end saves thinking on the back end.

Including "Catch-Up Time" After Travel

When you travel domestically or internationally, not only do you want to plan out your travel time, you'll want to plan "catch-up time" to do your e-mail and voice mail when you return. You may discover that you come home with all kinds of good ideas and perspectives that you want to capture and process, and so it's important to make room for these activities. You may get some of your best ideas 35,000 feet up in the skies!

People aren't realistic about scheduling catch-up time. They return from trips to face back-to-back meetings and hundreds of e-mail messages, and then wonder why they "fall off the wagon" every time they travel. The best way to handle this is to block out large chunks of time on your Calendar when you return so that you can empty all of your Collecting Points and catch up.

We have clients who inform their staff that they're on vacation from May 15 to May 25, but they come home on the 23rd and use two days to catch up. Get smart: plan the time you need for reentry so that you get caught up and don't have to miss a beat because of travel.

Using Out of Office Replies

When you travel, use your out of office (OOO) replies to clearly state what your response time will be so that recipients know when to expect a communication from you. "I'm on vacation and won't be responding to e-mail until May 28. Please send urgent requests to joshp@lucernepublishing.com. Thank you for your patience."

We once had a client who was going on an extended vacation, and whose OOO stated, "I am on extended vacation from July 25 to August 25. While I'm gone I will not be reading e-mail. If you need *such and such*, please contact henrys@cpandl.com. If you need *this and that*, contact suzanp@cpandl.com. If you require my attention, I will be returning on

Part Four:
Creating an
Integrated
Management
System—The
Prioritizing and
Planning Phase

Take Back Your Life!

August 26." This worked because it gave her colleagues clear information, and her staff were prepared to handle things in her absence.

Including 9-1-1 Interruptions

Our clients tell us, "My Calendar would be fine if I didn't get 9-1-1 interruptions." The term **9-1-1** refers to an emergency situation that you can't predict or expect. However, many of our clients can predict their 9-1-1 situations! One client said, "Every quarter, we get a virus, the system crashes, and we're down for two days. It's a real pain!" We suggested, "How about planning two days every quarter with no meetings, and when the 9-1-1 happens you can move your meetings to the unblocked time. And if the 9-1-1 doesn't happen, you have more time to play with!"

Our point of view is that if a 9-1-1 is predictable, it's not really a 9-1-1 and you can build it into your system. Identify the 9-1-1 situations you deal with and be realistic. You know that these events will happen, and so budget for them. You're going to spend the time one way or another.

If you can foresee a 9-1-1 situation, it's not really an emergency. Think about firefighters for a moment. Do you think a building on fire is a 9-1-1 to a firefighter? No, because firefighters plan for fires and crises. That's their job, and a 9-1-1 is not an emergency to them. Remember, true 9-1-1 situations are unexpected and unpredictable.

Now, you are likely to get a few true 9-1-1 situations, and so you can prepare for those as well. Carol includes two days a month of unstructured time to handle truly unexpected situations. Of course, those situations don't happen on the day she's booked for them, but she gets two days to reschedule meetings when it does happen. (That's her secret. Shhhhh, don't tell anyone because she's not giving them up!)

As you complete setting up your BaselineCalendar, consider your expected and unexpected 9-1-1 situations and how much time to book for them. This enables you to be realistic. If they happen, you have time. If they don't, you still have time.

Keeping Appointments with Yourself Is a Priority

Your BaselineCalendar will now have numerous appointments that you have booked with yourself; the question is "Are you going to keep them?" Our clients often give up their own appointments to attend meetings with other people. It seems much easier to support the requests of your staff, customers,

Chapter Twelve: The Prioritizing and Planning Phase

Part Four:
Creating an
Integrated
Management
System—The
Prioritizing and
Planning Phase

and family than it is to support your own priorities. We would like you to consider a second paradigm shift: moving from "other people are more important than I am" to "I am as important as others."

We hear our clients say, "I want to process my e-mail at work so that I don't have to do it at home." When you book appointments with yourself, such as an appointment to process your e-mail or exercise at lunch, you're making yourself a priority. However, when you cancel these appointments to accommodate the requests of others, you're not taking care of what you need to do to accomplish your objectives. You're sending a very clear message to yourself: *Everyone else's agenda is more important than mine.* If you keep reinforcing this message, you'll eventually become resentful and tired, and you'll start blaming your organization because you're not able to keep up with your own workload and needs. It's hard to be a Superman or Superwoman when you're stressed out and overwhelmed. Make yourself a priority, and then you can do a better job of taking care of others.

Our most successful clients make their own appointments a priority. They know that when they take good care of themselves, they'll take good care of their customers and staff. They're tenacious about sticking to their uninterrupted e-mail time, exercise time, planning time, and Strategic Next Action time. This practice separates those who are moderately productive from those who are extremely productive. Without exception, we've found that our most successful clients live by this discipline. It's the only way they can survive long term. Don't give up your appointments with yourself. They help you get your job done, and get it done in balance.

Using Colors on the Calendar to Create Differentiation

Color coding your appointments is extremely powerful because with it you, in one glance, can differentiate activities. In Microsoft Office Outlook 2007, categories can be associated with colors and these color categories can be applied to e-mails, contacts, appointments, tasks, and/or Journal entries. In this section we are going to discuss applying color categories to your appointments.

There are several ways of setting up your colors, once you know what your options are available you can choose what is going to work best for you. If you assign a category to an appointment, then it will changes the color of the appointment to match that category.

Part Four:
Creating an
Integrated
Management
System—The
Prioritizing and
Planning Phase

Take Back Your Life!

Carol uses her colors to distinguish between her Planning and Action Categories, as shown in Figure 12-2. Unfortunately, you only see shades of gray in this book, but in real life the colors you can choose are vibrant, distinctive, and positively cheery!

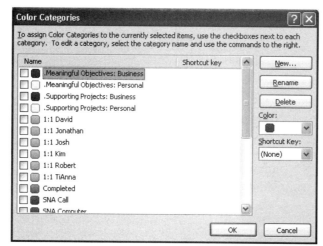

Figure 12-2   Carol's color-coded Planning and Action Categories.

Carol's color codes are listed as follows:

- Yellow: Meaningful Objectives: Personal and Supporting Projects: Personal

- Red: Meaningful Objectives: Business and Supporting Projects: Business

- Turquoise: 1:1 or group meetings with staff

- Green: Strategic Next Actions

- Gray: Travel time

- Pink: Completed. No actions remain that aren't tracked

To create color labels for your categories, follow these steps:

1. On the To-Do Bar, right-click the Subject line of any Task, click Categorize on the shortcut menu, and then select All Categories. You'll see the Planning and Action Categories you entered in Chapter 7.

Chapter Twelve: The Prioritizing and Planning Phase

Part Four:
Creating an
Integrated
Management
System—The
Prioritizing and
Planning Phase

2. In the Color Categories dialog box, highlight the first category by clicking it once. (Don't put a check mark in the box.)

3. Click the Color drop-down menu for a choice of colors, and select the color you want for that specific category. The box to the left of the category name will change from white to the color you select, as shown in Figure 12-3.

4. After you have chosen the colors for your categories, click OK.

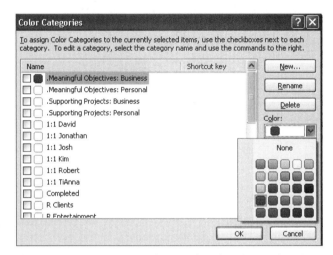

Figure 12-3   Assigning colors to the Planning and Action Categories.

When Carol looks at her week at a glance view on her Calendar, she can see right away which meetings relate to her objectives, which meetings relate to her 1:1s, and how much time she has for SNAs.

Another way to do this is to keep your Planning and Action Categories colors blank and create a set of bogus categories that you use only for Calendar appointments. See Figure 12-4. This way, you can customize how you want to use them; for example, Carol could have set up the following categories:

- z Client Meeting: Orange
- z Completed: Pink
- z Conference Call In Office: Green
- z Email Time: Yellow
- z Internal Management Meeting: Purple
- z Personal Appointment: Teal
- z Phone Call On Cell: Blue
- z Travel Time: Gray

Part Four:
Creating an
Integrated
Management
System—The
Prioritizing and
Planning Phase

Take Back Your Life!

If Carol sees a blue appointment, this immediately tells her that she can be in any location to complete the call, as long as she has cell phone coverage, which creates flexibility. However, if she's got a client meeting, the orange color signifies that she needs to show up at a specific location, and so she's got less flexibility. Gray travel time is useful because Carol can make calls during that period. The colors help her create this distinction.

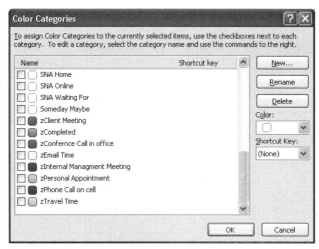

Figure 12-4   Color labels for the Calendar.

To create new categories for your Calendar and color them, follow these steps:

1. On the To-Do Bar, right-click the Subject line of any Task, click Categorize on the shortcut menu, and then select All Categories. You'll see the Planning and Action Categories you entered in Chapter 7.

2. In the Color Categories dialog box, click the New button.

3. In the Add New Category dialog box, in the Name box, enter the category you want to add.

4. In the Color drop-down menu, select a color.

5. Ensure the Shortcut key box is set to (None).

6. Click OK.

7. The category you just added should appear in the list. If a check mark appears to the left of the category, clear it.

Chapter Twelve: The Prioritizing and Planning Phase

Part Four:
Creating an
Integrated
Management
System—The
Prioritizing and
Planning Phase

Another way to color code is to distinguish between your objectives, labeling each appointment to represent the specific objective it links to. By using this system, you can see how much time you're spending working on different Meaningful Objectives and in some cases how much time you're spending outside of your objectives.

Another powerful way to use color is to distinguish between complete and incomplete activities. When Carol completes a meeting and captures the appropriate Strategic Next Actions on her To-Do Bar, she then changes the meeting color on her Calendar to pink so that she knows the meeting is completed and has no untracked actions.

At the end of the day, when Carol reviews the Calendar, the colors allow her to see immediately what's complete and what's incomplete. If an appointment is not complete, she tracks the unfinished action and marks it pink or renegotiates the appointment and moves it to a different day, or even back to the To-Do Bar. This creates a sense of momentum throughout the week, and it's a nice way to close the day.

As you can tell, there are several ways you can use color to highlight activities and/or objectives. Now that you know what your options are you can choose what is going to work best for your situation and work style. Our only caution with using colors is to use them consistently; otherwise, they become meaningless. Therefore, before you embark on using colors, be clear how you want to employ them, and ensure they provide value.

Handling Meeting Requests

After your BaselineCalendar is established, you'll have less time for additional meetings, causing you to be more discriminating. The McGhee Productivity Solutions (MPS) Meeting Request Model, shown in Figure 12-5, guides you through a series of questions that are designed to help you make more effective decisions regarding accepting meetings. Remember, you'll always have more requests than you can accept, and so you have to be more discerning about what you agree to do.

Part Four:
Creating an
Integrated
Management
System—The
Prioritizing and
Planning Phase

Take Back Your Life!

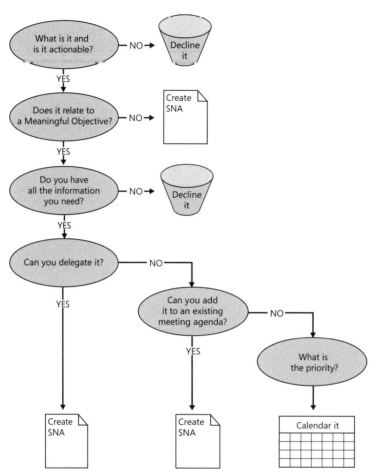

Figure 12-5   The Meeting Request Model shows you how to deal with meeting requests.

When we work with clients who have heavy meeting schedules—75 percent of their time is in meetings—we often go through each appointment on their Calendar and ask, "Does this directly impact one of your Meaningful Objectives?" This cleans out 5 to 8 percent of the meeting requests right away. Then we ask, "Can you delegate this?" and that cleans out another 2 to 5 percent. Often, agendas can be combined by moving two meetings into one, or the agenda of a meeting can happen on a conference call, saving travel time. Also, if you have an assistant working with you, consider having that person use this model to help prioritize your appointments for you. There are many ways to work more effectively with meetings. These are just a few ideas.

Chapter Twelve: The Prioritizing and Planning Phase

Part Four:
Creating an
Integrated
Management
System—The
Prioritizing and
Planning Phase

Following is a closer look at the MPS Meeting Request Model.

What Is It and Is It Actionable?

"What is it and is it actionable?" is a question designed to help you pause and reflect on what type of meeting you're dealing with. We're sure you've received meeting requests from colleagues that are unclear. You might be asking yourself, "Is it personal or business? Is it an off-site meeting or is it in the building? Is it a vendor meeting or an internal meeting? What is it?" Once you know what type of request it is, you may need more information or you need to decline it. If you think the meeting will be useful, move to the next question.

Does It Relate to a Meaningful Objective?

If the meeting request does not relate to one of your Meaningful Objectives, we suggest you look very closely at whether you should attend; perhaps someone else must attend, not you. Occasionally, there are special circumstances in which you'd accept an appointment that doesn't relate to one of your objectives, such as supporting a colleague in reaching a goal or attending company staff events. Remember, you're not measured on the meetings you attend; you're measured on achieving your Meaningful Objectives. We recommend you stay focused on the activities you say are important to you and don't get distracted by all the other requests on your time. If the request does relate to one of your objectives, move to the next question.

Do You Have All the Information You Need?

It's much easier to prioritize meeting requests when you have all the information available. Make sure you find out the following:

- What is the agenda?
- Who is attending?
- Is any supporting information required?
- Location and length of the meeting?
- Date by when meeting needs to happen?

This gives you valuable information, and if you don't have this data, you can create a Strategic Next Action to get it. Sometimes, when you ask recipients to be more specific, they realize a meeting is not the best forum for their needs and create alternative options.

Part Four:
Creating an
Integrated
Management
System—The
Prioritizing and
Planning Phase

Take Back Your Life!

If you have an administrator, you can ask that person to create a simple template using these questions and send the template to requesting parties. When internal staff realize they need to answer these questions prior to getting a meeting with you, they'll do a better job of providing this information ahead of time, and often the questions help them recognize that a meeting is not necessary. Once again, you're asking people to move their thinking to the front end instead of the back end, which saves cycles of action for everyone.

Can You Delegate It?

Clients frequently forget the option to delegate. Have you considered whether the meeting request could be passed to one of your direct reports? If someone can make decisions on your behalf, create an SNA to delegate the meeting to that person. If not, move to the next question.

Can You Add It to an Existing Meeting or Agenda?

Rather than set up a new meeting, can the agenda be added to an existing meeting that's already on your Calendar? If so, identify the SNA that you need to take to add the agenda. There's no point in creating an additional meeting if you don't have to! If this doesn't work, move to the next question.

Schedule It

If you have the time and it makes sense to schedule the meeting, accept the request. However, if your calendar is full, you'll need to assess whether you can push the meeting out or if you need to renegotiate your current appointments to make room for it. To make these decisions, you must be clear about your objectives and deadlines, and if you have an assistant, that person will need to be just as clear as you so that he or she can make these decisions on your behalf.

Much like the questions in the McGhee Productivity Solutions (MPS) Workflow Model, the questions in the Meeting Request Model are simple but profound, and they help you pause and think before making agreements. Our clients can reduce their time spent in meetings by 20 percent as a result of being more discriminating about which meetings they attend. It's worth taking a moment to make these decisions on the front end so that you can save time on the back end. Guard your calendar and don't spend time in meetings that don't directly impact your Meaningful Objectives.

Chapter Twelve: The Prioritizing and Planning Phase

Part Four:
Creating an
Integrated
Management
System—The
Prioritizing and
Planning Phase

Sustaining and Maintaining your IMS: The Weekly Review

After your IMS is set up, the most important habit to embrace is the Weekly Review. For this to happen gracefully, we want you to consider a third paradigm shift. This shift involves moving from being reactive to proactive and having this be a conscious choice. Most of our clients spend their days reacting to incoming data: e-mail, voice mail, meetings, and interruptions. This is fine; however, once a week during the Weekly Review appointment we want our clients to shift from being reactive to being proactive. **Proactive** means creating and causing action to occur; it means reviewing your Meaningful Objectives and Supporting Projects to establish what needs to be done to keep them on track, prioritizing your SNAs, and moving SNAs onto your Calendar to ensure they get done.

To make this point a little clearer we're going to use an analogy we talked about in Chapter 3. (See Figure 12-6.) Imagine an airport for a moment. The control tower gives you a 30,000-foot view, and with the help of a radar system you know exactly where the planes are, enabling you to ensure they land and take off safely. The tarmac gives you the ground-level view; planes are being guided into gates, trucks are loading bags and transferring them to baggage claim, and customers are picking up luggage. From the control tower you manage your Meaningful Objectives and Supporting Projects (Planning Categories), and through course correction you enable them to land and take off safely—this is a very proactive process. The tarmac is where you complete Strategic Next Actions (Action Categories) and work on more tactical reactive activities.

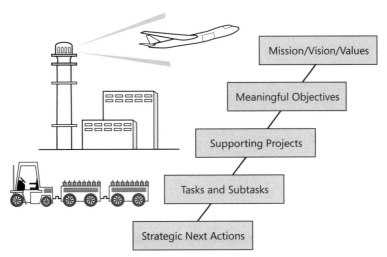

Figure 12-6 Proactively reviewing your Planning Categories gives you a 30,000-foot view.

323

Part Four:
Creating an
Integrated
Management
System—The
Prioritizing and
Planning Phase

Take Back Your Life!

As you can imagine, when you are on the ground moving bags, it's hard to pull yourself away to go to the control tower and manage the 30,000-foot view. Baggage claim is a very reactive environment; bags arrive and need to be placed on the correct carousels, customers are anxious when they can't find their suitcases, and it all appears so important. However, when you compare a lost bag with a plane crash, the two are not equal. That about sums up the Weekly Review process: with it, you can manage your objectives so that they land safely, and to do this you have to embrace the discipline of pulling yourself away from baggage claim and moving to the control tower.

Three Stages to Completing a Weekly Review

The purpose of the Weekly Review is to assist you to stay on track with your Meaningful Objectives and maintain work/life balance.

There are three stages to completing a Weekly Review:

1.   Ensuring your IMS is up-to-date and accurately reflects your current situation

2.   Reviewing your Planning Categories to course correct and create SNAs

3.   Prioritizing your Action Categories and moving appropriate SNAs onto the Calendar

During the Weekly Review you update your IMS so that it accurately reflects your current situation, you decide what you have to complete to stay on track with your Meaningful Objectives, and you prioritize and plan your SNAs onto your Calendar to get them done.

When you start your review, you need to decide which window of time you are going to plan: a week, two weeks, a month. In this chapter, we plan a week as an example; however, after you get the hang of the review you can choose the time frame you want to plan out. The entire process can take about 30 to 45 minutes to complete, but the first couple of times you do it, it can take an hour or more.

The ControlPanel, shown in Figure 12-7, is the view you use to complete your Weekly Review. In this view, you can see the Calendar, the Daily Task List, and the To-Do Bar. It's much like the cockpit of an airplane showing you all the dials to ensure you reach your destination safely. With this view, you can see everything you have to do in one place, which makes course correcting, prioritizing, and planning much easier.

Chapter Twelve: The Prioritizing and Planning Phase

Part Four:
Creating an
Integrated
Management
System—The
Prioritizing and
Planning Phase

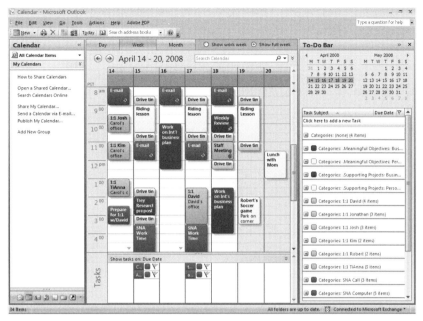

Figure 12-7   The ControlPanel.

1. Ensuring Your IMS Is Up-to-Date and Accurately Reflects Your Current Situation

The most important system in the control tower is the radar equipment, and it has to be accurate for you to guide planes to land and take off safety. Your IMS is no different: it has to be up-to-date and accurate for you to guide your Meaningful Objectives to completion; otherwise, it could be equally as disastrous.

Ensure All Your Collecting Points Are Empty   The first step in getting your IMS current is to ensure all your Collecting Points are empty. If you have any unprocessed data in your approved (and unapproved) Collecting Points, your IMS won't be up-to-date. After you've completed processing your Collecting Points, check your head to make sure you're not carrying around anything there by mistake! Also, check to see if you've picked up any loose papers, sticky notes, and meeting notes along the way, and process them as well. This is your time to capture anything you've collected and organize it into your Integrated Management System.

Picking Up Actions from Past and Future Calendar Weeks   Past and future Calendar appointments are another place clients often find untracked action steps. Go to your Calendar, show the full week (including

Part Four:
Creating an
Integrated
Management
System—The
Prioritizing and
Planning Phase

Take Back Your Life!

Saturday and Sunday), and review the past week. Go through each appointment one by one starting with last Saturday. Ask yourself, "Are there are any actions related to this appointment that aren't captured in my system?" Following are some examples:

- At a family dinner on Saturday night, you promised to organize a movie night, and then forgot to capture that in your To-Do List.

- Business meetings you attended, during which you created Strategic Next Actions but didn't capture them in your system.

- Conference calls you had where you talked about a follow-up but didn't type that into your To-Do Bar.

- Meetings you didn't attend that you need to reschedule.

Don't be too hasty with this process. Stay present and go through each personal and business appointment until you've completed the week.

After you've captured theses action items from your appointments, you can categorize them with the color you chose for completed tasks. This lets you know the appointment is complete and all the actions are tracked. The goal is to have your past week completely colored as completed at the end of this process so that you know everything that needed to be captured was captured and any appointments that needed to be moved were moved. Remember the old days when you used a highlighter to cross off items you completed and how good that felt; this is a bit like that—it's fun!

Now, look ahead to the coming week and review each appointment and ask, "Do I have all the PowerPoint slides I need? Do I have directions and the agenda? Am I prepared for that conference call?" Again, pick up any hidden actions and record them on your To-Do Bar or Calendar. You can continue into the future as far as you have the courage to go, ensuring that you're prepared for what you've planned.

Capturing Actions from OneNote, SharePoint, and Project onto Your To-Do Bar   Did you know that you can view action items from OneNote, SharePoint, and Project onto your To-Do Bar with just a few clicks? This keeps your To-Do List up-to-date and ensures all your actions are in one place. This is a very powerful feature.

To View Actions from OneNote on the To-Do Bar   OneNote and Outlook synchronize, so if you create a task in OneNote you can easily copy it onto the To-Do Bar. If you then complete a Task in Outlook, it will mark the Task as complete in OneNote, and vice versa. This makes it possible for you

When you're operating out of assumptions and paradigms that are incomplete, inaccurate or distorted, there is no way you are going to get maximum quality results. Align your expectations with reality, the way things really are, and with the timeless and universal principles that create the positive results you want to achieve.
—A. Roger Merrill

Chapter Twelve: The Prioritizing and Planning Phase

Part Four:
Creating an
Integrated
Management
System—The
Prioritizing and
Planning Phase

to keep your reference information in your Reference System and your actions in your Action System. You gotta love that!

To transfer a Task from One Note to the To-Do Bar follow these steps:

1. In OneNote, highlight the action you want to copy to the To-Do Bar.

2. On the OneNote toolbar, click the Task icon.

3. A Task flag will appear to the left of the item you highlighted, and the Task will appear in your To-Do Bar under Categories: (none) with a link to the OneNote page in the Notes section of the Task.

For more information visit *www.microsoft.com/onenote/default.mspx*.

To View Actions from SharePoint on the To-Do Bar   When you're working in SharePoint, you can assign yourself or another a task, and that task will automatically show up on your To-Do Bar. Since Outlook is synchronized with SharePoint, when you complete the SharePoint task in either environment, it will update the other when you are online. To assign a task to another person or to yourself follow these steps:

1. Under the tasks list in Sharepoint, click Add New Item.

2. Enter the title and any other items such as whom the task is assigned to, the priority, a description, and the start date and due date.

3. Click OK.

As the project owner, if you want to view the SharePoint task list in Outlook, (this is a viewing preference) follow these steps:

1. In your Web browser, open the tasks list on the SharePoint site.

2. If you cannot locate your tasks list, click View All Site Content, and then click the name of your tasks list.

3. On the Actions menu, click Connect To Outlook.

4. When you are prompted to confirm that you want to connect the tasks list to Outlook, click Yes. The task list is added to Other Tasks under the Navigation Pane In Outlook, under Tasks.

For more info visit *www.microsoft.com/sharepoint/default.mspx*.

To View Actions from Project Manager on the To-Do Bar   To view your actions on the To-Do Bar, you need to have Project Server 2007 installed along with the the Outlook add-in included with Project. Once these are installed, the integration with Outlook works well. A team mem-

Part Four:
Creating an
Integrated
Management
System—The
Prioritizing and
Planning Phase

Take Back Your Life!

ber can then choose to import their Project assignments into Outlook as either an Outlook task item or as a calendar item. To import project assignments to the To-Do Bar, be sure you have downloaded the add-in and then follow these steps:

1. In Outlook, select Tools then Options, and click the Project Web Access tab.

2. On the Project Web Access properties page, go to the Integrate With section and select Outlook Tasks.

3. Click OK.

For more information visit *http://office.microsoft.com/en-us/project/default.aspx*.

Once you have captured all your actions from your various collection points and you feel that you've truly captured and processed everything into your system, you can move on to step 2.

2. Review Your Planning Categories to Course Correct and Create SNAs

The Planning Categories consist of your Meaningful Objectives, Supporting Projects, and 1:1 categories. This is an opportunity to review these categories from the control tower instead of from the tarmac so that you can gain a different and much higher perspective. This is your opportunity to be proactive and to course correct.

Meaningful Objectives and Supporting Projects Categories   Most airplanes are on course only 25 percent of the time, and 75 percent of the time the pilot is course correcting to keep the plane on track. When you're reviewing your Meaningful Objectives and Supporting Projects, you're viewing them from the perspective of course correction as well. You're looking at the end result you want to accomplish (your destination), and then identifying where they are today against those end results (present location). After you have this data, you can look to see what course correction is needed to stay on track to your destination. This part of the Weekly Review allows you to stop and proactively check out your radar screen and make the necessary adjustments to ensure your objectives take off and land safely.

Go ahead and open each Meaningful Objective and corresponding Supporting Project task one at a time. Inside of each Meaningful Objective Task you will see your Supporting Projects and Metrics, and inside of your Supporting Project you will see your Project Plans and Metrics. Ask the following questions:

Chapter Twelve: The Prioritizing and Planning Phase

Part Four:
Creating an
Integrated
Management
System—The
Prioritizing and
Planning Phase

- What is the outcome for this Meaningful Objective/Supporting Project?

- What is the status of this outcome as of today?

- What course corrections do I need to make?

- Do I need to update my plan?

- What's the most Strategic Next Action to move forward and stay on track?

To answer these questions you are going to have to look through your project plans and metrics. This data gives you a clear idea of where the Meaningful Objectives and Supporting Projects stand. In an ideal world, you'd open the Supporting Project and find a hyperlink to an Excel worksheet or a Project document or OneNote that displays the plan along with what's completed and what's incomplete. You'd also find in the Task a hyperlink to the Metrics associated with your project. In an instant, you'd know where the project stood. Not all projects need this level of planning and measurement, if you don't, have this in place, do not be alarmed;only some of your Supporting Projects require this degree of planning.

After you've clarified the status of your Meaningful Objectives and corresponding Supporting Projects, you can update your project plans to ensure they are accurate.

Last, you will create Strategic Next Actions to move each of your Meaningful Objectives and Supporting Projects forward. Some of these SNAs may relate to discussions you need to have with your direct reports or boss, in which case you will add Tasks to your 1:1 categories. Or they may be SNAs you can do in less than two minutes, in which case you can complete them right away. Or they may be SNAs that you need to defer to an SNA category or to your Calendar. For now, we recommend leaving these in your SNA categories and later in this chapter we show you some options of how to move them to your Calendar or daily To-Do List. There are several ways of doing this, and therefore you will need to decide which method or combination of methods works best for you.

1:1 Categories The last planning category is your 1:1 categories. These categories give you some idea of how your key business and personal relationships are doing. These relationships in many ways are your support system for completing your objectives. Therefore, during the review you will be assessing, at a high level, if these relationships are working or not working and what you need to do to keep improving and growing them.

Part Four:
Creating an
Integrated
Management
System—The
Prioritizing and
Planning Phase

Take Back Your Life!

If you have several direct reports, 1:1 categories are critical because they give you a pulse on how well these staff are performing and what type of coaching or support you need to give them. You will likely have a 1:1 for your boss, several for your direct reports, and some for people in your personal life. When you look inside of your direct reports' categories, you're looking to review progress on their objectives, updates on discussion points, and to delete any items that have been completed. For the other 1:1 categories in your list, check for completed items and new agenda items you want to discuss. And if you don't have a scheduled 1:1 meeting time to discuss these agendas, create a Strategic Next Action to book an appointment!

When you get to the end of reviewing your Planning Categories you've reached a good check point to stop and reflect on your work/life balance. Ask yourself, "Am I experiencing a sense of well-being?" If not, decide what you need. It may be a small thing, such as a good night's sleep or a day of unstructured time. When you've discovered what it is, record the SNA to make sure it happens.

Now that you've reviewed the big picture and have a better idea of where all your objectives, projects and key relationships stand, it will be easier to drop to the tarmac and ensure that all your Strategic Next Actions are going in the right direction.

3. Prioritizing Your Action Categories and Moving Appropriate SNAs onto the Calendar

This is the section in the Weekly Review where the rubber meets the road and the real action takes place.

Your Action Categories consist of your Strategic Next Actions. You review these to delete SNAs that you've completed and to prioritize the SNAs that remain. You will be deciding which SNAs must be completed for you to stay on track and balanced.

The assumption we are going to make here is that you have completed processing and organizing your Collection Points and all your commitments and agreements have been recorded on your To-Do Bar. You have listed all your Meaningful Objectives and Supporting Projects and have created the appropriate SNAs for them. For this example, we are going to plan one week ahead, but when you do this on your own you have a choice regarding how often you plan and how far out you plan—it is entirely up to you and what best serves your situation.

Chapter Twelve: The Prioritizing and Planning Phase

Part Four:
Creating an
Integrated
Management
System—The
Prioritizing and
Planning Phase

In Figure 12-8, you can see the To-Do Bar on the right showing Strategic Next Action categories; the Calendar in the middle showing a week at a glance; and the Daily Task List below the Calendar. This is the view you will want to use when prioritizing and planning SNAs.

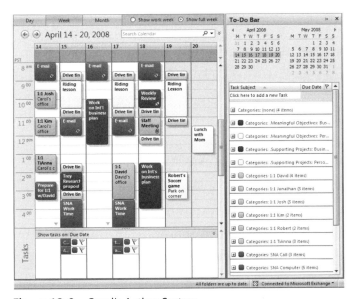

Figure 12-8 Carol's Action System.

Take a look at your Strategic Next Actions on your To-Do Bar and ask yourself the question "Which of these SNAs do I want to complete next week to stay on track with my Meaningful Objectives and be in balance?"

You have several options as to how you plan your SNAs onto your Calendar:

- You can move them off the To-Do Bar and onto the Calendar to complete at a specific time.

- You can leave them on the To-Do Bar, give them a due date, and they will automatically show up on the Daily Task List on that due date..

- You can leave them on the To-Do Bar, set a reminder, and they will pop up in the reminder window on the date and time you selected to remind you to complete them.

- You can leave them on your To-Do Bar and allocate SNA time on your Calendar to complete them during your SNA time.

As you can tell, there are many ways to prioritize and plan your SNAs and we talk in detail about each of these methods in the following subsections.

Part Four:
Creating an
Integrated
Management
System—The
Prioritizing and
Planning Phase

Take Back Your Life!

As you get familiar with them you will be able to decide which combination of options works best for you.

Moving SNAs Directly to the Calendar   Remember, there's a 75 percent greater chance that a Task will get done if it is on your Calendar instead of your To-Do Bar. Based on these statistics, we are great believers in moving Tasks onto the Calendar and off the To-Do Bar. To move an SNA from the To-Do Bar to the Calendar, follow these steps:

1. Right-click and drag the Task onto a specific date on the Calendar.

2. On the shortcut menu, select Move Here As Appointment With Attachment.

3. An Appointment dialog box opens for the Task, and the appointment's Subject line is prefilled with the Task name.

4. In the Appointment dialog box, verify the date, and choose the Start Time and End Time you want for the appointment.

5. Click Save And Close.

When you drag an SNA to the Calendar, be sure to select Move rather than Copy. Move means the task will be moved from the To-Do Bar to the Calendar and deleted from the To-Do Bar. This scares some of our clients. They ask, "What if I don't do it when it's on the Calendar. I want a backup on the To-Do Bar." This suggests that you have an option as to whether you complete the Tasks you have planned on your Calendar. The idea here is that once it is on the Calendar you have made a commitment to complete it, and completing it is necessary to staying on track with your objectives and therefore is important.

The To-Do Bar displays action items that you need to complete, but ones that do not need to be completed right away. The items on your Calendar are the priorities for that week. To give you more confidence that you will not miss anything, we suggest you categorize your appointments using a color when they are completed. At the end of the week any appointments that are not colored as completed indicate they are incomplete, and you can deal with them accordingly. You can simply drag the item to another day to ensure it gets completed, or if needed, you can drag it back to the To-Do List. Pretty simple, really.

Using the Daily Task List   Instead of moving an SNA onto the Calendar, you can mark it with a due date and the Task stays on the To-Do Bar and also shows up in the Daily Task List on the day it is due, as shown in Figure 12-9. However, this method does not make time on your Calendar to com-

Chapter Twelve: The Prioritizing and Planning Phase

Part Four:
Creating an
Integrated
Management
System—The
Prioritizing and
Planning Phase

plete the SNA, it just reminds you at the bottom of your Calendar that the Task needs to be done.

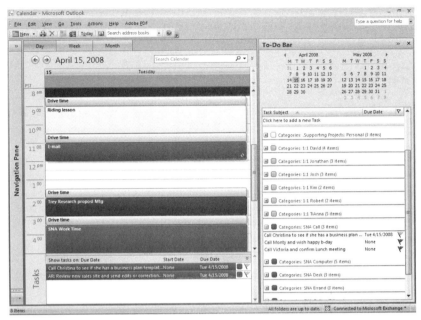

Figure 12-9 The Daily Task List.

If you have four days in a row of back-to-back meetings and your Daily Task List shows SNAs that need to be completed, you have a conflict because you have no time allocated to complete them. Therefore, you need to make sure you allocate SNA time each day or every other day so that SNAs come due on your Daily Task List and you have time scheduled to complete them, ensuring there's no conflict. It is also useful to note that if you don't complete a Task on time, it is automatically moves to the next day on the Daily Task List.

Using Reminders You can open up an SNA on your To-Do Bar and set a reminder date so that your SNA pops up in a reminder box on the day it is due. Figure 12-10 shows you where the reminder feature can be found in a Task. Like the preceding method, this creates conflicts on the Calendar if you do not have SNA time booked to complete these Tasks. It is useful to note that a reminder date can be different from a due date.

Part Four:
Creating an
Integrated
Management
System—The
Prioritizing and
Planning Phase

Take Back Your Life!

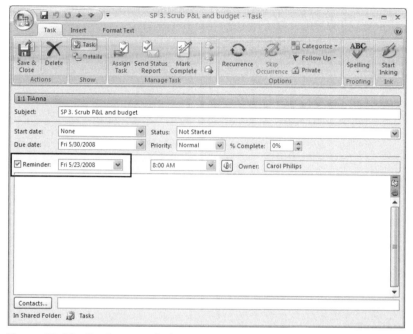

Figure 12-10   Setting a reminder.

Planning SNA Time on Your Calendar   You can schedule SNA time on your Calendar regularly throughout the week. For example, you could book one hour a day for Strategic Next Action time. Instead of moving your SNAs to a specific day, you leave them on the To-Do Bar and select due dates for the priority items. When you get to your Strategic Next Action appointment on the Calendar, you simply review your Strategic Next Action categories and complete the Tasks that have due dates for that day. Also, any SNAs with due dates show up on your Daily Task List, and that also reminds you to do them during your SNA time.

Carol's preference is to move her SNAs onto her Calendar, and then mark them in pink when they're completed. She has a tendency to get distracted, and if she goes into her Strategic Next Action categories to find the appropriate next actions, she ends up crossing off completed Tasks, updating lists, and so on. To avoid this behavior, she moves the SNAs she needs to complete onto the Calendar, which keeps her focused and more productive.

Carol also uses the Daily Task List to keep track of her Waiting For and Follow Up SNAs. If Carol delegates a Task and tracks it in one of her 1:1 categories, she gives it a due date several days before it is due. This then shows up in her Daily Task List. During her one hour of e-mail processing time, she

Chapter Twelve: The Prioritizing and Planning Phase

Part Four:
Creating an
Integrated
Management
System—The
Prioritizing and
Planning Phase

looks through her Daily Tasks List at her Waiting For and Follow Up items. From the Daily Task List she can open the Task, and then open the e-mail message and send it back to the staff member asking that person if the Task is going to be completed on time. This takes less than two minutes and enables her to stay on top of all her delegated and follow-up items.

The Weekly Review is the most important activity you can adopt after you've read this book. The three stages we just outlined in this section are summarized in Figure 12-11. We recommend you create a recurring one-hour weekly appointment to complete this review.

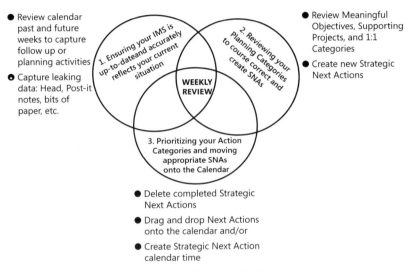

Figure 12-11 Making the Weekly Review a habit.

Making the ControlPanel Your Default View

Your Calendar now represents your top priorities for the week, and these are your most important agreements to keep. Therefore, you'll want to continually review your ControlPanel to make sure you honor these agreements. We recommend that you make the ControlPanel your default view so that it opens whenever you start Outlook. (Don't worry; you'll still be able to get to your Inbox!)

As you look at your week at a glance Calendar, you'll see how much available time you have. If your week is back to back with appointments, you'll know that you won't have time for chatting by the water cooler or getting distracted. However, if your Calendar is open, you'll know you have time to "shoot the breeze," work on SNAs that are on your To-Do Bar, or get a little distracted and have fun doing it!

Part Four:
Creating an
Integrated
Management
System—The
Prioritizing and
Planning Phase

To make the ControlPanel your default view in Outlook, follow these steps:

1. On the Tools menu, click Options.

2. In the Options dialog box, on the Other tab, click Advanced Options.

3. In the Advanced Options dialog box, in the General section, click Browse.

4. In the Select Folder dialog box, click Calendar, and then click OK.

Scheduling Your Weekly Review

The Weekly Review may take you about an hour to complete and we suggest you do it weekly. You need to pick a regular time to complete the review. Carol does her review from 9:30 to 10:30 on Friday mornings, when her mind is fresh and her energy is good. She tried it at 4 P.M. on a Friday, but found it too difficult to do it so late in the day. She also experimented with Monday morning, but worried about her tasks over the weekend, and so Friday morning works best for her.

Pick one hour on your Calendar that works for you and label it Weekly Review and make it a reoccurring appointment.

Making Your Weekly Review a Priority

The Weekly Review process is simple and the rewards are well worth the effort. However, it does take discipline. Each week, clients learn something about themselves while doing their review. For example, they may see where they planned too much in a day, and where things took longer than they thought. They may discover what kinds of tasks they avoid and how they avoid them. It's a self-revealing process that helps clients to pause and reflect, which they don't get to do during the week very often.

However, this may not be the easiest discipline to adopt. You have to stop and move your focus from the tarmac to the control tower, where you'll gain the higher perspective you need to ensure all your planes take off and land safely. To do this, you have to pry yourself away from putting bags on carousels and dealing with annoyed customers who have lost their bags (doing e-mail and handling last-minute interruptions and deadlines) and walk over to the control tower. You have to make that paradigm shift from being reactive to proactive. It is a choice that can help you achieve your personal and professional objectives while maintaining an experience of freedom and balance.

Nothing can add more power to your life than concentrating all your energies on a limited set of targets.

—Nido Qubein

Part Four:
Creating an
Integrated
Management
System—The
Prioritizing and
Planning Phase

Motivation is what
gets you started.
Habit is what keeps
you going. —**Jim
Ryan**

What to Do When You Fall Off the Wagon?

You are likely to fall off the wagon at some point, for any number of reasons, such as going on holiday, taking on new projects, changing jobs, undergoing reorganization, or getting the flu. You must remember that this is a process of practice and learning. All you have to do is climb back on one more time than you fall off. And the best way to get back on track again is to spend time doing a Weekly Review.

To support you in this process—we created a webinar series specifically for individuals who read this book to help you stay on the wagon The series covers the fundamental concepts in this book: managing your collecting system, using the Four Ds to empty your Inbox, and completing the Weekly Review. For additional information or to download the webinar, visit our Web site at *www.mcgheeproductivity.com*. Select Products and TBYL webinars, and then click the TBYL Refresher Webinar Series link, where you can read an overview or purchase the Webinar.

We also created a software product to help you remember to use these methods more easily day to day, and you can find this on our Web site at *www.mcgheeproductivity.com*. Select TBYL Outlook Add-in to read the overview or download it.

Using an IMS takes vigilance and discipline. It's not for the faint of heart—but nothing worth doing ever is. You'll be consistently improving your productivity, and because the results are immediate, you'll find yourself continually encouraged.

Coming Full Circle

In the beginning of the book, we described how the definition for **productivity** and the **MPS Cycle of Productivity** were the cornerstones for your IMS. Now that your system is set up, we want to revisit with you how this works.

The first step in the MPS Cycle of Productivity is "Identify Meaningful Objectives...with execution plans." This step starts on your To-Do Bar, with your Planning Categories.

The second step in the cycle is "Create Strategic Next Actions...without dependencies." Each week, you'll be capturing SNAs in your Action Categories that support you in moving forward with your Meaningful Objectives and Supporting Projects.

Part Four:
Creating an
Integrated
Management
System—The
Prioritizing and
Planning Phase

Take Back Your Life!

The third step in the cycle is "Schedule and Complete Strategic Next Actions...creating integrity." Each week, you'll transfer your priority Strategic Next Actions from the To-Do Bar to the Calendar so that you can complete them. This creates and builds personal integrity and credibility.

The fourth and last step in the cycle is "Review and Course Correct...being accountable." This takes place during the Weekly Review where you evaluate whether the completion of your Strategic Next Action moved you toward your Meaningful Objectives and Supporting Projects and assess what on-course/off-course adjustments are required to stay on track. This creates personal accountability and responsibility. Then, the cycle begins again!

The Weekly Review process enables you to move the MPS Cycle of Productivity forward consciously and proactively week after week after week. As long as you keep the cycle going, you'll eventually unlock your Tasks and Subtasks, Supporting Projects, and Meaningful Objectives, and finally you'll achieve your Mission/Vision/Values. In other words, if you consistently complete Strategic Next Actions that link to and drive your Meaningful Objectives, you'll improve your productivity and quality of life. That is what the Weekly Review is all about: staying on track and maintaining a clear, positive focus on your Meaningful Objectives.

What Changes Will You Make?

Go to your To-Do List and open the Task you labeled IMPROVING PRODUCTIVITY. This is the Task you created to capture the changes you want to make as a result of the Three Phases for Creating an Integrated Management System. Under the heading "Prioritizing and Planning," list the changes that you want to make as a result of learning about this phase. For example, Carol's choices are shown in Figure 12-12.

Chapter Twelve: The Prioritizing and Planning Phase

Part Four:
Creating an
Integrated
Management
System—The
Prioritizing and
Planning Phase

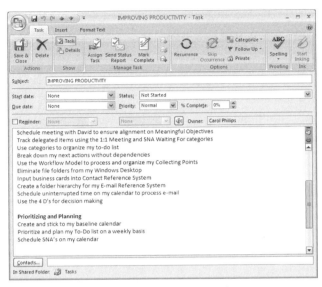

Figure 12-12   What changes will you make?

For inspiration, here's what some of our clients have to say:

- "Use the Calendar to schedule Tasks as well as appointments."

- "Take the time to update my IMS each week."

- "Review Meaningful Objectives and Supporting Projects and create Strategic Next Actions."

- "Plan my Strategic Next Actions onto my Calendar."

- "Use the Due Date column on the To-Do Bar."

- "Set up color categories."

- "Book travel time on the Calendar."

- "Schedule and do the Weekly Review ."

Success Factors for Prioritizing and Planning

Here are some factors to keep in mind so that you can be successful when you're prioritizing and planning.

- You will always have more to do than you can do—paradigm shift number 1.

- Realize "I am as important as others"—paradigm shift number 2.

Part Four:
Creating an
Integrated
Management
System—The
Prioritizing and
Planning Phase

Take Back Your Life!

- Move from being reactive to proactive—paradigm shift number 3.

- Create a BaselineCalendar that accurately reflects the reoccurring activities you need to complete to support your objectives.

- Use color coding to create distinctions and add value to your Calendar.

- Schedule uninterrupted time to complete your Weekly Review. Make this appointment a priority. If necessary, set it up to do with a colleague or your executive administrator. It's the most important practice you can do. It's the glue that holds your system together.

- Use your Calendar and Daily Task List as the central location to track all of your planned commitments.

- Keep your appointments with yourself so that you can take care of yourself and do a better job of taking care of others.

- Empty your Collecting Points consistently so that the information in your IMS is current.

- Review and prioritize your Planning Categories so that you're managing the 30,000-foot view and gaining a higher perspective on your Meaningful Objectives, Supporting Projects, and 1:1 Meetings.

- Prioritize your Action Categories, planning your Strategic Next Actions onto your Calendar to ensure that they get done. This enables you to be realistic about how much time it takes to get the job done, and it supports you in moving toward your objectives.

- Review your Calendar for work/life balance, and identify what you need to do to maintain and sustain equilibrium.

You have to continually improved your system to maintain it. The Weekly Review ensures that you keep your system up-to-date and that you operate within the limits of your Calendar. This keeps you realistic about what you can accomplish. Remember, you can't do everything, but you can do anything, as long as it fits into your Calendar. Respecting your Calendar makes it easier to respect your agreements.

We've used our IMSs for more than 28 years, and we continually fine-tune them to make them better and more effective. Have fun with your IMS. Integrate as much of your personal and business life into it as you can.
The more you use your IMS, the more useful it will become. Remember, using your IMS isn't about doing more, it's about improving the quality of your life, counting the rain drops and smelling the roses.

You've Read the Book. What's Next?

We hope the information in this book inspired you to increase your productivity and improve your work-life balance. If the content was valuable, there are a number of other activities you can do to reinforce what you've learned, go deeper into the methodologies, and increase your contribution to those around you.

- Accept our free offer. We've created a special page on our Web site *just for readers of this book* to access a free learning aid. The product we're currently offering is a webinar from the Take Back Your Life! Refresher Webinar Series called *Prioritizing and Planning your Calendar.* This webinar assists you to complete your Weekly Review, which is the most important habit you can adopt to sustain your productivity. Based on customer feedback, we suggest you view this webinar the first time you plan to do your Weekly Review. To download the webinar, go to *www.mcgheeproductivity.com/ireadthebook.*

- Install our Take Back Your Life! Outlook Add-In software. This software saves you time, supports you in implementing key concepts from the book such as the MPS E-mail PASS model, and provides coaching tutorials. To download, go to *www.mcgheeproductivity.com* and click on the Products section.

  - ❏ View our Take Back Your Life 101 E-mail webinar series. (To download go to *www.mcgheeproductivity.com* and click on the Products section.)

  - ❏ Module 1: Storing E-Mail So You Can Find It Fast. This effective e-mail reference system can save you as much as 50 minutes a day.

  - ❏ Module 2: Writing E-Mail That Gets Results. Learn how MPS' high-impact PASS model uses all parts of the e-mail to reduce volume and speed action.

  - ❏ Module 3: Getting to Zero in Your Inbox. Discover how the MPS E-Mail Processing Model™ can reduce e-mail in your inbox by 80 percent.

- Attend a Take Back Your Life! Seminar. McGhee Productivity Solutions (MPS) offers a variety of customized seminars available to corporations and educational and community groups. They include:

  - ❑ Take Back Your Life for Executive Administrators
  - ❑ Take Back Your Life for Executives
  - ❑ Take Back Your Life for Senior Managers
  - ❑ Take Back Your Life for Sales and Customer Service
  - ❑ Take Back Your Life for Individual Contributors

  For more information visit *www.mcgheeproductivity.com*, or contact us at: info@mcgheeproductivity.com

- Host a Take Back Your Life! Keynote. John Wittry and Sally McGhee are available for keynote speeches. Topics include:

  - ❑ Getting your e-mail to zero—eliminating the e-mail problem
  - ❑ Creating a culture of true productivity
  - ❑ Getting the *right* things done, not just getting things done
  - ❑ Increasing productivity while maintaining balance

  For more information contact: info@mcgheeproductivity.com

We value your comments! Let us know how we can make our products and services more effective for you by sending an e-mail to talkback@mcgheeproductivity.com.

When you look back over your life, we guarantee you won't recall all the times you did your e-mail at the crack of dawn, during meetings, and at home. You'll remember who you were and the difference you made to those around you. Make yourself a priority, and use your IMS to serve you, your family, your company, and your community. In the long run, you'll be more successful! Remember, it's not just about getting more done. It's about living and experiencing the *quality* of your life and sharing that with others.

Go forth, and take back *your* life!

McGhee Productivity Solutions
www.mcgheeproductivity.com
info@mcgheeproductivity.com
303-573-0723

Index

Take Back Your Life! 4Outlook Add-in

Built-in MPS protocols speed and simplify e-mail and task management.

This next-step software from McGhee Productivity Solutions and Standss Limited saves you time and steps as you process and organize your e-mail, calendar and tasks. With the time-saving template and prompts, you can:

- **Turn** action items into tasks or appointments
- **File** reference information appropriately
- **Write** effective e-mail using the proven MPS PASS™ model
- **Access** coaching for your Weekly Review

Multiple tools work to your advantage, including:

MPS PASS Model Implementation. A PASS model template is automatically inserted in each new e-mail or response. *Your culture of productivity is supported with every message.*

MPS 4Ds for Decision Making™. Empty your inbox! You can now create a categorized task or calendar appointment from any e-mail with a single click. Filing reference e-mails is equally simple. *Inbox processing is faster than ever.*

Reference System Maintenance. As business or personal objectives are placed into the Task Pad, you can simply create corresponding e-mail and My Documents folders to support your efforts. *Consistency is achieved across all storage locations to keep you focused.*

Follow-up System for Sent E-mails. When you click "send," you automatically create a task with a follow-up reminder. *Sorting through sent items for that one important message is over...forever.*

Coaching on Key MPS Methods and Protocols. We've built coaching into the software for your Weekly Review, Writing Effective E-Mail and MPS 4Ds for Decision Making. *You can stay on task and on track effortlessly.*

Integrated Management System View. A direct response to a customer request: now you can view your e-mail inbox preview pane along with your Calendar and Task Pad. *You can see it all...simultaneously.*

The **MPS Take Back Your Life! 4Outlook Add-In** makes it easier than ever to implement what you've learned in this book. Versions are available for both the 2007 and 2003 versions of Microsoft Office Outlook. To purchase the software or for more information, visit www.mcgheeproductivity.com/ireadthebook.html.

Special discounts available to readers of *Take Back Your Life!*

Visit http://www.mcgheeproductivity.com/ireadthebook.html for complete details.